England's Queens

About the Author

Elizabeth Norton gained her first degree from the University of Cambridge and her Masters from the University of Oxford. She is the author of ten books on the Tudors and the queens of England.

England's Queens

From Boudica to Elizabeth of York

ELIZABETH NORTON

AMBERLEY

For my son, Dominic

First published 2011
This edition first published 2015

Amberley Publishing
The Hill, Stroud
Gloucestershire, GL5 4EP

www.amberleybooks.com

British Library Cataloguing in Publication Data.
A catalogue record for this book is available from the British Library.

ISBN 978 1 4456 4233 8 (paperback)

Typeset in 10pt on 12.75pt Celeste OT.
Typesetting and Origination by Amberley Publishing.
Printed in the UK.

Contents

1. The Early & Mythical Queens 7
Boudicca, Cartimandua, Guinevere, Cordelia, Bertha, Etheldreda, Cynethryth

2. The Anglo-Saxon Queens 23
Redburga, Osburga, Judith of Francia, Wulfrida, Ealswitha, Ecgwyna,
Elfleda, Edgiva, St Elgiva, Ethelfleda of Damerham, Elgiva of Wessex,
Ethelfleda *Eneda,* St Wulfrida of Wilton, Elfrida, Elgiva, Emma of
Normandy, Aldgyth, Elgiva of Northampton, Edith Godwin, Edith
Swanneck, Edith of Mercia

3. The Norman Queens 75
Matilda of Flanders, Matilda of Scotland, Adeliza of Louvain, Matilda of
Boulogne, Matilda, Empress

4. The Plantagenet Queens 111
Eleanor of Aquitaine, Berengaria of Navarre, Isabella of Gloucester,
Isabella of Angouleme, Eleanor of Provence, Eleanor of Castile, Margaret
of France Isabella of France, Philippa of Hainault, Anne of Bohemia,
Isabella of Valois

5. The Lancastrian Queens 196
Mary de Bohun, Joan of Navarre, Catherine of Valois, Margaret of Anjou

6. The Yorkist Queens 219
Elizabeth Woodville, Anne Neville, Elizabeth of York

Genealogical Tables 243
Notes & Bibliography 247
List of Illustrations 263
Index 268

1

The Early & Mythical Queens

England has always been a place of queens. The earliest known lived nearly 2,000 years ago. Early queens, such as Boudica and Cartimandua, are historical figures, whilst others, such as Cordelia and Guinevere, are mythical. In both historical documents and romantic legends, the early queens of Britain played a prominent role. With the coming of the Anglo-Saxons in the fifth century, England itself came into existence. At first, the English were divided into a number of smaller kingdoms, all of which had queens of their own, before finally, in the ninth century, the kings of Wessex triumphed, uniting the country of England as it still exists today.

From the period before the ninth century, numerous queens are known, some merely as a name and some in more detail. The first Anglo-Saxon queen, for example, can be considered to be the legendary Rowen, the daughter of Hengist, one of the first Saxon settlers. Rowen married the British king, Vortigern, in return for the grant of the kingdom of Kent to her father, and she later assisted her countrymen in obtaining more of the island at the expense of the British. A more significant queen is Sexburga, Queen of Wessex, who, in 672, on the death of her husband, ruled the kingdom as a reigning queen. It would be impossible to detail the lives of every early and mythical queen. Several queens did leave a tangible record, and whilst not queens of England as such, as the country of England did not exist in their time, their stories are remarkable.

The earliest named queens are the contemporaries BOUDICA and CARTIMANDUA, two queens who lived shortly after the Roman conquest of Britain. Boudica, or Boadicea as she is sometimes incorrectly known (*c.* AD 30–60/61), is the better known of the two women.

Britain was conquered by the Emperor Claudius in AD 43, making much of southern and eastern Britain part of the Roman Empire. Before the conquest, Britain had been divided into a number of tribal groups or kingdoms. Following the conquest, some tribes were placed under direct Roman control. Others remained in the hands of their existing rulers, who were friendly to Rome and became client kings. One such client king was Prasutagus, leader of the Iceni, a tribe based in East Anglia. Prasutagus remained on good terms with Rome throughout his life, and according to his near contemporary Tacitus, on his death, he

> had made the emperor his heir along with his two daughters, under the impression that this token of submission would put his kingdom and his house out of reach of wrong. But the reverse was the result, so much so that his kingdom was plundered by centurions, his house by slaves as if they were the spoils of war. First, his wife Boudicea was scourged, and his daughters outraged. All the chief men of the Iceni, as if Rome had received the whole country as a gift, were stripped of their ancestral possessions, and the king's relatives were made slaves.

Prasutagus had expected his friendly relationship with Rome to continue after his death, but the conquerors had other ideas and decided to take the kingdom back into direct control.

If the Romans had assumed that the Iceni would simply accept this treatment, they had reckoned without Boudica, Prasutagus's widow. According to the chronicler Cassius Dio, Boudica was a particularly terrifying specimen and 'in stature she was very tall, in appearance most terrifying, in the glance of her eye most fierce, and her voice was harsh; a great mass of the tawniest hair fell to her hips; around her neck was a large golden necklace; and she wore a tunic of divers colours over which a thick mantle was fastened with a brooch'. Boudica was outraged at the whipping she had received at the hands of the invaders, the rape of her daughters and the attack on her kingdom, and setting herself up as the ruler of her people, she exploded out of her territory, intent on driving the Romans from Britain.

The Iceni were not alone in their hatred of Rome, and Boudica was joined by a neighbouring tribe, the Trinovantes, and other disaffected Britons. The Trinovantes had been driven from their lands so that a new city of Camulodunum (modern Colchester) could be built for Roman settlers. It was to Camulodunum that Boudica and her army went first. Boudica was fortunate in the timing of her rebellion, as the Roman governor of Britain, Gaius Suetonius Paullinus was far away, campaigning against the Druids on Anglesey. This meant that Britain was largely undefended; the inhabitants of Camulodunum begged for aid from Catus Decianus, a procurator stationed nearby, but he sent them only 200 troops with which to defend the town. The Romans were completely unprepared for any attack and the city had no walls or defences. As Tacitus put it, 'surprised, as it were, in the midst of peace, they were surrounded by an immense host of barbarians'. On reaching Camulodunum, Boudica's forces stormed the city, burning and plundering, before destroying the hated symbol of Roman rule, the Temple of Claudius. To the terror of the Roman settlers, Boudica's forces also routed a legion commanded by Petilius Cerialis, which arrived to try to restore order.

Boudica showed the Romans at Camulodunum no mercy, and flushed with success, she and her army moved on towards a second large Roman settlement, Londinium (modern London). The Roman governor, Paullinus, had, by that time, marched with a small number of troops to Londinium, ahead of Boudica's forces. On arrival, he realised that it would be impossible to defend the town and 'he resolved to save the province at the cost of a single town'. As the townspeople wept and implored him to stay, Paullinus marched away, taking with him anyone who was able to fight and leaving everyone else to Boudica's fury. Londinium suffered the same fate as Camulodunum, and in both cities, archaeological excavations often reveal a burned layer that testifies to the completeness of the city's destruction. Tacitus did not give a detailed description of the attack on Londinium, but Dio, writing what is likely to be a considerably embellished account, claimed that, in both cities, Boudica's treatment of the inhabitants was terrible:

They hung up naked the noblest and most distinguished women and then cut off their breasts and sewed them to their mouths, in order to make the victims appear to be eating them; afterwards they impaled the women on sharp skewers run lengthwise through the entire body. All this they did to the accompaniment of sacrifices, banquets, and wanton behaviour, not only in all their other sacred places, but particularly in the grove of Andate. This was their name for Victory, and they regarded her with most exceptional reverence.

With the destruction of Londinium, Boudica moved northwards, destroying the town of Verulamium (modern St Albans) before setting off in pursuit of Paullinus.

Tacitus claimed that 70,000 people were killed by Boudica's forces in the three cities; whilst this is almost certainly an exaggeration, the numbers involved were immense. Dio claimed that Boudica's army numbered 120,000 people, and again, whilst this is likely to be exaggerated, her forces considerably outnumbered Paullinus's. This discrepancy in numbers made Boudica believe that she was invincible, and she made the grave mistake of allowing Paullinus, with his well-trained Roman army, to select the place where their battle would take place.

Boudica's force was confident of victory, and her soldiers brought their families to watch the expected slaughter, with women and children sitting in wagons positioned behind the British lines. According to Tacitus, before the battle began, Boudica, riding in a chariot with her daughters, moved up and down the line declaring,

It is not as a woman descended from noble ancestry, but as one of the people that I am avenging my lost freedom, my scourged body, the outraged chastity of my daughters. Roman lust has gone so far that not our very persons, not even age or virginity, are left unpolluted. But heaven is on the side of righteous vengeance; a legion which dared to fight has perished; the rest are hiding themselves in their camp, or are thinking anxiously of flight. They will not sustain even the din and the shout of so many thousands, much less our charge and our blows. If you weigh well the strength of the armies, and the causes of the war, you will see that in this battle you must conquer or die. This is a woman's resolve, as for men, they may live and be slaves.

Boudica's words were stirring, and in order to further encourage her troops, she released a hare from the folds of her dress in divination, which everyone watched run in an auspicious direction. This was enough for Boudica's troops, and they marched against the Romans. Whilst the Britons had superiority in numbers, they were undisciplined and untrained and no match for the highly organised Romans. The result was a dramatic defeat, and when the Britons attempted to flee, they found themselves hemmed in by their own wagons, leading to a bloodbath where even the women, children and horses were brutally killed. According to Tacitus, 80,000 Britons died that day and only 400 Romans. The numbers may not have been quite so dramatic, but it was a heavy defeat and the end for Boudica. Tacitus claims that she killed herself soon afterwards by poison, whilst Dio suggested that she escaped and was attempting to build a new army when she fell ill and died.

Whilst Boudica's revolt ended in defeat and her death, she made her point, and her rebellion was considered a terrible disaster by Rome. Dio claimed that 'moreover, all this ruin was brought upon the Romans by a woman, a fact which in itself caused them the greatest shame'. For the Romans, the idea of a female ruler was unnatural, but this was not so for the Britons. Whilst Boudica's queenship was conferred on her through marriage, her contemporary, Cartimandua, was a queen in her own right.

Cartimandua was the queen of the Brigantes, a tribe who occupied land that extended north to Dumfriesshire and south to Derby. As the hereditary ruler, it was Cartimandua with whom the Romans dealt following their conquest of Britain, and she came to terms with them, ruling as a client queen. Cartimandua is known only from Tacitus's works. She first came to his attention due to her somewhat notorious role in the capture of the British leader Caratacus, the son of King Cunobelinus of the Catuvellani tribe.

At the time of the Roman invasion, Caratacus refused to surrender and eventually joined with the warlike Silures, in what is now modern Wales, in order to wage a guerrilla campaign against the Romans. In AD 51, he was defeated in battle and fled. Forced to enter Cartimandua's territory, he appealed to her for aid. According to Tacitus, this was a near-fatal error of judgement. Cartimandua, eager to please her Roman friends, had him put in chains and handed over to Rome. Caratacus was taken to Rome to feature prominently in a victory parade but escaped execution by persuading the emperor to release him. He retired to a prosperous existence in Rome, a fate that Cartimandua may also have eventually enjoyed.

A few years later, Cartimandua faced a threat to her throne. She had been sharing power with her husband, Venutius, a famous warrior, but in AD 57, the marriage failed:

> A quarrel broke out between them, followed instantly by war, and he [Venutius] then assumed a hostile attitude also towards us [Rome]. At first, however, they simply fought each other, and Cartimandua by cunning stratagems captured the brothers and kinsfolk of Venutius. This enraged the enemy, who were stung with shame at the prospect of falling under the dominion of a woman. The flower of their youth, picked out for war, invaded her kingdom. This we had foreseen; some cohorts were sent to her aid and a sharp contest followed, which was at first doubtful but had a satisfactory termination.

Cartimandua had relied on Roman military aid before, when there had been an earlier disturbance amongst the Brigantes, and she had no qualms in appealing for aid again following her split with her husband. Venutius had a following amongst the Brigantes, but it was Cartimandua, with Roman assistance, who won the day.

Cartimandua was not so fortunate in AD 69. At some point after her divorce from Venutius, she replaced him with a second husband, Vellocatus, who had been Venutius's armour-bearer. This marriage increased hostility towards Cartimandua amongst the Brigantes, and in AD 69, Venutius once again invaded her territories. The Romans came to Cartimandua's aid, and though they managed to rescue her, they were unable to maintain her rule. With her flight, Cartimandua lost control of her kingdom and disappears from history. As a loyal ally of Rome, it is possible that she ended her days in the capital of the empire itself, but this can only be speculation. Boudica and Cartimandua, in spite of information about their lives being limited, are very much historical figures. Other early queens of Britain can only be considered legendary.

One mythical queen is CORDELIA, the youngest daughter of the famous King Lear. William Shakespeare immortalised Cordelia as Lear's loyal daughter, but the main details of Cordelia's life come from the twelfth-century writer Geoffrey of Monmouth, who created so much of the folklore that has been passed down in England.

According to Geoffrey of Monmouth, Lear was one of the great early kings of Britain, ruling the country for sixty years. He had no sons, but three daughters 'of whom he was dotingly fond': Goneril, Regan, and Cordelia. Cordelia, as the youngest, was her father's favourite. As he grew old, Lear decided to divide his kingdom between his three daughters in accordance with a trial of his own devising. He asked each of his daughters in turn which of them loved him the most. When his eldest two daughters answered that they loved him more than life itself and more than any other living thing, he immediately granted them each one third of his kingdom and the promise of good husbands. He then turned to his youngest daughter:

> But Cordeilla, the youngest, understanding how easily he was satisfied with the flattering expressions of her sisters, was desirous to make trial of his affection after a different manner. 'My father,' said she, 'is there any daughter that can love her father more than duty requires? In my opinion, whoever pretends to it, must disguise her real sentiments under the veil of flattery. I have always loved you as a father, nor do I yet depart from my purposed duty; and if you insist to have something more extorted from me, hear now the greatness of my affection, which I always bear you, and take this for a short answer to all your questions; look how much you have, so much is your value, and so much do I love you.'

Cordelia's answer was honest, but it was not wise. Lear, furious, declared that he would give his youngest daughter no part of his kingdom and expend no efforts in securing an honourable husband for her. He then married his elder daughters respectively to the Dukes of Cornwall and Albany and gave them each one half of the kingdom. Cordelia was very beautiful and able to find a husband for herself, marrying Aganippus, King of the Franks, soon afterwards, without receiving any dowry from her father.

Cordelia's two sisters loved their father rather less than they had claimed. In his old age, Lear decided to stay with his eldest daughter, taking with him sixty servants. Lear's household was a source of great annoyance to Goneril, and after two years, she had had enough, demanding that Lear reduce his household by half. Enraged, Lear went to stay with Regan, only to find that she too demanded a reduction in his household, ordering him to retain only five men. Lear then tried to return to Goneril, but she refused to receive him unless he dismissed all but one of his servants. With this, Lear finally realised how unjustly he had treated his youngest daughter and travelled to Francia to be with her.

When Lear arrived in his daughter's kingdom, Cordelia was shocked to hear how low he had fallen and provided him with clothes and money and a retinue of forty servants. She and her husband invaded Britain on Lear's behalf, installing him again as king, where he reigned for a further three years until his death. Cordelia was widowed during this time and, following her father's death, took the throne alone as the sole ruler of Britain. She ruled peacefully and well for five years, but her two nephews resented being ruled by a woman and rebelled against her, imprisoning Cordelia in one of their fortresses and dividing the kingdom between themselves. In grief, Cordelia, seeing that all was lost, killed herself. The story of Cordelia is a myth, and it is unlikely that there ever was a historical King Lear, or his daughter, Queen Cordelia. Guinevere, who, according to legend, would have been one of the last British queens, is also mythical.

GUINEVERE, the famous wife of King Arthur, was developed as a character in the Arthurian romances over the medieval period. Her husband was a historical figure, and the early British chronicler Nennius noted that, at the time of the Anglo-Saxon incursions in the fifth century, 'the magnanimous Arthur, with all the kings and military forces of Britain fought against the Saxons. And though there were many more noble than himself, yet he was twelve times chosen their commander, and was as often conqueror.' According to Nennius, the real Arthur was a military commander of some strength, winning his twelfth and final victory at the hill of Badon, where he killed 900 Saxons with his own hand. Little more is known about the historical Arthur, but the fictional Arthur and his queen are well developed. By the late medieval period, Arthur was always depicted as a romantic and chivalrous figure, presiding over his Knights of the Round Table from his capital at Camelot.

Geoffrey of Monmouth provided the first full details of the legendary King Arthur. There is little information about Guinevere, although he notes that, once Arthur had taken control of his kingdom, 'he took to wife Guanhumara, descended from a noble family of Romans, who was educated under duke Cador, and in beauty surpassed all the women of the island'. All accounts of Guinevere note her beauty and, also, her treacherous conduct towards Arthur. Geoffrey states that Arthur resolved to leave Britain in order to carry out a military campaign. Before he sailed, he appointed his nephew, Mordred, as regent of Britain and committed Guinevere to his governance. As he was approaching Rome itself, Arthur heard that Mordred 'by tyrannical and treasonable practices set the crown upon his own head; and that queen Guanhumara, in violation of her first marriage, had wickedly married him'. On hearing this, Arthur returned to England, where he met Mordred in battle. Mordred was killed, and Arthur, mortally wounded, was forced to resign his crown and travel to the Isle of Avalon to seek a cure. Guinevere, in despair, ended her life as a nun.

By the late medieval period, Guinevere was renowned as an adulteress who became the lover of the famous Sir Lancelot. Sir Thomas Malory in his *Morte d'Arthur* provided one of the fullest depictions of the relationship between the queen and her lover. According to Malory, Lancelot rescued Guinevere when she was kidnapped by a knight whilst out riding. One night, following this,

> Sir Launcelot took his sword in his hand and privily went unto a place whereas he had espied a ladder toforehand, and that he took under his arm and bare it through the garden, and set it up to the window. And there anon the queen was ready to meet him. And then they made either to other their complaints of many divers things. And then Sir Launcelot wished that he might come in to her. Wit ye well, said the queen, I would as fain as ye that ye might come in to me. Would ye, madam, said Sir Launcelot, with your heart that I were with you? Yea, truly said the queen. Now shall I prove my might, said Sir Launcelot, for your love.

Lancelot spent some time that night with the queen and the affair between the couple was passionate. Arthur's nephews, Mordred and

Agravaine, learned of the affair some time later, and since both hated Guinevere and her lover, they watched the couple closely. Finally, Agravaine brought the matter to the King's attention, and Arthur, devastated by the news, declared that he would only believe it if he had proof. Arthur resolved to lay a trap for the couple, informing them both that he was going hunting and would be out all night. That night, as expected, Lancelot went to Guinevere's chamber. Agravaine, Mordred, and twelve other knights tried to arrest him. Fearing that he would be killed, Lancelot 'took the queen in his arms, and kissed her, and said, Most noble Christian queen, I beseech you, as ye have ever been my special good lady, and I at all times your true poor knight unto my power, and I never failed you in right nor in wrong, since the first day that king Arthur made me knight, that ye will pray for my soul if that I here be slain'. Guinevere declared that she did not wish to live if Lancelot were dead.

Lancelot escaped from the trap laid for him. Arthur, however, furious at the betrayal, ordered that Guinevere be burned as a traitor. On the appointed day, Guinevere was led out to die. As she prepared for death, Lancelot rushed forward and killed a number of knights before carrying her away to safety. Arthur immediately declared war on Lancelot, attacking his castle in an attempt to take both Guinevere and her lover. It was only with the Pope's intervention that matters were resolved, and Lancelot brought Guinevere out to her husband with the promise that she would be safe and not shamed. Lancelot then travelled to the Continent and was followed by Arthur, intent on continuing their war. Whilst abroad, Arthur learned that Mordred had seized his crown and had attempted to marry Guinevere, who had remained in Britain. He returned to confront him, killing him before being mortally wounded himself. Guinevere was devastated when she heard of Arthur's death and, eschewing a possible future with Lancelot, became a nun, spending the rest of her life attempting to atone for her sins.

Guinevere, the sinful queen of King Arthur, is a mythical rather than a historical figure. In both Geoffrey of Monmouth's account and the *Morte d'Arthur*, Guinevere was the cause of the final confrontation between Arthur and Mordred. She turned to religion as a way of expiating her guilt. Early queens were often associated with religious devotions; for example, Bertha, Queen of Kent, who, unlike Guinevere, is very much a historical figure.

BERTHA (539–c. 612), the wife of King Ethelbert of Kent, is usually credited with having brought Christianity to England. She was the daughter of Charibert I, King of Paris, and his wife, Ingerberg, and the great-granddaughter of the great King Clovis of the Franks, who, at the instigation of his wife, Clotild, had converted to Christianity. Whilst Bertha was raised as a Christian, her father was rather less committed to piety than his grandmother had been. According to the historian Gregory of Tours, Bertha had a disturbed childhood, and her father's marital troubles led to him being the first Frankish king to be excommunicated:

King Charibert married a woman called Ingoberg. He had by her a daughter, who eventually married a man from Kent and went to live there. At that time Ingoberg had among her servants two young women who were the daughters of a poor man. The first of these, who wore the habit of a religious, was called Marcoverfa, and the other Merofled. The king fell violently in love with the two of them. As I have implied, they were the daughters of a wool-worker. Ingoberg was jealous because of the love which the king bore them. She made a secret plan to set their father to work, in the hope that when Charibert saw this he would come to despise the two girls. When the man was working away Ingoberg summoned the king. Charibert came, hoping to see something interesting, and, without approaching too near, watched the man preparing wool for the royal household. He was so angry at what he saw that he dismissed Ingoberg and took Merofled in her place.

Charibert later tired of Merofled and married her sister instead, leading to the couple's excommunication. According to Gregory, he also had a further wife called Theudechild. Betha must have been glad that her own marriage, which was an arranged one, proved more lasting than that of her parents.

By the time of Charibert's death in 567, Ethelbert and Bertha were married. From Ethelbert's point of view, it was an excellent match, and it provided him with links to the prestigious Merovingian kings of Francia. Bertha's religion was important to her, and her father secured a promise that she be allowed to practice Christianity before she sailed to Kent. Once in Kent, she was given a converted Roman building to use as a chapel, and she and her chaplain, Bishop Liuthard, set about trying to convert the King. Bertha saw the conversion of England as her duty. According to the Anglo-Saxon historian Bede, in 596, Pope Gregory decided to begin the conversion of England by sending a churchman, Augustine, and some monks to preach in England. They arrived in Ethelbert's kingdom of Kent, an ideal landing place given the queen's Christian beliefs:

> On receiving this message, [that Augustine and the monks had arrived] the king ordered them to remain in the island where they had landed, and gave directions that they were to be provided with all necessaries until he should decide what action to take. For he had already heard of the Christian religion, having a Christian wife of the Frankish royal house named Bertha, whom he had received from her parents on condition that she should have freedom to hold and practice her faith unhindered with Bishop Liudhard, whom they had sent as her helper in the faith.

Ethelbert agreed to meet with Augustine's embassy, and it is likely that Bertha influenced this decision. She certainly allowed Augustine to use her chapel to perform Mass, preach, and baptise those that he managed to convert. Finally, Ethelbert, who had at first been highly wary of Christianity, came to be baptised, no doubt, to Bertha's pleasure.

She still wished to convert England to Christianity and was instructed to attempt this in a letter that she received from Pope Gregory in 602:

> We bless Almighty God, who hath graciously vouchsafed to reserve for your reward the conversion of the people of the Angles. For, as through the memorable Helena, the mother of the most pious Constantine, Emperor of the Romans, the hearts of the Romans were kindled to the Christian faith; so, by the zeal of your glory, we are confident the mercy of God is operating among the people of the Angles.

Bertha died some years before Ethelbert, and her husband had remarried by the time of his death in 616. He chose to be buried with Bertha in the Church of St Peter and St Paul that had been built in his kingdom. Bertha will always be remembered as prominent in the conversion of England, and whilst her own son, Eadbald, turned his back on his mother's religion for a time and even married his stepmother after his father's death, he was soon re-converted. Both Bertha and her daughter Ethelberga, who was responsible for the conversion of Northumbria through her marriage to the Northumbrian king, can be considered the first of a long line of pious and evangelical Anglo-Saxon queens. St Etheldreda is another.

ST ETHELDREDA, or Ethelthryth, (*c.* 636–679) was the daughter of King Anna of East Anglia. According to Bede, her father was pious and sent his stepdaughter, Sæthryd, and his daughter Ethelberga to be educated at the Frankish monastery at Brie, where both eventually became abbesses. Anna was also renowned for his patronage of monasticism. Etheldreda showed evidence of her family's piety early in her life, as described in the *Liber Eliensis*:

> [She] was always pleasant, sweet and gentle to everybody. But something very wonderful and laudable is that, favouring sobriety and chastity from the very earliest stages of her infancy, she used to keep making her way to the thresholds of churches, sometimes following in her parents' footsteps, sometimes alone, and was happy to pray to God assiduously, while neglecting the pastimes of girls.

Etheldreda, like her eldest sister, who became queen of Kent, was not originally intended for the church, and her father arranged for her to marry Tondbert, a prince of the South Gyrwas. Etheldreda was furious when she heard of her betrothal and resisted for a long time, declaring that she wished to remain a virgin. Her parents insisted, and she reluctantly agreed. When he died shortly after the wedding, Etheldreda was married to King Egfrid of Northumbria. Etheldreda had no vocation for either marriage or queenship and, before her first marriage, had made a vow of perpetual chastity. Etheldreda was able to persuade both her husbands to respect this and, whilst she lived with Egfrid for twelve years, she remained a virgin.

Etheldreda was always unhappy in her second marriage, and according to Bede,

> for a long time Etheldreda begged the king to allow her to retire

from worldly affairs and serve Christ the only true king in a convent. And having at length obtained his reluctant consent, she entered the convent of the Abbess Ebba, King Egfrid's aunt, at Coludesbyrig, where she received the veil and clothing of a nun from the hands of Bishop Wilfrid. A year later she was herself made Abbess in the district called Ely, where she built a convent and became the virgin mother of many virgins vowed to God and displayed the pattern of a heavenly life in word and deed.

As a mark of her piety, Etheldreda refused to wear the expensive linen to which her rank entitled her and, instead, wore only woollen clothes. She refused to wash in hot water, except on the eve of great festivals. Etheldreda ate only one meal a day and remained in church praying for most of every night. She was believed to have the gift of prophesy and prophesied her own death.

Etheldreda's hard life affected her health and she developed a tumour in her jaw, which eventually caused her death. Bede claims she bore the pain of the tumour with good humour, often saying, 'I realise very well that I deserve this wearisome disease in my neck, on which, as I well remember, when I was a girl, I used to wear the needless burden of jewellery. And I believe that God in His goodness wishes me to endure this pain in my neck so that I may be absolved from the guilt of my needless vanity. So now I wear a burning red tumour on my neck instead of gold and pearls.'

Etheldreda lived with her tumour for some time before finally asking her physician, Cynifrid, to attempt to cure her. She seemed to improve for two days before dying suddenly. Etheldreda's death was lamented by her nuns, and she was succeeded as abbess by her sister, Sexburga, Queen of Kent. Sixteen years after her death, it was decided to open her grave and place her body in a fine white-marble sarcophagus. When her tomb was opened, her body was found to be perfectly preserved and the wound where her tumour had been opened entirely healed. This would have been proof of her sanctity enough, but more was to follow: as her body was prepared for its reburial, a voice called out from the sky, 'Glory to the Name of the Lord!' Etheldreda was also said to cure those who prayed to her, and she was declared a saint soon after her death, with Bede declaring that she was 'all the more a queen because a bride of Christ'.

Whilst the early Anglo-Saxon period produced a high number of deeply pious and saintly queens, not all queens are remembered as favourably. The most notorious of the early queens is Cynethryth, the wife of King Offa of Mercia.

CYNETHRYTH (died after 798) is the only Anglo-Saxon queen to have minted her own coins and must have been powerful, although no details of her family background survive. Offa came to the throne of Mercia in 757 and reigned for nearly forty years. He was a remarkable man and William of Malmesbury claimed that 'he was a man of a great mind, and one who would endeavour to effect whatever he had preconceived'. He was also formidable, and the chronicler Roger of Wendover stated that he was 'a terror and a fear to all the kings of England'. By the time of his death, Offa had established his authority over most of England. His prestige was so great that, during his reign, he entered into an alliance with the Frankish emperor, Charlemagne, and there was talk of marriages between the families of the two men in around 789 or 790.

Cynethryth had a great deal of influence over her husband, and her notoriety rests on her role in the murder of King Ethelbert of East Anglia. According to Roger of Wendover, Ethelbert visited Mercia hoping to marry one of King Offa's daughters:

> Now Offa, who was a most noble king, and of a most illustrious family, on learning the cause of his arrival, entertained him in his palace with the greatest honour, and exhibited all possible courtesy, as well to the king himself as his companions. On consulting his queen Quendritha, and asking her advice on this proposal, she is said to have given her husband this diabolical counsel, 'Lo,' said she, 'God has this day delivered into your hands your enemy, whose kingdom you have so long desired; if, therefore, you secretly put him to death, his kingdom will pass to you and your successors for ever.' The king was exceedingly disturbed in mind at this counsel of the queen, and, indignantly rebuking her, he replied, 'Thou hast spoken as one of the foolish women; far from me be such a detestable crime, which would disgrace myself and my successors'; and having so said, he left her in great anger.

Offa left his wife to dine with his visitor, but Cynethryth had no intention of abandoning her plan. She caused a room to be prepared for Ethelbert and, next to the bed, had a deep pit dug over which she placed a fine chair surrounded by curtains. As Cynethryth had planned, when Ethelbert retired to bed, he sat on the chair and fell into the pit where the queen's followers waited. Covering him with pillows, clothes and curtains, the murderers smothered the King. Shortly afterwards, Offa annexed East Anglia to his own kingdom.

Whilst Cynethryth is remembered as Ethelbert's murderer, in reality, it was Offa who must have been primarily responsible for the deed, and he was certainly the one to benefit most from it. Cynethryth was, however, a powerful queen, and she witnessed a number of her husband's charters. Little else is known about her life. She bore her husband one son and at least four daughters, one of whom was Queen Edburga of Wessex, a woman as notorious as her mother. Cynethryth outlived Offa, retiring to become the Abbess of Cookham following his death.

In the period before the ninth century, England, and the area of Britain that would become England, had many hundreds of queens. In 802, Egbert became King of Wessex, and the dynasty that he and his wife Redburga founded ruled a united England for over 200 years. Their descendants still sit on the throne today, and it is from Redburga that an unbroken line of English queenship can truly be traced.

2

The Anglo-Saxon Queens

The early Anglo-Saxon period was characterised by a number of small competing kingdoms. The kingdom of Wessex began the process of creating a united England, and the ninth-century kings of Wessex can be considered the first kings of England.

In 802, Egbert came to the throne of Wessex. Whilst he never attained direct control over the whole of what is now known as England, he attained ascendancy over Cornwall, East Anglia, Mercia and Northumbria during his reign, as well as subduing the Welsh. Egbert was the overlord of most of what would become England, and he and his wife were the ancestors of all but four future monarchs of England.

According to the ninth-century writer Asser, the role of the queen was deliberately kept in obscurity during the ninth century:

> The West Saxons did not allow the queen to sit beside the king, nor indeed did they allow her to be called 'queen', but rather 'king's wife'. The elders of the land maintain that this disputed and indeed infamous custom originated on account of a certain grasping and wicked queen of the same people, who did everything she could against her lord and the whole people, so that not only did she earn hatred for herself, leading to her expulsion from the queen's throne, but she also brought the same foul stigma on all queens who came after her.

The queen in question was Edburga, or Eadburh, daughter of Offa of Mercia and the wife of Egbert's predecessor, King Beohtric. Edburga was politically influential and ultimately murdered her husband, before fleeing the kingdom, leading the people of Wessex to reject the office of queen altogether.

There is no contemporary record of Egbert's queen, although one later medieval document suggests that he was married to a woman called REDBURGA, or Rædburgh, and that she was a kinswoman of the great Frankish emperor Charlemagne. This is possible, as Egbert was exiled to Francia in around 800, staying at Charlemagne's court before returning to Wessex to take the throne in 802. Egbert retained contact with the Frankish royal family, and according to the *Annals of St Bertin*, he corresponded with Charlemagne's son and successor, Louis the Pious, shortly after Easter 839. The most that can be said for Redburga is that it is not impossible that she was a kinswoman of Charlemagne who married Egbert during his exile.

Given the strength of feeling against her predecessor, Edburga, Redburga would never have used the title of queen and, instead, would have been called 'lady'. Redburga bore her husband children, although only one, Ethelwulf, survived to adulthood. She had little involvement in Ethelwulf's upbringing, which was entrusted by Egbert to Bishop Helmstan. Ethelwulf was not Egbert and Redburga's eldest son, and he was originally groomed for a career in the church. According to the chronicler William of Malmesbury, he had previously been subdeacon of Winchester, but the deaths of all other legitimate heirs led to him returning to the secular world with the agreement of the Pope. There is no evidence that Redburga survived her husband, who died in 839.

Redburga's successor as queen is equally shadowy. Osburga, or Osburgh, was the first wife of King Ethelwulf. Ethelwulf was a mature man at his accession in 839 and, given the likely date of his parents' marriage, may have been approaching forty. Osburga and Ethelwulf's marriage occurred some years before Ethelwulf's accession, and he immediately made their eldest son king of Kent, implying that he was nearing adulthood. Osburga bore Ethelwulf five sons and a daughter. Her youngest and favourite child, Alfred, was born in 849 at the royal manor at Wantage in Berkshire. This date suggests that she was of a similar age to her husband, reaching the menopause shortly after this time.

Osburga was the daughter of Oslac, Ethelwulf's butler. The office of butler was not as lowly as it sounds to modern ears, and Oslac was an important nobleman at court, retaining his position after his son-in-law's accession to the throne. Oslac was a kinsman of two legendary chieftains of the Isle of Wight, the brothers Stuf and Wihtgar, who were famous for their extermination of the last native Britons on the island.

In addition to her noble birth, Osburga was renowned for her piety and her near-contemporary Asser, recorded that she was 'a most religious woman, noble in character and noble by birth'. Ethelwulf shared his wife's interest in religion, and their youngest son was sent on two pilgrimages to Rome in his early childhood. Unusually for a woman of her time, Osburga was educated and was given some responsibility for the upbringing and education of her children. According to a famous story told by Asser, Alfred had a particular interest in English poetry, of which Osburga was aware:

One day, therefore, when his mother was showing him and his brothers a book of English poetry which she held in her hand, she said 'I shall give this book to whichever one of you can learn it the fastest'. Spurred on by these words, or rather by divine inspiration, and attracted by the beauty of the initial letter in the book, Alfred spoke as follows in reply to his mother, forestalling his brothers (ahead in years though not in ability): 'Will you really give this

1. Extract from the manuscript of the ninth-century writer Asser, who recorded details of Queen Edburga, wife of King Beohtric.

book to the one of us who can understand it the soonest and recite it to you?' Whereupon, smiling with pleasure she reassured him, saying: 'Yes, I will'. He immediately took the book from her hand, went to his teacher and learnt it. When it was learnt, he took it back to his mother and recited it.

The absence of Osburga's daughter, Ethelswitha, from the family group in this story implies that it took place after 853 when the princess married Burgred, King of Mercia, at Ethelwulf's manor at Chippenham. The wedding may have been Osburga's last public appearance as the King's wife, and she disappears from the records soon afterwards. By 853, Osburga was approaching fifty, elderly for the ninth century, and it is likely that she died before her husband made his second marriage to Judith of Francia.

JUDITH OF FRANCIA (b. 843/44) was the daughter of Charles the Bald, King of the Franks, and his wife, Ermentrude. Judith's parents were married on 13 December 842, and Judith, the eldest of the couple's eleven children, was born around a year later. In order to preserve the royal bloodline, it was very unusual for Carolingian princesses to be allowed to marry, and from her infancy, Judith knew that her likely future lay in a nunnery. She was not particularly pious, and this fate may have alarmed her. Her actual fate was no less terrifying, and it was only due to exceptional circumstances that Charles the Bald was prepared to make his daughter available for marriage.

In 851, Viking raiders landed in Devon. Later that year, the Vikings spent the winter in England, setting up camp on the Isle of Sheppey. Shortly afterwards, a great Viking army, with 350 ships, entered the mouth of the River Thames and ravaged Canterbury, putting the King of Mercia to flight. The attacks continued throughout the year. In 855, the Vikings returned and overwintered at Sheppey, demonstrating that they were likely to remain a threat for some time. The Vikings induced horror in England and on the Continent, and the fury and violence of the raids was the worst that anyone could remember. In spite of this, Ethelwulf coped with the early Viking raids and enjoyed an impressive military reputation. During the summer of 856, the Vikings attacked the Seine valley in Francia, the first raid in a decade of attacks on Charles the Bald's kingdom. Charles was eager

2. Viking warriors. Scene from a viking-age picture stone from Stenkyrka, Gotland, Sweden.

to ally himself with the powerful King Ethelwulf. In 855, Ethelwulf passed through Francia on his way to Rome on a pilgrimage with his youngest son, Alfred. On his return in 856, he was invited to visit Charles's court, spending three months in the company of his fellow monarch whilst an alliance was negotiated. During his negotiations with Charles, Ethelwulf made it clear that the price of his support would be a marriage with Judith. By 856, Ethelwulf was at least fifty years old. Charles had misgivings about the match and insisted on a number of safeguards intended to secure his daughter's position as the child bride of an elderly king.

According to the *Annals of St Bertin*, Judith and Ethelwulf were married at Charles's palace at Verberie on 1 October 856. Whilst Ethelwulf had been able to insist upon the marriage, it was Charles who dictated the terms, and in the days before the wedding, he took the unusual step of ordering Bishop Hincmar, one of his advisors, to devise a marriage ceremony in which a coronation could be incorporated. Immediately after the marriage, a crown was placed on Judith's head by Ingmar, Bishop of Reims, who then honoured her as queen. Even more unusually, Judith was anointed with consecrated oil, something that was designed to enhance her status as Ethelwulf's wife and prioritise her children over those of the unconsecrated Osburga following Ethelwulf's death. As far as Charles was concerned, this was the best safeguard that he could give his daughter, but it was viewed very differently when the ceremony was reported in England.

Ethelwulf and Judith set out for England soon after their marriage. According to the chronicler William of Malmesbury, on their return, they found Ethelbald, Ethelwulf's eldest son in revolt against his father. The revolt was due to Ethelwulf's marriage and the status that had been given to Judith and her future offspring. Ethelbald refused to receive his father in Wessex, and in order to avoid further conflict, it was agreed that the kingdom would be divided, with Ethelbald taking the richer western section of the kingdom, relegating his father to the eastern and central portions. This was a major blow to Ethelwulf, but he treated Judith kindly, and 'although the whole dispute was on account of his foreign wife, he [Ethelwulf] treated her with the greatest deference, and even defied the tradition of the West Saxons and set her beside himself on the throne'. Ethelwulf died in 858, leaving Judith a widow at the age of fourteen.

Judith must have expected to be summoned back to her father, where a lifetime in a nunnery awaited her, but within weeks of Ethelwulf's death, her life had taken a very different course, and she married her eldest stepson, Ethelbald. For Ethelbald, marriage to an anointed queen conferred additional throneworthiness on his future sons. Judith was given more prominence in her second marriage than in her first, and she witnessed a surviving charter from the reign, named only behind her second husband and his younger brother, Ethelbert, who was sub-king of Kent. In the charter, Judith was described as queen and signed her name above the bishops and other noblemen in attendance at her husband's court, a prominence unheard of in a ninth-century queen of Wessex.

Both Ethelbald and Judith were aware of hostility towards their marriage. Whilst Judith was some years younger than Ethelbald, she was still his stepmother and, in the eyes of the church, effectively his mother. Judith's contemporary Asser voiced the disgust felt by many when he recorded that Ethelbald, 'against God's prohibition and Christian dignity, and also contrary to the practice of all pagans, took over his father's marriage-bed and married Judith, daughter of Charles, King of the Franks, incurring great disgrace from all who heard of it'. Such a marriage was incestuous, and Asser believed that it was the reason for the troubles and lawlessness of Ethelbald's reign. In any event, Judith's second marriage lasted no longer than her first as Ethelbald died in 860, leaving the throne of Wessex to his brother, Ethelbert.

Soon after Ethelbald's death, Judith sailed for Francia, immediately finding herself immured in the nunnery at Senlis by her father, who had no plans for her to make a further marriage. After her freedom as

Ethelbald's wife and as a powerful English queen, the nunnery must have felt like a prison, and in 862, Judith eloped with Count Baldwin of Flanders. The circumstances surrounding Judith's third marriage do not survive. It is likely that Baldwin was politically motivated, hoping both to secure access to Judith's cross-channel contacts and to make an alliance with her powerful father.

Charles was furious when he discovered his daughter's actions and ordered the Archbishop of Reims to excommunicate them. The pair travelled to Rome to ask for the intercession of Pope Nicholas I himself. The church generally disapproved of the remarriage of widows, but Nicholas, charmed by Judith and her husband, reversed the sentence of excommunication and granted them his personal protection. This forced Charles to recognise his daughter's marriage. Judith's third marriage proved longer than her first two, and she bore her husband children, disappearing into obscurity as Countess of Flanders. It is likely that she lived to see her children reach adulthood because, in 884, Judith's eldest surviving son, Baldwin II, married the daughter of her stepson and brother-in-law, Alfred the Great, a match that was almost certainly arranged using Judith's English connections.

King Ethelbert died unmarried in 871 and was succeeded by his brother, Ethelred I. Ethelred's accession coincided with a major upsurge in Viking attacks, and whilst they had previously consisted of a series of isolated raids, in the autumn of 865, a Viking army landed in East Anglia intent on conquest. By 867, the Vikings had subdued Northumbria and had forced the Mercians to buy peace. By the winter of 871, they had turned their attention towards Wessex, and they spent that winter in Reading, in the heart of Ethelred's kingdom. Ethelred spent most of his brief reign fighting against the Viking onslaught and, early in 871, met the Vikings in battle at Ashdown, winning a major victory. Two weeks later, Ethelred was defeated in the battle at Basing. He died suddenly soon afterwards and was buried at Wimbourne.

Very little is known about Ethelred's queen. A charter of Ethelred's for 868 was witnessed by a 'Wulfryth Regina', and this Queen Wulfthryth, or WULFRIDA, is likely to have been his wife. The fact that Wulfrida was described as a queen and witnessed a charter suggests that she had some political prominence; of her ninth-century predecessors, only Judith of Francia was similarly described in such a document. It has also been suggested that the use of the title of 'Queen' hints that Wulfrida may have been crowned. It is not impossible that Ethelred would have wanted his own children to enjoy the status of having a crowned mother, as his father and eldest brother had done. However, no details survive of any such ceremony, and this can only be speculation.

With the exception of the charter, Wulfrida is completely obscured. Wulfrida is an English name, and she was presumably the daughter of an Anglo-Saxon nobleman, perhaps, given the similarity in their names, the sister of Wulfhere, ealdorman of Wiltshire. Wulfhere witnessed immediately after Wulfrida in the charter and was given a position of prominence in other charters of Ethelred's reign, implying that he was held in high regard by the King. He was also the only one of Alfred the Great's ealdormen to defect to the Vikings, perhaps an attempt to assert his nephews' rights over their uncle.

If Wulfrida survived her husband, she would have seen her two young sons passed over in the succession in favour of their adult uncle, Alfred. Alfred, who sought to promote the claims of his own children, was suspicious of his nephews, and in his Will, he bequeathed them only estates in the eastern and less important portion of his kingdom, leaving the crown to his eldest son, Edward the Elder. In 902, Wulfrida's eldest son, Ethelwold, landed in Essex and persuaded the Vikings to attack Wessex, in the hope of gaining the throne for himself. He was killed in battle in Kent, and his younger brother later came to terms with the King. The descendants of Ethelred and Wulfrida remained at the forefront of the Anglo-Saxon nobility and they were the ancestors of a number of later Anglo-Saxon queens.

The life of Wulfrida's successor as queen, EALSWITHA, or Eahlswith, (d. 902) is better documented. Ealswitha, the wife of Alfred the Great, was the daughter of Ethelred, known as Mucil, ealdorman of the Gaini. The Gaini was an old tribal group absorbed into the kingdom of Mercia, and Mucil was an important figure at the Wessex court, attesting two charters of King Ethelred I in 868. Ealswitha's maternal lineage was even more impressive, and her mother, Edburga, was a member of the Mercian royal family. According to Asser, Ealswitha's mother was a 'notable woman, who remained for many years after the death of her husband a chaste widow, until her death'.

Alfred married Ealswitha due to her prominent family and royal connections, and at the same time as their betrothal in 868, he was also created heir apparent by his elder brother, Ethelred I. At around the same time, Ethelred and Alfred received an appeal from their brother-in-law, King Burgred of Mercia, for aid against the Viking army, and the marriage was celebrated during this campaign. According to Asser, the ceremony was held in the presence of a number of witnesses and accompanied by feasting that lasted both day and night. It is possible that Ealswitha met her husband for the first time at her wedding, and if this is the case, the omens were not good. Following the feasting, Alfred 'was struck without warning in the presence of the entire gathering by a sudden severe pain that was quite unknown to all physicians'. Alfred's illness continued, on and off, for twenty years.

Alfred became king of Wessex in 871. In accordance with tradition, Ealswitha was never called queen, instead being referred to by the title 'lady'. In spite of this, Ealswitha was a prominent figure, and during the reign of her son, she was referred to as 'the true lady of the English' in order to emphasise her high rank. Ealswitha played no political role during Alfred's reign and was content to remain

3. Head of Alfred the Great from a silver penny.

4. A passage from a letter from Alfred the Great to Bishop Werferth.

in a domestic sphere, accompanying her husband and children into exile in January 878 in order to avoid capture by the Vikings. This was a traumatic time for Alfred and Ealswitha, as the Viking leader, Guthrum, declared that Alfred had abandoned his kingdom and forfeited his crown. Alfred spent the first half of 878 as a fugitive on the Isle of Athelney. From here, Alfred carried out guerrilla attacks on Guthrum, defeating him in battle at Edington later that year.

Ealswitha returned to Wessex with Alfred when he regained his throne. There is little record of her activities during Alfred's reign, and she may have devoted her energies to the Church. Certainly, she had the pious example of her own mother to draw upon, and Alfred was also deeply religious, founding two religious houses during his reign: Athelney for monks and Shaftesbury Abbey for nuns. That Ealswitha was involved in the foundation of these houses is suggested by the fact that her daughter, Ethelgiva, was appointed abbess at Shaftesbury and lived there with other nuns of noble status. Ealswitha's piety can also be seen after Alfred's death, as she founded the Convent of St Mary at Winchester (known as Nunnaminster) during her widowhood. Asser referred to Ealswitha as Alfred's 'excellent wife', suggesting that she conformed to contemporary ideals of queenly piety.

There is little evidence to show the nature of the relationship between Alfred and Ealswitha. According to Asser, Alfred's mysterious illness plagued the first two decades of their marriage, and he did not 'have even a single hour of peace in which he does not either suffer from the disease itself or else, gloomily dreading it, is not driven to despair'. Alfred's illness, coupled with the ever-present threat of Viking invasion, cannot have made him a cheerful man to live with. Ealswitha bore a number of children, with five surviving to adulthood. Ethelfleda, Ealswitha's eldest child, married Ealdorman Ethelred of Mercia, succeeding as ruler of Mercia herself after her husband's death. The couple's second daughter, Ethelgiva, as previously mentioned, became the Abbess of Shaftesbury, whilst the youngest, Elfrida, married Count Baldwin II of Flanders. Ealswitha also bore two surviving sons, Edward, who succeeded his father as king, and Ethelweard.

Asser informs us that Edward and Elfrida were raised at court under the care of tutors and nurses and were a credit to their parents:

> To the present day they continue to behave with humility, friendliness and gentleness to all compatriots and foreigners, and with great obedience to their father. Nor, amid the other pursuits of this present life which are appropriate to the nobility, are these two allowed to live idly and indifferently, with no liberal education, for they have attentively learned the Psalms, and books in English, and especially English poems, and they very frequently make use of books.

Alfred insisted on an education akin to that which he received in his mother's household during his childhood, and Edward and Elfrida's curriculum was focused both on religious instruction and works of English literature. Although not raised at court, Ealswitha's other children also received good educations and Ethelweard could read English and Latin.

Alfred and Ealswitha were married for over thirty years. Alfred died in 899 and, in his Will, paid Ealswitha the tribute of leaving her three estates and a share of £400 to be divided between her and her daughters. Ealswitha often visited her son's court and witnessed a charter in 901. She died on 5 December 902 and was buried in the New Minster at Winchester beside her husband. It was rare for Anglo-Saxon queens to be buried with their husbands, and this is a further indication that Ealswitha enjoyed a happy life and a long and contented marriage, in spite of the turbulent times in which she lived. Her relationship with Alfred was more lasting than the marriage of Ealswitha's successor as queen, Egwyna.

Egwyna is sometimes referred to as the concubine of Edward the Elder, rather than his first wife. In the ninth and tenth centuries, marriage had not been entirely formalised and the repudiation of wives was common. It was also possible for a relationship that had not been officially sanctioned by the Church to have the status of a marriage, and it is likely that Egwyna and Edward were married, although not in any religious ceremony.

Few details about Egwyna survive. The later medieval chronicler Florence of Worcester claimed that she was of noble birth, although no details of her parentage survive. William of Malmesbury recounted a romantic legend to explain the attachment between Edward and Egwyna:

> There was in a certain village a shepherd's daughter, a girl of exquisite beauty, who gained through the elegance of her person what her birth could never have bestowed. In a vision she beheld a prodigy: the moon shone from her womb, and all England was illuminated by the light. When she sportively related this to her companion in the morning, it was not so lightly received, but it immediately reached the ears of the woman who used to nurse the sons of the king. Deliberating on this matter, she took her home and adopted her as a daughter, bringing up this young maiden with costlier attire, more delicate food, and more elegant demeanour. Soon after, Edward the son of king Elfred, travelling through the village, stopped at the house which had been the scene of his infantile education; indeed, he thought it would be a blemish on his reputation to omit paying his salutations to his nurse. Becoming deeply enamoured of the young woman from the instant he saw her, he passed the night with her. Pregnant from this single intercourse, she realised her dream when she brought forth her son, Ethelstan.

William of Malmesbury also recorded that, when Egwyna's son, Athelstan, claimed the throne, he met opposition on the grounds that he was born of a concubine. This, along with the story that Egwyna was a lowly born shepherd's daughter, sounds like slander, designed to debase Athelstan's claims in favour of another candidate. Egwyna and Edward's relationship was more lasting than a single night, and it is more plausible that she was a noblewoman, perhaps selected by Edward as a suitable bride whilst he was still some way off inheriting the crown. The marriage took place before 893, and Edward's father, Alfred the Great, considered it a valid relationship and delighted in his grandson.

Athelstan was knighted in his youth by his grandfather, Alfred the Great, and was sent to be raised in Mercia by his aunt, Ethelfleda. Egwyna also does not appear to have participated in the upbringing of her second child, a daughter who was married to King Sihtric of Northumbria. This daughter has been identified as St Edith of Polesworth, a queen who retired to a Mercian nunnery when she was widowed. The choice of a Mercian religious house suggests that she may have been raised in the kingdom by her aunt alongside her brother. Egwyna's fate is not known. It is possible that she died young. Alternatively, she may have been repudiated by Edward. What is certain is that he took a second wife shortly after coming to the throne. Egwyna played no role in the reign of Athelstan and was almost certainly dead by 925 when he became king.

Edward the Elder's second marriage was made entirely for political reasons. Within months of his accession, he had married ELFLEDA, or Ælfflæd, the daughter of Ealdorman Ethelhelm. Ethelhelm was the youngest son of Ethelred I and his wife, Queen Wulfrida, and the marriage was arranged in order to neutralise support for Elfleda's uncle Ethelwold's rebellion. Edward considered his second marriage to be more legitimate than his first, and he designated Elfleda's eldest son, Elfweard, as his successor in Wessex, allocating the lesser kingdom of Mercia to his eldest son, Athelstan. It was only Elfweard's death within days of his father that left Athelstan as king of Wessex. In 933, Elfleda's younger son, Edwin, also rebelled against Athelstan, an event that again supports the assumption that Elfleda's marriage was more legitimate that Egwyna's. There is some evidence that Elfleda was crowned at the same time as her husband on 8 June 900. Elfleda's family were prominent enough to insist on this, and an English coronation *ordo* (essentially, an order of service) from around this period includes the coronation of both a king and a queen, suggesting that this might have been for Edward and Elfleda.

Elfleda and Edward were married for around eighteen years and produced eight surviving children. Given the high infant mortality rates of the time, this implies that Elfleda may have borne almost a child a year during her marriage, suggesting that the couple were often together. Elfleda's eldest son, Elfweard, was Edward's favourite child. Elfleda spent the years of her marriage childbearing and raising her daughters, and four of her six surviving daughters made prestigious foreign marriages. Edward the Elder arranged the marriage of Elfleda's second daughter to Charles the Simple, King of the Franks, and her younger daughters were married respectively to Hugh, Duke of the Franks, Otto I, Emperor of Germany, and Conrad of Burgundy. Elfleda's remaining two daughters became nuns.

Around 919, Elfleda was repudiated by Edward in order to allow him to make a prestigious third marriage. She was sent to the nunnery at Wilton, where she became a nun, taking two of her daughters with her. Repudiation was a common way for a king to dispose of an unwanted wife, and Elfleda may simply have accepted her lot. Certainly, there is evidence that she was pious, and at some point during her time as queen, she commissioned embroideries to adorn the tomb of St Cuthbert.

Elfleda survived Edward, remaining at Wilton following his death. If she had harboured hopes of leaving her nunnery, these were dashed with the death of her eldest son, Elfweard, and the succession of Athelstan. It is possible that the rumours surrounding Athelstan's illegitimacy originated with Elfleda, and she undoubtedly supported

5. The coffin of St Cuthbert, one of the most important medieval saints of England, venerated by many English queens. Elfleda, Edward the Elder's queen, is known to have been pious, and at some point during her time as queen, she commissioned embroideries to adorn the tomb of St Cuthbert.

the attempts of her second son, Edwin, to claim the crown in preference to his half-brother. With Edwin's murder on Athelstan's orders in 933, Elfleda lost any remaining hope of political power. The date of her death is not recorded, but she remained at Wilton, where she was buried.

Elfleda was not the only wife to survive Edward the Elder, and his third wife, EDGIVA, or Eadgifu, (*c.* 899–966/67) played a role in the succession dispute following his death. Edgiva was the daughter of the wealthy Kentish ealdorman Sigehelm, who was killed fighting the Vikings at the Battle of the Holme in 902. She may have been her father's heiress and, certainly, inherited estates from him in Kent. Edgiva's wealth and connections recommended her to Edward the Elder, and he married her in 919, shortly after his divorce from Elfleda. Edgiva was only around twenty years old, and Edward, who allowed her no political role during their brief marriage, was over twice her age. In spite of this, the couple spent much time together, and in a marriage of only around five years, Edgiva bore four children.

Edward died in July 924, and following the early death of his second son, Elfweard, he was succeeded by Athelstan, the son from his first marriage and a man several years older than Edgiva. Edgiva is all but invisible during the reign of her eldest stepson, and she may have devoted herself to raising her children: sons Edmund and Eadred, and a daughter, Edgiva, who married the continental nobleman Louis of Aquitaine. Edgiva's second daughter, Edburga, had been dedicated as an infant to the convent at Nunnaminster and was venerated as a saint following her death in around 950.

When Athelstan came to the throne, he had two living stepmothers with sons of their own. Following Elfweard's death, Edwin, Elfweard's younger brother, was Athelstan's most immediate threat, and it is not improbable that Athelstan sought to come to terms with Edgiva, whose sons were infants. It is possible that she secured Athelstan's promise to name her eldest son, Edmund, as his heir. Certainly, when Athelstan died in 939, Edmund's accession was undisputed, and Edgiva was finally able to come to prominence as the mother of the king.

During the reigns of both Edmund I and Edgiva's second son, Eadred, she was usually known by the title *Mater Regis*, mother of the king. As Edmund's mother, Edgiva entirely overshadowed both his queens. Edgiva witnessed a number of charters during the reigns of her sons and was always prominently placed, a further indication of her high status and power. Both of her sons made grants of land to her. In 943, for example, Edmund I granted Edgiva estates in Kent. In 953, Eadred granted his mother thirty hides at Felpham in Sussex. Eadred, in particular, was concerned for his mother's welfare, and in his Will, he bequeathed land to her at Amesbury, Wantage, and Basing, as well as other estates in Sussex, Surrey, and Kent.

Edmund died in 946 and was succeeded by Eadred, who never married and relied upon his mother as his leading councillor. Edgiva is remembered as a patron of the early religious reform movement in England, and under Eadred, she played a valuable role in assisting the leading churchmen in the kingdom. The Viking invasions of the late ninth century had impoverished the Church. Many monasteries had been burned or deserted during the period, and those that survived often failed to live up to the defining principles of monasticism: community life, celibacy, and personal poverty. Edmund I appointed a churchman called Oda as Archbishop of Canterbury in 942, and he immediately set about reforming the Church, advocating the strict observance of holy vows. Edgiva was very interested in this movement and was associated with another leading churchman, Dunstan, who came to prominence during Edmund's reign. According to the *Life of Dunstan*, Dunstan was in high favour at court under Edmund, and 'he dwelt a long time among the nobles in the royal palace, holding in holy governance a pair of reins, namely of the contemplative rule and of the practical life'. Dunstan's prominence led to jealousy amongst the noblemen at court, and they sought his ruin, persuading the King to strip him of his office. Edgiva may have played a role in persuading her eldest son to bring Dunstan back into favour and to appoint him as Abbot of Glastonbury. She certainly played a similar role in relation to another leading churchman, Ethelwold. Ethelwold was a monk of Glastonbury who expressed a desire to continue his studies at a continental monastery, petitioning King Eadred for his passport. Edgiva recognised the value of keeping him in England and persuaded her son to refuse. According to Ethelwold's biographer, Wulfstan of Winchester,

Swayed by his mother, he [Eadred] decided to give the holy man a place called Abingdon. Here there had of old been a small monastery, but this had by now become neglected and forlorn. Its buildings were poor, and the estate consisted of only forty hides of land.

Ethelwold wanted to establish a strict monastic rule at Abingdon, as he had known at Glastonbury, and Edgiva was an enthusiastic patron:

> The king also gave his royal estates in Abingdon, the hundred hides, with excellent buildings, to the abbot and the monks to increase their everyday provisions, and he gave them much monetary help from his royal treasury; but his mother sent them presents on an even more lavish scale.

Edgiva spent much of Edmund and Eadred's reigns patronising the Church. Eadred was always willing to listen to his mother's advice, and Edgiva was one of the most powerful of the Anglo-Saxon queens. It is possible that ill health played a part in Eadred's reliance on his mother. He died in November 955.

The death of Eadred saw Edgiva's fortunes wane. Following a succession dispute between Eadwig and Edgar, the sons of Edmund I, Eadwig came to the throne. Edgiva, along with her ally Dunstan, supported her younger grandson, Edgar, and soon after Eadwig's accession, Edgiva was deprived of her lands and possessions. Dunstan was exiled to Ghent by the young king. Eadwig was not able to establish his authority as king for long, and by 958, Edgar had created his own kingdom north of the Thames. Eadwig died soon afterwards, and with the accession of her younger grandson, Edgar, Edgiva was once again restored to her lands and possessions. To Edgiva's satisfaction, Dunstan was appointed as Archbishop of Canterbury, and the religious reform reached its peak under King Edgar.

Edgiva was unable to return to a political position of prominence under Edgar. By the late 950s, she was elderly by the standards of her time and she retired to a religious life, rarely visiting court. She remained an important member of the royal family and, in 966, attended Edgar's refoundation of the New Minster at Winchester, a great ceremonial occasion. Edgiva was friendly with Edgar's wife, the equally reform-minded Elfrida, and in her Will, she bequeathed to her five hides of land in Essex to be presented on her behalf to the abbey at Ely. The date of Edgiva's death is nowhere recorded, but it appears to have been around 966 or 967, when she was approaching seventy.

The first of Edgiva's eclipsed daughters-in-law, the first wife of Edmund I, was ST ELGIVA, or Ælfgifu (d. 946). It is unclear when she married the King, but her eldest son, Eadwig, was born around 940/41. Elgiva's father's name is not recorded, but her mother was called Wynfleda. Nothing else is known of her background or of how she came to marry the King.

Throughout her marriage and even after her death, Elgiva was associated with holiness. According to Florence of Worcester, in 943, when Elgiva was pregnant with Edgar, St Dunstan heard voices on high praising the child that would be born. A second story, told by William of Malmesbury, implies that Elgiva had some role in the upbringing of her sons. Edgar was out hunting one day when he stopped to sleep under an apple tree, next to a river. He was woken by the sound of the puppies inside his pregnant dog barking whilst their mother slept. Edgar was astonished and looked up at the tree to see two apples fall, one after the other, into the river. He then heard a voice say 'well is thee' and two pitchers travelled past him down the river. Edgar was amazed by this and returned home to tell his mother what had happened. Elgiva offered to pray for guidance and, a few days later, came to Edgar with an answer to his vision. She told Edgar,

'The barking of the whelps while the mother was sleeping implies, that after your death, those persons who are now living and in power, dying also, miscreants yet unborn will bark against the church of God. And whereas one apple followed the other, so that the voice, 'well is thee', seemed to proceed from the dashing of the second against the first, this implies that from you, who are now like a tree shading all England, two sons will proceed. The favourers of the second will destroy the first, when the chiefs of the different parties will say to each of the boys, 'well is thee', because the dead one will reign in heaven, the living one on earth.'

Elgiva continued that the two pitchers symbolised the Viking attacks that would follow after Edgar's death. This story, with its reference to the Viking attacks and the succession dispute after Edgar's death, is unlikely to have occurred, and in any event, Edgar would only have been three at most when Elgiva died. However, it does demonstrate the holy way in which she was viewed in the medieval period.

William of Malmesbury described Elgiva as a saintly person during her lifetime, recording that 'she was devoted to good works and endowed with such piety and sweetness of temper that she would secretly redeem with her own money culprits who had been openly condemned by a strict verdict of the courts'. She also gave away her fine clothes to beggars. Elgiva was loved and 'with Ælfgifu [Elgiva] even the envious could only praise her physical beauty and her skill in handiwork, as there was nothing they could criticise'.

Elgiva and her husband Edmund died in the same year: 946. Edmund died on 26 May and had remarried by the time of his death, so Elgiva's death must have occurred in the early months of 946. She was buried at the royal nunnery at Shaftesbury and, according to the near-contemporary *Chronicle of Æthelweard*, was immediately considered a saint, and 'at her tomb, with the help of God, down to the present day, very many miracles take place in the monastery known by the common people as Shaftesbury'. St Elgiva made a deeper mark in England than her successor, Ethelfleda of Damerham, who, but for a reference in the *Anglo-Saxon Chronicle*, would be entirely forgotten.

The *Anglo-Saxon Chronicle* described ETHELFLEDA, or Æthelflæd, of Damerham, (died after 975) as Edmund's queen at the time of his death. Edmund and Ethelfleda must have married soon after St Elgiva's death, and Ethelfleda was married, at most, for a matter of weeks before she became a widow. Edmund probably selected Ethelfleda due to her wealth and family connections, as she was the daughter of Elfgar, ealdorman of Essex. On her father's death, her brother-in-law, Brihtnoth, became ealdorman in his place, and this, coupled with Ethelfleda's personal wealth and possession of a number of estates in Essex, suggests that she and her sister were their father's heiresses.

Ethelfleda first appears in the sources when, on 26 May 946, Edmund I was murdered at the royal manor of Pucklechurch in Gloucestershire. During the night, Liofa, a robber, entered the manor intent on plunder. Edmund came upon Liofa attacking his steward and, as he intervened, was stabbed to death. There is no evidence that Ethelfleda remarried, so she was a widow for at least thirty or forty years, making a Will some time after 975. In her Will, Ethelfleda left lands to the King, which may have been the return of her dower. She also left extensive bequests to her kin, including estates to her sister and brother-in-law. Ethelfleda's Will suggests that she, like the majority of her predecessors and successors as queen, was pious: many of her bequests were made to her family for life with the remainder passing to religious foundations. The date of Ethelfleda's death is nowhere recorded.

If Ethelfleda of Damerham is little recorded, her successor as queen enjoyed no such anonymity during her own lifetime, and she is amongst the most slandered of all queens of England: ELGIVA OF WESSEX, a descendant of Ethelred I and his wife, Wulfrida. The tenth-century chronicler Ethelweard is likely to have been her brother, and Elgiva's father was therefore Ealdorman Eadric, who died in 949. Elgiva's father died when she was still a small child and it was her mother, Ethelgiva, who was the dominant force in her upbringing. Like her husband, Ethelgiva was a descendant of King Ethelwulf, and she had a more immediate royal connection as a descendant of the niece of Queen Ealswitha. Elgiva was raised in the south of England, where her family had important connections and lands.

The death of King Eadred in 955 was due to a long illness, and his only close family were his nephews, Eadwig and Edgar. In 955, Eadwig was, at most, fifteen and Edgar was twelve. When Eadwig became king, factions had already split his court, with St Dunstan and Queen Edgiva openly in support of Edgar, and Elgiva and her family in support of Eadwig. This accounts for the hostility towards Elgiva and her mother in the *Life of St Dunstan,* and the chronicler claimed of Ethelgiva that 'a certain woman, foolish, though she was of noble birth, with her daughter, a girl of ripe age, attached herself to him [Eadwig], pursuing him and wickedly enticing him to intimacy, obviously in order to join and ally herself or else her daughter to him in lawful marriage'. It is not impossible that Ethelgiva sought to marry the King herself, but she was some years older than the teenage king, and it is unlikely. More plausibly, marriage to Elgiva was the price of her family's support.

St Dunstan and the other members of his faction considered Elgiva to be a dangerous influence on the King, and they were determined to blacken her name, refusing even to acknowledge her as Eadwig's wife. According to the *Life of St Dunstan,* Elgiva and her mother were nothing more than common harlots, and the chronicler claimed that, during Eadwig's coronation feast, it was noticed that the young king had disappeared. Dunstan and his kinsman, Bishop Cynesige, were asked to find him and bring him back. They went straight to Eadwig's bedchamber, where

> they found the royal crown, which was bound with wondrous metal, gold and silver and gems and shone with many-coloured lustre, carelessly thrown on the floor, far from his [Eadwig's] head, and he himself repeatedly wallowing between the two of them [Elgiva and Ethelgiva] in evil fashion, as if in a vile sty. They said 'Our nobles sent us to you to ask you to come as quickly as possible to your proper seat, and not to scorn to be present at the joyful banquet of your chief men.' But when he did not wish to rise, Dunstan, after first rebuking the folly of the women, drew him by the hand from his licentious reclining by the women, replaced the crown, and brought him with him to the royal assembly, though dragged from the women by force.

It is highly unlikely that events happened as Dunstan described, as, by the time of the coronation, Elgiva and Eadwig were already married. In spite of this, even as late as the twelfth century, Eadwig was remembered as a 'wanton youth', and Elgiva as a harlot and a strumpet.

The picture painted of both Eadwig and Elgiva is not the entire story. Elgiva's brother, the chronicler Ethelweard, provided the only contemporary favourable account of Eadwig, claiming that 'he for his great beauty got the nick-name "All-fair" from the common people. He held the kingdom continuously for four years, and deserved to be loved.' Whilst the majority of leading churchmen supported Edgar and thus refused to recognise Eadwig and Elgiva's marriage, Ethelwold, Abbot of Abingdon, who would later work closely with Edgar's own queen, recognised Elgiva's position. In one charter of Abingdon, Elgiva witnessed as the King's wife, and in her Will, she left a number of bequests to Ethelwold's foundations and to the churchman personally, suggesting a debt of gratitude for his support during the troubled days of her marriage.

At first, Eadwig and Elgiva had the upper hand, exiling or seizing the goods of their enemies. However, in 957, Eadwig found himself deserted by the Northumbrians and Mercians, who chose Edgar as their king, dividing the kingdom at the Thames. Elgiva's family connections helped to secure the south for Eadwig, but the King's position was fatally weakened. The *Anglo-Saxon Chronicle* for 958 records that Archbishop Oda, an ally of St Dunstan, divorced Eadwig from his wife on the grounds of consanguinity. The couple were related at least three times, both with Elgiva's double descent from King Ethelred I and her relationship to Queen Ealswitha. However, the much closer marriage of Edgar's own grandfather, Edward the Elder, to Elfleda and, of course, the marriage of Elgiva's own parents were unchallenged, demonstrating that the consanguinity between Edgar and Elgiva should not, on its own, have been enough to warrant their separation. Elgiva was exiled to the Continent for the remainder of Eadwig's reign. Eadwig did not, in any event, have long to live, dying suddenly on 1 October 959 and leaving the remainder of his kingdom to Edgar.

Elgiva's thoughts on her separation from Eadwig are not recorded, but the fact that she never remarried suggests that she loved him. She made her peace with Edgar during her widowhood and returned to England by the mid-960s. In 966, she received two grants of land from her brother-in-law, which was, perhaps, the grant of her dower and an acknowledgement of her position as a former queen. As further proof of her rehabilitation, Elgiva attended the refoundation of the New Minster at Winchester in that same year. Elgiva remained on good terms with Edgar and her Will, which was made at some point between 966 and 975, included bequests to Edgar and one of his sons. Elgiva also made large grants to religious foundations, and it is not unlikely that she retired to a religious house for her last years. The date of her death is nowhere recorded, but she remained devoted to her husband until the end, requesting that she be buried with him.

As the examples of Elgiva and her earlier predecessors as queen, Egwyna and Elfleda, show, divorce was common amongst tenth-century kings. Elgiva's brother-in-law, King Edgar, was a serial monogamist, marrying three wives in quick succession. Around the time that he seized the throne of Mercia from his brother, he took his first wife, ETHELFLEDA, or Æthelflæd, the daughter of an ealdorman named Ordmer. Ethelfleda's nickname of *Eneda* translates as 'swan' or 'fair'. Edgar always had an eye for a beautiful woman, and Ethelfleda's charms recommended her to him. Edgar also sought an alliance with Ethelfleda's family in order to strengthen his position in Mercia.

No stories survive surrounding Ethelfleda *Eneda* and she played no political role. She bore one child, Edward, before Edgar's accession in 959. With his accession to the entire kingdom, the support of Ethelfleda's family was no longer required by Edgar, and the couple were divorced so that he could find a more politically prominent bride. Nothing more is heard of Ethelfleda, and it is likely that she died young. She played no role in her son's brief reign.

Once he had become King of England, Edgar looked for an alliance with an important noble family. His first choice was a beautiful young nun called Wulfhilde, who lived at Wherwell Abbey under the governance of her aunt, the Abbess. Edgar went to the Abbey and persuaded the Abbess to support his suit. Wulfhilde, who had no desire to marry the King, was tricked into a meeting with him by her aunt. When she entered the room, Edgar met her passionately, terrifying the girl, and she fled the room. Both Edgar and the Abbess were furious, and they locked her in her room until she would agree to marry. Wulfhilde managed to flee through the abbey sewers, forcing Edgar to abandon his suit and propose to her cousin, ST WULFRIDA OF WILTON, instead.

Wulfrida is almost certainly the young nun of Wilton Abbey who was mentioned in the *Life of St Dunstan*. According to the *Life*, Edgar fell in love with a young nun and made her his mistress. The *Life* does not consider Wulfrida to have been Edgar's wife, claiming that she was merely his concubine. However, there is evidence to suggest some sort of marriage, although it is unlikely to have been made with a church ceremony. It is possible that Wulfrida was not, at the time of her marriage, actually a nun, and William of Malmesbury claimed that Wulfrida 'had merely put on the veil as her own idea in her sudden fear of the king, before, as the story continues, the king snatched away the veil and dragged her to his bed'.

Nun or not, Wulfrida and Edgar were married by around 961, and she bore the King a daughter, Edith. According to William of Malmesbury, following this birth, 'Wulfthryth [Wulfrida] did not develop a taste for repetitions of sexual pleasure, but rather shunned them in disgust', retiring with her daughter to Wilton Abbey, where she became Abbess. It is indeed possible that Edgar and Wulfrida quickly found that they were not compatible and that their separation was mutually agreed. However, Wulfrida's retirement coincides with the beginnings of Edgar's relationship with his third wife, Elfrida, and it is more likely that she was divorced by the changeable king. Whether a voluntary exile or not, Wulfrida and Edith spent the rest of their lives at Wilton, with Edith succeeding her mother as Abbess before dying at the age of twenty-three. Both were venerated as saints after their deaths, a far cry from the reputation enjoyed by Edgar's third wife, Elfrida.

ELFRIDA, or Ælfthryth, (c. 940–1000/01) was the third wife of King Edgar, and whilst his other wives are shadowy and insignificant figures, Elfrida was a queen. She was the daughter of Ordgar, a West Country thegn. Her mother was of royal descent, and Elfrida, who was the family's only daughter, was born around 940. In 956, Elfrida made an advantageous marriage to Ethelwold, the eldest son of the powerful nobleman Athelstan Half-King. The Half-King had gained his nickname from his immense power, and he was the most prominent man in the country after the King. His prestige was so great that his wife was chosen as the foster mother for the young Edgar following the death of his mother, St Elgiva. In the summer of 956, the Half-King retired to Glastonbury Abbey to become a monk, allowing for the succession of Elfrida's husband to his father's lands and titles.

Elfrida bore her first husband two sons but played no role in their upbringing, and this may have been due to the frosty relations occasioned by the beginning of her relationship with Edgar. William of Malmesbury tells us that before Elfrida's marriage, Edgar heard reports of her beauty and sent Ethelwold to visit her and report if she was worthy of marriage to the King. Ethelwold, falling in love with her on sight, persuaded Elfrida to marry him, informing the King that she was very plain and not a suitable bride:

When Edgar's heart was disengaged from this affair, and employed on other amours, some tattlers acquainted him how completely Æthelwold had duped him by his artifices. Driving out one nail with another, that is, returning him deceit for deceit, he showed the earl a fair countenance, and, as in a sportive manner, appointed a day when he would visit this far-famed lady. Terrified almost to death with this dreadful pleasantry, he hastened before to his wife, entreating that she would administer his safety by attiring herself as unbecomingly as possible; then first disclosing the intention of such a proceeding. But what did not this woman dare? She was hardy enough to deceive the confidence of her miserable lover, her first husband, to adorn herself at the mirror, and to omit nothing which could stimulate the desire of a young and powerful man. Nor did events happen contrary to her design; for he fell so desperately in love with her the moment he saw her, that, dissembling his indignation, he sent for the earl into a wood at Warewelle, under pretence of hunting, and ran him through with a javelin.

A similar story is told by Gaimar, who recorded that Elfrida and Edgar began an affair before Ethelwold's death. Both stories imply that Edgar had already become king before Elfrida's first marriage, which was not correct, and must cast doubt on their truthfulness. Ethelwold died in 962 and Elfrida and Edgar only married in 964, again calling into question the claims that they organised Ethelwold's murder.

Elfrida played a much more political role as queen than either of Edgar's previous wives, and she received a dower from Edgar at the time of their marriage. Edgar's reign is remembered for religious reform and Elfrida played a prominent role in this movement. On his accession, Edgar appointed St Dunstan as his Archbishop of Canterbury and he quickly became his chief councillor. Other leading churchmen were prominent under Edgar, including Ethelwold, Abbot of Abingdon, who was appointed Bishop of Winchester. The tenth-century religious reform sought to regulate monasticism and bring it back to the stricter rule of St Benedict. Even before her marriage, Elfrida showed an interest in the reform and the *Liber Eliensis* claims that

a woman called Ælfthryth [Elfrida] pleaded with King Edgar that he sell to the blessed Æthelwold ten hides at Stoke, which is near Ipswich; and two mills which are situated in the southern part. Her entreaties availed with him. For the bishop gave the king one hundred mancuses for that land and the mills, [and] he afterwards presented [the same land and mills] to Æthelfryth.

This demonstrates both that, even before her marriage, Elfrida had an interest in the reform movement, and that she was already closely associated with Bishop Ethelwold.

In 964, shortly after their marriage, Edgar called a council which produced a famous document, the *Regularia Concordia*. This document set out the rules by which monks and nuns were expected to live. Elfrida, as queen, was given a specified political role, with Edgar declaring 'that his queen Ælfthryth, should be the protectress and fearless guardian of the monasteries; so that he himself helping the men and his consort helping the women there should be no cause for any breath of scandal'. Elfrida was placed in direct control of all the English nunneries.

Elfrida is remembered as one of the most prominent of all the Anglo-Saxon queens. Edgar made great efforts to assert the legitimacy of his third marriage over his two previous unions, and he always presented Elfrida as his queen rather than as merely his wife. Elfrida was a prominent figure at the great royal gathering at the New Minster at Winchester in 966. The charter drawn up to witness the event saw Edgar witness first, followed by the powerful St Dunstan. Immediately after Dunstan, witnessed Edgar and Elfrida's infant son, Edmund, who was strikingly described as the 'legitimate son of the king'. Edward, Edgar's son by Ethelfleda *Eneda*, witnessed next and was described only as the 'son of the king'. Elfrida was the fifth witness and described as the 'legitimate wife of the king'. It is obvious that Edgar intended to demonstrate that his third wife and her children were his legitimate family. Elfrida's eldest son by Edgar, Edmund, died in 971, and she transferred her ambitions to her youngest child, Ethelred, who was born between 967 and 969. Elfrida was crowned with Edgar at the Roman city of Bath in 973, a ceremony intended to highlight his imperial ambitions and dominance of the whole island of Britain.

Edgar was still a young man at the time of his coronation, and it was a shock to everyone when, on 8 July 975, he died suddenly. His only possible successors were his two young sons, Edward and Ethelred. Edward cannot have been more than fourteen or fifteen years old, and Ethelred around seven. Factions developed and Elfrida, naturally, supported her own child. St Dunstan settled on Edward. This led to the succession dispute allegedly foretold by Edgar's mother, St Elgiva, when she interpreted her son's childhood dream.

Dunstan won the succession battle and Edward was crowned king in around March 976, to Elfrida's fury. There was little she could do, except retreat with her son to her house at Corfe whilst Dunstan took over the governorship of England. In 978, matters suddenly changed, and when a meeting of Edward's council was called at Calne, the upper floor on which the councillors stood collapsed, causing everyone, except Dunstan, who was standing on a rafter, to fall to the floor below, killing or maiming the majority of the King's supporters. This was the opportunity that Elfrida had been waiting for.

On 18 March 978, King Edward happened to be in the area of Corfe Castle and decided to pay a visit to his stepmother and half-brother, attended by only a small escort. A number of different accounts describe the events at Corfe of that day. The fullest contemporary account is that contained in the *Life of St Oswald,* which claims that, when Edward arrived at Corfe,

> there came out to meet him, as was fitting, nobles and chief men, who stayed with the queen, his mother. They formed among them a wicked plan, for they possessed minds so accursed and such diabolical blindness that they did not fear to lay hands on the lord's anointed. Armed men surrounded him on all sides, and with them also stood the cupbearer to perform his humble office. The revered king indeed had with him very few thegns, for he feared no one, trusting 'in the lord and the might of his power'.

As Edward accepted a drink, one of Elfrida's thegns seized his hand, wounding him, as the King shouted, 'What are you doing – breaking my right arm?' Edward was then violently stabbed before his horse bolted, causing the King to fall from the horse with his foot trapped in the stirrup. Edward died as he was dragged along the ground behind his horse. The earliest accounts of the murder do not specifically accuse Elfrida of complicity, although one early version of the *Anglo-Saxon Chronicle* states that 'here King Edward was killed in the evening-time on 18 March at Corfe passage'. Elfrida was widely known to live at Corfe, and the fact that this was the scene of Edward's death is striking. By the early eleventh century, whilst Ethelred was still alive, the blame was already commonly attributed to those about the Queen, and in the mid-eleventh century, the *Life of St Dunstan* by Osbern specifically laid the blame at Elfrida's door, declaring that Edward was 'killed by a stepmother's deceit'. It is impossible now to judge just what Elfrida's involvement in the murder was, but the surviving evidence is damning. It was also Elfrida and her young son who had the most to gain. Shortly after the murder, Ethelred was crowned king.

Ethelred II was no more than twelve years old at his accession, and Elfrida was the power behind the throne. She appears regularly on charters between 979 and 984, demonstrating that she attended councils during her son's minority. She generally witnessed using the title 'king's mother' and was placed directly below the King himself. Elfrida continued to co-operate with Bishop Ethelwold, and the pair kept the King under their control well past his fifteenth and sixteenth birthdays; ages at which an Anglo-Saxon monarch could expect to attain his majority. It was Ethelwold's death on 1 August 984 that finally allowed the King to assert his own authority, and by the end of the year, Elfrida had ceased to attend council meetings and had retired to her own estates, probably against her will.

Even in her old age, Elfrida remained a prominent political figure. At some point between 995 and her death, she became involved in a lawsuit over land. During Edgar's reign, Elfrida had persuaded him to return a large estate at Taunton to the see of Winchester. She also retained an interest in the business, as is recorded in her only surviving letter, written during her old age:

Ælfthryth [Elfrida] sends humble greetings to Archbishop Ælfric and Earl Æthelweard. I bear witness that Archbishop Dunstan assigned Taunton to Bishop Æthelwold, in conformity with the Bishop's charters. And King Edgar then relinquished it, and commanded every one of his thegns who had any land on the estate that they should hold it in conformity with the bishop's wish or else give it up. And the king said that he had no land to grant out, when he durst not, for fear of God, retain the headship himself; and moreover he then put Ruishton under the Bishop's control. And then Wulfgyth rode to me at Combe and sought me. And I then, because she was my kinswoman, and Ælfsyth because he [Leofric] was her brother, obtained from Bishop Æthelwold that they [Wulfgyth and Leofric] might enjoy the land for their lifetime, and after their deaths the land should go to Taunton, with produce and men, just as it stood. And with great difficulty we two brought matters to this conclusion. Now I have been told that Bishop Æthelwold and I must have obtained the title deed by force. Now I, who am alive, am not aware of any force any more than he would be, if he were still alive. For Leofric had a new title deed; when he gave it up he thereby manifested that he would engage in no false dealings in the matter. The Bishop Æthelwold told him that none of his successors could dispossess him. He then commanded two documents to be written, one he kept himself, the other he gave to Leofric.

Whilst the outcome of the dispute is not recorded, it shows a touching loyalty to the memory of Bishop Ethelwold, Elfrida's greatest friend. As she aged, Elfrida continued to show an interest in the Church, founding two nunneries. Her name always remained linked to the death of Edward the Martyr, and it irked her to see him popularly honoured as a saint within months of his death. The exact date of Elfrida's death is not recorded, but she lived to a good age for the period, reaching around sixty. She died on 17 November in 1000 or 1001.

Elfrida will always be remembered as the murderer of Edward the Martyr. She was undoubtedly one of the greatest and most prominent of all Anglo-Saxon queens and one of the most powerful women in medieval England. This is in direct contrast to her first daughter-in-law, Elgiva. The date of Ethelred's first marriage is not recorded, but his eldest four sons attested a charter in 993, suggesting that the marriage must have been by the mid-980s at the latest.

Elgiva is mentioned in no contemporary sources and attested no charters. Her existence can be glimpsed by the fact that four sons, Athelstan, Egbert, Eadred and Edmund had been born by 993, a fifth son, Eadwig, by 997, and a sixth, Edgar, by 1001. Two daughters, Elgiva and Edith, also survived to adulthood, and it is safe to assume that she was entirely occupied in childbearing during her marriage. Later records claim that Elgiva was either the daughter of Ealdorman Thored of York or, perhaps, an unidentified man named Ethelbert. No Ealdorman Ethelbert has been identified for the period and so Thored is more likely to have been her father. By 992, Thored had vanished from the sources, implying that he had died. In 1002, Ethelred remarried, and it is likely that Elgiva was repudiated in order to make way for a more prominent match. Alternatively, she may have died. Elgiva was entirely overshadowed by Elfrida, and she was never recognised as queen.

Whilst Ethelred II's first wife is entirely obscure, no such anonymity surrounds his second wife, EMMA OF NORMANDY (c. 980s–1052). She was the eldest of the nine children of Richard I, Duke of Normandy, and his second wife, Gunnor, and was born between 980 and 990. Emma's father died whilst she was still young, but her mother was a formidable woman. According to the chronicler Wace, Gunnor 'was very beautiful, well educated and very courtly. Her father and mother were Danish and she was born of noble Danes, with good lineage on both sides. She was kind and friendly, very generous and honourable; she knew all a woman could know about woman's work'. Richard was, at first, unwilling to marry Gunnor, and Emma was born of a union unsanctioned by the church. Gunnor was the dominant influence on her children's upbringing, and she imbued in Emma a love of Scandinavian culture, as well as ensuring that her daughter was fluent in her native language, Danish. Gunnor ruled as regent for her son Richard II following his accession as Duke of Normandy in 996.

Viking raids were a major concern to Ethelred II during his reign and this brought him into contact with Normandy. The Dukes of Normandy were descended from Vikings, and this, coupled with Gunnor's Danish origins, ensured that Normandy was largely sympathetic to the raiders. A letter from the Pope to Ethelred in 991 shows the strained relations between England and Normandy, and in it, the Pope stated the agreement that 'Richard is to receive none of the king's men, or his enemies, nor the king any of his, without their seal'. Normandy harboured Viking ships and the agreement of 991 failed to stop hostilities between the two countries. During the 990s, Ethelred carried out an unsuccessful raid on Normandy, presumably a reprisal for a Viking attack.

The death of Ethelred's mother, Elfrida, left the office of queen vacant, and in the hope of securing a more lasting peace with his troublesome neighbours, the King proposed a marriage alliance. England in the early eleventh century was a stable and wealthy country and the offer of marriage was a good one for the teenage Emma. In late 1001, Ethelred moved his court to Kent to await Emma's coming. She arrived a few weeks later, early in 1002, and the couple married that spring at Canterbury. From the first, it was intended that Emma would be treated as a queen, and she was crowned soon after her wedding. There is also some evidence that Richard II was able to insist on Emma's children taking priority over Ethelred's elder sons in the succession, as Charles the Bald had done in the ninth century with Judith of Francia. According to the *Life of King Edward who rests at Westminster*, when Emma was pregnant with her first child, 'all the men of the country took an oath that if a man child should come forth as the fruit of her labour, they would await in him their lord and king who would rule over the whole race of the English'.

Ethelred was considerably older than Emma and had a number of adult children. The couple never became close and Emma bore her husband only three children in a marriage of fourteen years.

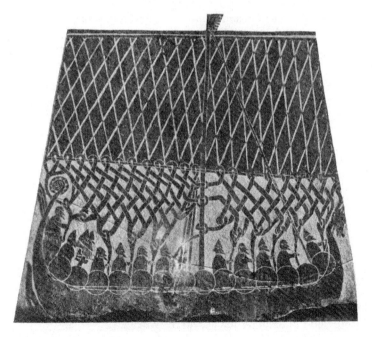

6. A Viking ship. Scene from a viking-age picture stone from Stenkyrka, Gotland, Sweden.

She was based at Winchester, and she owned property there, living within her own household. She is likely to have been responsible for the upbringing of her stepdaughters, and also for raising her own children: Edward, born in 1004 or 1005, Godgiva, born in around 1007, and Alfred, born by 1013. Emma rarely appears in sources for Ethelred's reign, and with the large age gap between herself and her husband, it would have been difficult for her to establish herself politically. She was also perceived in England to have Danish sympathies. In 1003, the *Anglo-Saxon Chronicle* recorded that the city of Exeter was destroyed by the treachery of Emma's French reeve, who helped the Vikings gain access to the city. Emma did witness some of Ethelred's charters, an honour that was not granted to his first wife, but in the main, she had little public role.

Ethelred's long reign was continually troubled by Viking raids. The biggest crisis came in 1013, when Sweyn Forkbeard, King of Denmark, landed in England, intent on conquest. Ethelred sent Emma to Normandy with her daughter, Godgiva. This was both for Emma's own protection and in order to allow her to appeal personally to her brother for aid. Emma was soon joined by her sons, Edward and Alfred and, shortly afterwards, by Ethelred himself, who had abandoned his kingdom to Sweyn. It was a relief, in February 1014, when, following the sudden death of Sweyn, the family were invited to return to England and Ethelred recovered his throne. It cannot have been an easy homecoming, and within a year, Ethelred's eldest son, Edmund, was in open rebellion against his father. Sweyn's son, Cnut, was also active in the kingdom. Ethelred died quietly in London on 23 April 1016, beset on all sides. Emma was with him.

Ethelred's death left Emma in a perilous position, whilst Cnut and Edmund fought over the country. She, at first, threw in her lot behind her stepson, Edmund, who was immediately proclaimed king. In spite of this, she was under no illusions about the danger that she faced, and soon after Ethelred's death, her children returned to Normandy. Emma remained in London and was horrified to find herself a prisoner of Cnut when he took possession of the city. Edmund's death late in 1016 left Cnut as king of the entire kingdom, and in mid-1017, he ordered Emma to be 'fetched' as his wife.

Emma provided her own account of her marriage to Cnut, and she sought to portray it as a marriage of equals. The *Encomium Emmae*

Reginae, a book commissioned by Emma herself, provides an account of events once Cnut was secure in his new kingdom:

> [He] lacked nothing except a most noble wife; such a one he ordered to be sought everywhere for him, in order to obtain her hand lawfully, when she was found, and to make her a partner of his rule, when she was won. Therefore journeys were undertaken through realms and cities and a royal bride was sought; but it was with difficulty that a worthy one was found, after being sought far and wide. This imperial bride was, in fact, found within the bounds of Gaul, and to be precise in the Norman area, a lady of the greatest nobility and wealth, but yet the most distinguished of the women of her time for delightful beauty and wisdom, inasmuch as she was a famous queen. In view of her distinguished qualities of this kind, she was much desired by the king, and especially because she derived her origin from a victorious people, who had appropriated for themselves part of Gaul in despite of the French and their prince. Why should I make a long story of this? Wooers were sent to the lady, royal gifts were sent, furthermore precatory messages were sent. But she refused ever to become the bride of Knutr, unless he would affirm to her by oath, that he would never set up the son of any wife other than herself to rule after him, if it happened that God should give her a son by him. For she had information that the king had had sons by some other woman; so she, wisely providing for her offspring, knew in her wisdom how to make arrangements in advance, which were to be to their advantage. Accordingly the king found what the lady said acceptable, and when the oath had been taken, the lady found the will of the king acceptable, and so, thanks be to God, Emma noblest of women, became the wife of the very mighty King Knutr.

This is how Emma wanted to present her marriage to the world. In reality, Emma never even left London, let alone returned to Normandy, and as Cnut's prisoner, she had little bargaining power. In spite of this, she was valuable to Cnut: marriage to the English queen helped cement his position as King of England. The marriage also neutralised Norman support for Emma's sons by Ethelred, and it is therefore not impossible that Cnut did agree to make any son born to Emma his heir in preference to his elder children by his first wife, Elgiva of Northampton. Elgiva was still living at the time of Cnut's second marriage to Emma, and unlike his predecessors as king, Cnut did not actually go to the trouble of repudiating his previous wife, instead, to both women's anger, maintaining them both as his wives throughout his reign.

Whilst Emma was not Cnut's only wife, she was his only queen, and in 1017, she shared his coronation. She quickly gained political power; aged around thirty at the time of their marriage, she was several years older than Cnut and was able to influence him. In Cnut's charters of 1018–19, Emma's name often appeared low down in the list of witnesses. After 1019, she tended to witness directly behind the King himself, demonstrating her rapidly increasing political power. A letter written by Wulfstan, Archbishop of York, addressed the couple jointly, highlights Emma's importance.

Emma bore Cnut two children, Harthacnut and Gunhild, between 1018 and 1020. Harthacnut, as the son of his legitimate wife, was Cnut's favourite child, and in 1023, he was sent to Denmark to be raised as the future king of his father's ancestral kingdom. Gunhild made an advantageous marriage to the eldest son of the Holy Roman Emperor. For Emma, her time as Cnut's queen was much more satisfying than her marriage to Ethelred, and she was given much more freedom to act. She and Cnut were often together and they jointly took part in conspicuous patronage, together presenting a shrine to Abingdon Abbey, for example. They are depicted as jointly presenting a cross to the New Minster, Winchester, on the frontispiece of the manuscript the *Liber Vitae*. In 1023, Emma was present at the most important church event of Cnut's reign, the reburial of St Alfheah at Canterbury. She and Cnut acted together throughout Cnut's reign in their attempts to establish a new Danish dynasty in England.

Emma also took political action without Cnut. She was always uncomfortably aware of the position of Cnut's other wife, Elgiva, and of her sons, Sweyn and Harold. When Harthacnut was sent to Denmark, Emma took steps to further secure his position. According to the chronicler Snorri Sturlsson, Harthacnut was placed under the guardianship of Earl Ulf before he sailed, and upon arrival in Denmark, Ulf produced a letter bearing Cnut's seal which stated that the King wished his son to become king of Denmark, to rule beside him. This was very far from Cnut's own intention, and according to the chronicler, 'it was Queen Emma who had been the originator of this plan, and it was she who had this letter written and sealed, having obtained the King's seal by trickery. But the King himself knew nothing about this'. Emma's plan was successful and she secured her son's election as king of Denmark during his father's lifetime, ensuring that Harthacnut's elder half-brothers were barred from asserting their own claims to the kingdom.

Emma was an active and visible figure throughout Cnut's reign and she was reluctant to relinquish power. She was at Winchester when Cnut died suddenly at Shaftesbury on 12 November 1035. She was entirely unprepared for the death of her still young and, apparently, healthy husband. Cnut's surviving son by Elgiva of Northampton, Harold Harefoot, was his only son present in England, and he took the initiative, rushing to Winchester and taking Cnut's treasure from Emma before attempting to secure the crown for himself. Emma immediately threw her support behind Harthacnut and a council at Oxford agreed that her son was Cnut's heir, offering the compromise that Harold should rule as regent until Harthacnut returned from Denmark. Emma set about trying to protect her own child's position, both by slandering Harold and his mother, Elgiva, and by buying support in England. Harthacnut, however, had no desire to leave his primary kingdom of Denmark and, by 1036, with Harold's position daily increasing in strength, Emma decided to take drastic action and recall one of her elder sons to England to take up the throne in their half-brother's stead.

A letter exists, summoning Edward and Alfred to England from Normandy. Emma herself, in the *Encomium Emmae Reginae*, maintained that this letter was a forgery produced by Harold in order to trick her sons into leaving the safety of Normandy. This is not impossible, but it is more likely that the summons came from Emma herself, desperate to maintain her position in England at any cost.

Emma, queen in name only, imparts motherly salutations on her sons, Edward and Alfred. Since we severally lament the death of our lord, the king, most dear sons, and since daily you are deprived of more and more of the kingdom, your inheritance, I wonder what plan you are adopting, since you are aware that the delay

arising from your procrastination is becoming from day to day a
support for the usurper of your rule. For he goes round hamlets
and cities ceaselessly, and makes the chief men his friends by gifts,
threats and prayers. But they would prefer that one of you should
rule over them, than that they should be held in the power of him
who now commands them. I entreat, therefore, that one of you
come to me speedily and privately, to receive from me wholesome
counsel, and to know in what manner this matter, which I desire,
must be brought to pass. Send back word what you are going to do
about these matters by the present messenger, whoever he may be.
Farewell, beloved ones of my heart.

This was the first direct contact that Emma had had with her elder
sons for twenty years. Whilst Emma requested that only one of her
sons come to her, Edward and Alfred, who had spent their entire
adulthoods in exile and as the penniless guests of their family in
Normandy, were both determined to make an attempt on the English
throne.

Edward set out directly from Normandy and arrived safely at
Winchester for what must have been a difficult reunion with the
mother that he had not seen for so long. Alfred, who, as the younger
son, did not receive the financial backing of his Norman kin, took
a more circuitous route, travelling first to Flanders before sailing
for England. Upon arrival, he was intercepted by the powerful Earl
Godwin, who had been Emma's strongest supporter in the days
following Cnut's death. Godwin, who was well aware of Harold's
increasing prominence in Harthacnut's absence, entertained the
young prince at his house at Guildford before treacherously handing
him over to Harold's men. Alfred was taken as prisoner to Ely where,
on Harold's orders, his eyes were put out. He was then delivered to
the monastery, dying soon afterwards. On hearing of his brother's
murder, Edward returned to Normandy, leaving Emma alone in
Winchester. Alfred's death and Edward's departure signalled the final
blow for Emma's hopes, and in 1037, Harold seized the crown, exiling
Emma to Flanders.

The fact that Emma chose to go to Flanders rather than Normandy
suggests that relations between herself and her eldest son, Edward,
and her Norman kin, were poor and that they objected to her marriage

to Cnut and support for Harthacnut. Emma was made welcome in Flanders, although it was, perhaps, the most difficult time of her life. Whilst in exile, she received news that Gunhild, the only one of her five children that she had raised to adulthood herself, had died in Germany after only three years of marriage. Following her exile, Emma turned once again towards Harthacnut for support, and finally, in 1040, he sailed from Denmark, bringing a large fleet to Flanders.

Emma was overjoyed to see her youngest son, and the pair planned to mount an invasion of England. Whilst they were still in Flanders, word arrived that Harold had died and that Harthacnut had been proclaimed king. Harthacnut and Emma sailed at once, and Emma was able to establish herself as the power behind the throne, always witnessing immediately after the King in charters. Emma and Harthacnut also jointly issued a writ granting land at Hemingford to Ramsey Abbey, again demonstrating Emma's political prominence. During the reign, Emma commissioned what is, essentially, her autobiography, the *Encomium Emmae Reginae,* which she used to justify her actions throughout her lifetime. Emma became increasingly concerned about her youngest son's health, and loath to find herself alone and unprotected as she had been in 1035, in 1041, she persuaded Harthacnut to recall Edward to England to share in his rule. The *Encomium* presents this as a triumph of Emma's enlightened policy and ended with this comment:

> Obeying his brother's command, he [Edward] was conveyed to England, and the mother and both sons, having no disagreement between them, enjoy the ready amenities of the kingdom. Here there is loyalty among the sharers of rule, here the bond of motherly and brotherly love is of strength indestructible.

When Harthacnut died suddenly in 1042, Edward was proclaimed king in his place, just as Emma had hoped.

Edward the Confessor, who had spent most of his life waiting to become king of England, was in no mood to share his throne with his mother. Soon after his coronation in 1042, he deprived her of all her lands and treasures. According to William of Malmesbury, this was something that Edward had been planning for some time, and his 'royal spirit was woken to hostility against his mother by the memory of past events. She had not been very generous in her treatment of her son, while he was passing through his teenage years, and so he ordered all his mother's effects to be ransacked, down to the last pennyworth'. Emma was furious and, whilst she had not been entirely loyal to her son for much of his life, she had at least ensured his safety by arranging for him to leave for Normandy in 1016. She had also been instrumental in securing Harthacnut's recognition of him as his successor. Emma was powerless to act against her son, and Edward returned to her only those possessions that were sufficient to meet her needs. After 1043 Emma virtually disappears from the sources, and it is likely that she returned, defeated, to Winchester. Her last public appearance was at London in 1045, when she witnessed a charter granting privileges to Westminster Abbey. Emma died at Winchester on 14 March 1052 and was buried beside Cnut in the Old Minster there.

Emma of Normandy spent over fifty years as queen of England and is the most famous of all the Anglo-Saxon queens. Another woman who briefly became queen of England in between Emma's two marriages led an equally turbulent life, but unlike her famous contemporary, Aldgyth is barely remembered at all.

ALDGYTH has been described as a lady of 'distinguished lineage', although details of her parentage do not survive. Her family were based in the north Midlands and she was a kinswoman of Cnut's first wife, Elgiva of Northampton. Whilst she was still young, Aldgyth married Sigeferth, a Danish nobleman from the Five Boroughs. By 1015, King Ethelred, whose kingdom had been subject to Viking attacks for many years, was not feeling very favourable towards Scandinavians. William of Malmesbury states that, in 1015, he decided to take action against Aldgyth's powerful husband:

A grand council of Danes and English was assembled at Oxford, where the king commanded two of the noblest Danes, Sigeferd and Morcard, accused of treachery to him by the impeachment of the traitor Edric [Eadric Streona], to be put to death. He had lured them, when deceived by his soothing expressions, into a chamber, and murdered them, when drunk to excess, by his attendants prepared for the purpose. The cause of their murder was said to be, his unjustifiable desire for their property. Their dependents, attempting to revenge the death of their lords by arms, were defeated, and driven into the tower of St Frideswide's church, where as they could not be dislodged, they were consumed by fire.

Aldgyth was present at the council, and she must have been terrified as events unfolded. Eadric Streona, her husband's murderer, was a favourite of the King, and there was nothing that any of Sigeferth's followers could do to avenge their lord. In order to obtain Sigeferth's lands, it was necessary to neutralise Aldgyth, and Ethelred had her taken by armed guard to Malmesbury Abbey, where she was to be imprisoned for life.

Sigeferth and Aldgyth were childless, and Aldgyth, as Sigeferth's widow, had a strong claim to both his property and to the loyalty of the people of his estates. She was also a famous beauty, and Edmund, the eldest son of Ethelred, who was already estranged from his father, resolved to visit her secretly. According to William of Malmesbury, Edmund immediately fell in love with Aldgyth and the couple married without the consent of his father. For Aldgyth, the marriage was an opportunity to regain all that she had lost, and Edmund, 'at the instigation of his wife, he asked of his father the possessions of Sigeferth, which were of large extent among the Northumbrians, but he could not obtain them; by his own exertions, however, he procured them at last, the inhabitants of that province willingly submitting to his power'. By taking Sigeferth's lands for himself, Edmund showed himself in open rebellion to his father for the first time.

Aldgyth's connections were very important to Edmund in establishing his position in 1015. It is unlikely that the couple spent much time together following their wedding, and in the summer of 1015, Cnut, the son of Sweyn Forkbeard who had previously deposed Ethelred, landed in England and carried out raids in Kent and Wessex. Edmund made attempts to halt Cnut's progress, moving south from the Five Boroughs, leaving Aldgyth behind. With the death of Ethelred on 23 August 1016, the citizens of London chose Edmund as their king. He was immediately locked in a fight for his kingdom against Cnut and, whilst initially successful, he was defeated by the Danes at the Battle of Ashingdon. This defeat prompted Edmund to come to terms with Cnut, and at a meeting, it was decided that they would divide the kingdom amongst themselves, with Edmund taking Wessex and Cnut the rest of the country.

Aldgyth's whereabouts are not known during Edmund's brief reign, although it is likely that, following the agreement with Cnut, she took up residence in Wessex. She bore Edmund two sons during their brief marriage, Edward and Edmund, and they may have been twins. Edmund II's reign was very brief, and he died on 30 November 1016. It is possible that he died from wounds inflicted during his defeat at Ashingdon, but murder cannot be ruled out. William of Malmesbury, writing in the twelfth century, believed that the King was killed by Eadric Streona, the murderer of Aldgyth's first husband, on the orders of Cnut. If this is the case, then it appears that Edmund suffered a particularly horrifying death because, as he sat to answer a call of nature, assassins hidden in the privy 'drove an iron hook into his posteriors'.

With Edmund's death, Cnut became king of the whole of England. It is unclear what became of Aldgyth. Her two sons were considered a major threat by Cnut and, unwilling to be seen to be a murderer of infants, he sent them to the King of Sweden with secret instructions that they be put to death. The Swedish king took pity on them and spared their lives, allowing the boys to ultimately take refuge in Hungary. Aldgyth may perhaps have accompanied them. The children were taken in by the King of Hungary and raised as princes, with Edward marrying Agatha, sister of the Queen of Hungary. Whilst Aldgyth disappears from history, her son, Edward the Exile, remained a prominent figure, and during the reign of his childless uncle, Edward the Confessor, he was recalled with his family to England. Edward the Exile died soon afterwards, but following the Norman Conquest in 1066, his children found their way to Scotland, where the eldest daughter, Margaret, married the King of Scots. Their daughter, Matilda, married Henry I of England, and it was through this marriage that Aldgyth became an ancestress of future monarchs of England.

Aldgyth was not the only member of her family to become queen, and around the time of her marriage to Edmund II, her kinswoman, ELGIVA OF NORTHAMPTON, married his greatest rival, Cnut. Elgiva was born into a prominent and powerful Midlands family. He uncle, Wulfric Spot, was the founder of Burton Abbey. Her father was Ealdorman Elfhelm of southern Northumbria and her mother was a noblewoman called Wulfrun. Like their kinswoman, Aldgyth, Elgiva's family had Danish sympathies, and in 1006, when Elgiva was probably approaching twenty, her father was murdered and her two brothers blinded by Ethelred's great favourite, Eadric Streona, on the orders of the King.

Elgiva and Cnut, the son of the Danish king, Sweyn Forkbeard, began a relationship in around 1013. Sweyn invaded England in 1013, and he left his son at Gainsborough to guard the Danish fleet, whilst he attacked Mercia. For Cnut, a marriage with Elgiva, the daughter of a prominent local family, made political sense, and it provided him with kinship links across the local area. Elgiva and her surviving family, who had no reason to love King Ethelred, were happy to throw in their lot with the invaders. Elgiva bore Cnut two sons, and possibly also a daughter, and it is likely that she and her children remained in the Midlands during the events of 1016 as Cnut claimed the throne of England. Elgiva and Cnut's marriage was not sanctioned by the church, and she is often referred to as only the King's mistress. However, it is clear that the couple were committed to their relationship. Elgiva's eldest son was named Sweyn, after his paternal grandfather, and her younger son was named Harold, after Cnut's grandfather. The use of family names was important to Cnut, and his third son, by Emma, was left with only the name of Cnut's great-grandfather, Harthacnut.

There is no record of Elgiva's whereabouts between 1016 and 1029. She cannot have been happy to hear of Cnut's second marriage to Emma of Normandy. In spite of this, she was not actually repudiated by Cnut and his marital relations can be seen as something approaching polygamy. It is possible that Cnut brought Elgiva south following his accession, and a daughter of Cnut is supposedly buried in the church at Bosham in Sussex, not far from the royal court at Winchester. This daughter would have been Elgiva's, and it is not impossible that she was based at Bosham.

Cnut decided to make Sweyn, his eldest son by Elgiva, his successor in Norway, a recently conquered kingdom, and he sent them there to act as his regents in 1029. It was very unusual for a tenth-century woman to receive an official appointment as regent, and Elgiva's role is a demonstration of Cnut's confidence in her. Unfortunately,

Elgiva's regency was not a success, and in Norway, 'Ælfgifu's time' is remembered as an age of wretchedness and oppression. This was not entirely Elgiva's fault, as her rule coincided with a period of poor harvests and famine, though she is remembered in Norway for her harsh and autocratic behaviour. She and Sweyn arrived with a large force of Danes and used them to ensure obedience to their rule. The chronicler Snorri Sturlsson commented that Elgiva 'instituted new laws in the land concerning many matters. They were patterned after Danish laws, but some were much harsher'. Elgiva's laws were bitterly resented, and they caused an upsurge of nationalism in Norway.

The previous king of Norway, Olaf Tryggvason, had begun to attract a cult by the time that Elgiva and Sweyn arrived in Norway. Elgiva was well aware of the dangers of this cult, and she sought to dispel it, attending the ceremonial exhumation of Olaf's body in 1031 to determine whether or not the deceased king was indeed a saint. According to Snorri Sturlsson, the coffin appeared brand new and the body smelled fresh:

Then the bishop bared the countenance of the king and its aspect had changed in nowise, and there was a ruddiness on his cheeks as though he had only recently fallen asleep. Those who had seen King Olaf when he fell now saw a great change in that his hair and nails had grown almost as much as they would have if he had been alive all the time since he fell. Then King Svein [Elgiva's son] approached to view the body of King Olaf, and so did all the chieftains present.

Then Alfifa [Elgiva] said, 'mighty little do bodies decompose when buried in sand. It would not be the case if he had lain in earth.' Then the bishop took a pair of sheers and cut the king's hair and trimmed his whiskers. He had had long whiskers as people in those days used to have.

Then the bishop said to the king and Alfifa, 'now the hair and the beard of the king are as they were when he died, but it had grown as much as you can see here cut off.'

Then Alfifa replied, 'that hair would seem to me a holy relic only if fire does not burn it. We have often seen wholly preserved and undamaged hair of persons who have lain in the ground longer than this man has.'

Therefore the bishop had fire put in a censer, blessed it, and put incense on it. Then he laid King Olaf's hair into the fire, and when all the incense was burned, the bishop took the hair out of the fire, and it was not burned. The bishop had the king and the other chieftains view it. Thereupon Alfifa bade him lay the hair into fire that had not been blessed. Then Einar Thambarshelfir bade her be silent and used hard language against her. So then, by the bishop's pronouncement, the consent of the king, and the judgment of all the people, King Olaf was declared a true saint.

The recognition of Olaf as a saint was the beginning of the end of Elgiva's rule in Norway. In 1032, Olaf's son entered Norway with an army to challenge Sweyn. When Sweyn and Elgiva attempted to raise an army, many of the leading men of the country refused to join, and it was only with difficulty that they defeated their rival. By winter 1033, Elgiva and Sweyn found it impossible to remain in Thrandheim, the centre of their administration. For nearly two years, they clung on to power in southern Norway, but in 1035, they were finally forced to flee to Denmark with Olaf's son, Magnus, being proclaimed king in Sweyn's place.

Soon after Elgiva arrived in Denmark, she heard that Cnut had died in England. This loss was shortly followed by the death of Sweyn, and Elgiva returned to England to support her surviving son, Harold. Emma's son, Harthacnut, was designated as Cnut's successor but Harold had designs on the crown. Although it was agreed that Harold would rule England as regent for Harthacnut until he could return from Denmark, Elgiva was desperate for her son to win the crown, and she began working on his behalf soon after her arrival in England. She held feasts and gave gifts to the leading men of England in return for their support of Harold's candidacy. Her rival, Emma of Normandy, was working equally hard in support of her own son, and it is likely that the rumours spread about Elgiva and her sons stemmed from Emma. The later chronicler Florence of Worcester, for example, had heard that Elgiva was a concubine of Cnut's and that 'this same Ælfgifu wished to have a son by the king, but could not, and therefore ordered to be brought to her the newly born infant of a certain priest, and made the king fully believe that she had just born him a son'. This story refers to the birth of Sweyn and Harold was accused of being the son of a shoemaker. The stories were slander, but Elgiva's efforts paid off, and in 1037, Harold was declared King of England.

Harold I's brief reign is poorly recorded, and he is an obscure figure. It is possible that Elgiva, who already had experience of ruling through one son, was the power behind the throne and, in the Will of Bishop Elfric of Elmham, Harold was referred to as 'my royal lord' and Elgiva as 'my lady', suggesting some sort of joint rule. Elgiva's time as queen mother was short-lived, as Harold died on 17 March 1040. Harthacnut and Emma sailed for England to claim the throne, and Elgiva made herself scarce. England would not have been a comfortable place under the rule of the son of her rival, and it is possible that she ended her life in Denmark.

Like Elgiva of Northampton, many of the eleventh-century English queens were Anglo-Danish in sympathy or origin, and the last powerful Anglo-Saxon queen, EDITH GODWIN (c. 1020s–1075) was no exception. She was one of the nine children of the powerful Earl Godwin, a self-made man who appears to have been a descendant of Ethelred I and who came from minor Sussex nobility. Through both intelligence and good fortune, he rose to power under Cnut, becoming a leading advisor to the King and his sons. By 1018, he had been made an earl and been given Cnut's sister-in-law, Gytha, as his wife. Edith was the couple's eldest daughter. The date of her birth is nowhere recorded, but it must have been between 1020 and 1030.

Edith was educated at the royal nunnery at Wilton, which provided her with a privileged lifestyle and a first-class education. At Wilton, Edith was educated with the daughters of other noble houses and prepared for a prestigious marriage rather than the life of a nun. She is described in contemporary sources as having been skilled in Latin prose and verse and fluent in French, Irish and Danish. William of Malmesbury described Edith as 'a woman whose bosom was the school of every liberal art, though little skilled in earthly matters: on seeing her, if you were amazed at her erudition, you must admire also the purity of her mind, and the beauty of her person'.

When Edward the Confessor succeeded his half-brother, Harthacnut, as King of England in 1042, he was around forty years old and, having spent most of his life in Normandy, was an unknown quantity in England. Whilst for Edward, Earl Godwin would always be the murderer of his brother, Prince Alfred, he was forced to rely on him as the leading man in the kingdom, and in 1045, Godwin persuaded the King to marry Edith. That this was not the King's free choice would later become apparent, but in 1045, Godwin and his sons were at the height of their power, with Edith's two eldest brothers, Sweyn and Harold, receiving earldoms in 1043 or 1044. There was little Edward could do but take Edith as his wife. William of Malmesbury claimed that Edward always kept Edith at a distance and refused to consummate the marriage, due to his hatred of her family. Edith also claimed that her marriage was not consummated in order to portray Edward as a saint and, also, to explain away her childlessness. It seems unlikely that Edward, who, as the last male member of his immediate family, badly needed an heir, would have ignored this consideration simply out of a dislike of his wife, and it is apparent that one party was simply infertile. The fact that Edward had no recorded illegitimate children, unusual for a medieval king, also points towards this conclusion.

Edith found Edward's court uncultured compared to her comfortable life at Wilton. In the *Life of King Edward who rests at Westminster*, which she commissioned, it was claimed that Edward spent most of his time hunting. Edith's husband was a disappointing specimen, and she took steps to make him appear more kingly:

Moreover, it was quietly, and only for the occasion – in any case, it should be distinctly said with no mental pleasure – that he displayed the pomp of royal finery in which the queen obligingly arrayed him. And he would not have cared at all if it had been provided at far less cost. He was, however, grateful for the queen's solicitude in these matters, and with a certain kindness of feeling used to remark on her zeal most appreciatively to his intimates.

Edith loved finery and selected expensive clothes for Edward. She also made the royal palaces appear more regal, ordering a throne draped in gold fabrics and covering the floors in Spanish carpets.

In the *Life*, Edith was determined that she should be presented as a queen and her chronicler obliged:

[Edward] stooped with great mercy to the poor and infirm, and fully maintained many of these not only daily in his royal court but also at many places in his kingdom. Finally, his royal consort did not restrain him in these good works in which he prepared to lead the way, but rather urged speedier progress, and often enough seemed even to lead the way herself. For while he would give now and then, she was prodigal, but aimed her bounty to such good purpose as to consider the highest honour of the king as well. Although by custom and law a royal throne was always prepared for her at the king's side, she preferred, except in church and at the royal table, to sit at his feet, unless perchance he should reach out his hand to her, or with a gesture of the hand invite or command her to sit next to him. She was, I say, a woman to be placed before all noble matrons or persons of royal and imperial rank as a model of virtue and integrity for maintaining both the practices of the Christian religion and worldly dignity.

Although the *Life*, on its surface, is intended to glorify the memory of Edward the Confessor, in reality, Edith wanted to safeguard her own reputation. As queen, she had little political power and was only kept in place by the position of her kin, her childlessness making her particularly vulnerable.

Edith's fortunes during Edward's reign were closely linked to those of her family. In 1051, Edward finally felt strong enough to depose the Godwins. He publicly accused Godwin of the murder of his brother, Alfred. The crime had been preying on Edward's mind since his accession, and whilst Edith, in the *Life*, sought to lay the blame for Edward's suspicions on the Norman influence at court, it was well known that Godwin was involved in Alfred's murder. With the King and the nobility against him, Godwin fled to Bosham in Sussex and, taking his wife and younger children with him, sailed to exile in Flanders. Godwin's second son, Harold, took ship to Ireland.

With the removal of the Godwins, Edward was free to act against Edith. In the *Life*, Edith claimed that Edward was persuaded by his Norman Archbishop of Canterbury, Robert of Jumierges, to separate from her:

For, in order that not a single member of the earl's family should remain at the king's side to provide for the country's well-being, he used every device to secure that even the queen herself, the earl's daughter, should be separated from the king, against the law of the Christian religion. This plan the king, although not opposing, yet did mitigate, giving out as reason for the separation this honourable pretext, that she was to await the subsidence of the storms over the kingdom in the monastery of Wilton, where she had been brought up. And so, with royal honours and an imperial retinue, but with grief at heart, she was brought to the walls of Wilton convent, where for almost a year in prayers and tears she awaited the day of salvation. Such grief more deeply moved and wounded the crowd of courtiers than even the departure of the earl himself. And no wonder! For she was in all the royal counsels, as we might say, a governess and the fount of all goodness, strongly preferring the king's interests to power and riches.

Edith's account of her exile from court is very far from the truth, and it is clear that Edward wanted to divorce her. Florence of Worcester claims that Edith was repudiated due to Edward's hatred of her father. Far from being sent with queenly honours to the comfortable Wilton Abbey, she was unceremoniously evicted from the palace and sent on foot with only one female attendant to Wherwell Abbey, where she was placed in the custody of the abbess, Edward's half-sister. Edward confiscated Edith's property and had no intention of ever taking her back. It is no wonder that Edith spent a whole year weeping.

In spite of his hopes of divorcing Edith and making a new marriage, Edward was forced to take her back the following year when Godwin returned to England with an army. This was a triumph for Edith, although relations must have been frosty between her and Edward following her return. From the mid 1050s, Edith was in a much stronger position at court, and she witnessed fourteen of the twenty-two charters surviving from the period. In the charters, Edith always witnessed immediately after Edward and always as queen. Even the sudden death of her father at Easter 1053 did not alter her position, and her brothers, Harold and Tostig, filled their father's place as Edward's chief advisors.

With the exception of providing an heir, Edith fulfilled most of the duties expected of her as queen. She was conspicuously pious and was involved in good works, rebuilding Wilton Abbey in stone towards the end of the reign, an action intended to complement Edward's building of Westminster Abbey. In spite of her good works, Edith's piety generally appears to have been coupled with her own self-promotion, and in the *Life*, she had it recorded that Wilton was more prudently and modestly planned than Westminster, ensuring that it was finished more quickly. Edith also became more political and had strong links to her brothers, who virtually ruled England during the 1050s and 1060s. Tostig was Edith's favourite brother and it was rumoured that in 1064, at his request, she arranged the murder of Gospatric, a rival to Tostig's position as Earl of Northumbria.

Edith was present at Edward's death on 4 January 1066, and she later claimed that he commended her and the kingdom to her brother Harold's protection. She was careful never to say that the King named her brother as his heir. The chronicler William of Poitiers later claimed that Edith, 'a woman of manly wisdom, loving good and eschewing evil, wished to see the English governed by William [of Normandy] whom her husband, King Edward, adopted as a son and made his heir'. This was the Norman viewpoint, attempting to justify Edward's cousin, William, Duke of Normandy, as his legitimate heir. The fact was that Edward the Confessor had no certain heir. His nephew, and closest male relative, Edward the Exile, had died some years before, leaving a young son, Edgar Ætheling, who was far too young to have built up his own party. In 1066, Edith's own brother, Harold, claimed the throne. In October 1066, William of Normandy defeated and killed Harold at the Battle of Hastings, and it was William who ended the year as King of England. For William, it was of paramount importance to present himself as Edward's legitimate heir, and he came to Edith at Winchester soon after his victory. Edith was determined to maintain her position as queen, and she submitted to William. This had tangible benefits as, in 1066, according to the Domesday Book, she was the richest woman in England. Edith retained most of her lands following the Conquest.

Edith lived at Winchester after the Conquest and played no part in her family's continued struggle against Norman rule. She was welcome at court and, in March 1071, attended the consecration of the Bishop of Durham. She enjoyed a comfortable retirement, dying at Winchester on 19 December 1075. In accordance with his desire to honour the widow of the Confessor, William arranged for her to be buried with great ceremony beside her husband in Westminster Abbey.

Edith Godwin was the last prominent Anglo-Saxon queen, and the last to retain her status in England, but she was not quite the last Anglo-Saxon queen. The first of Edith's two successors as queen was her sister-in-law and namesake, Edith Swanneck.

EDITH SWANNECK was the first wife of Harold II, the last Anglo-Saxon king of England. She is often called Harold's mistress rather than his wife, and the relationship was not solemnised in church. In spite of this, as with many earlier Anglo-Saxon queens, she can be considered Harold's spouse rather than simply a concubine.

Few details of Edith Swanneck's parentage or background survive, but she was apparently a great heiress, and according to the Domesday Book, in 1066, she held nearly 280 hides of land in eastern England worth over £520 a year. Edith's mother was a woman named Wulfgyth, who made her Will in 1046, but no other details of her family survive. It is likely that Harold and Edith formed a relationship around 1044, when Harold was created Earl of East Anglia by Edward the Confessor. A primary consideration for Harold would have been to secure good local connections. Edith's beauty also recommended her to him, and her nickname 'Swanneck' implies great beauty. She was described in the Domesday Book as 'Edith the Fair' and 'Edith the Beautiful', further testaments to her good looks.

Edith and Harold were married for over twenty years and had six surviving children: Godwin, Edmund, Magnus, Wulf, Gytha and Gunhild. The names show a marked Scandinavian bias, and it is possible that Edith, like Harold, came from an Anglo-Scandinavian family. Edith was based in Canterbury during her marriage and, according to the Domesday Book, possessed four dwellings there. An unbaptised infant of Edith and Harold's was also buried in the cathedral there, close to the tomb of St Dunstan.

Harold and Edith were probably still married in January 1066 when he became king. Shortly afterwards, Harold married Edith of Mercia, repudiating Edith Swanneck. Edith Swanneck sought sanctuary at Waltham Abbey during the turbulent days of her ex-husband's reign, when he was faced first with an invasion by Harold Hardrada, King of Norway, and then by William of Normandy. On 14 October 1066, Harold was killed at the Battle of Hastings and a number of sources attest that it was Edith Swanneck who was summoned to the battlefield in order to identify the King's body. This must have been a deeply traumatic task for Edith, but she did as she was asked, identifying Harold's mutilated corpse through certain 'intimate' marks on his body. Once he had been identified, he received an honourable burial in Waltham Abbey.

Following the Battle of Hastings, Edith Swanneck disappears from the records. She was dispossessed of her lands and most of her children fled abroad. There was very little left for Edith in England, and it is possible that she accompanied her sons to Ireland. Alternatively, she may have joined Harold's mother, Gytha, at Exeter, and assisted the older woman in rebellion against the new Norman rule. Edith's children led adventurous lives across Europe. Her sons, Godwin, Edmund and Magnus, fled to Dermot, King of Ireland. With the Irish king's support, they launched unsuccessful raids on Somerset in 1068 and 1069 before disappearing from history. Edith's final son, Wulf, is recorded as a hostage in Normandy on the death of William I, and it is likely that he was captured soon after the Conquest. Edith's daughter, Gytha, came under the protection of her cousin Sweyn, King of Denmark, and married Vladimir II, Grand Prince of Kiev. Edith's second daughter, Gunhild, was left behind at Wilton Abbey when her family fled and forced to become a reluctant nun. In 1093, she was abducted by the Norman Count Alan the Red, marrying him shortly afterwards. Count Alan had been granted a number of Edith's estates after the Conquest, and it is possible that he sought marriage to her daughter in order to impose his authority there. The date of Edith Swanneck's death is not known. A similar obscurity shrouds the later life of the woman who supplanted her as Harold's wife.

EDITH OF MERCIA was queen of England for only a few brief months and left little mark on the kingdom. She was the daughter of the powerful Earl Elfgar of Mercia. Her grandmother was the famous Lady Godiva, who reputedly rode naked through the streets of Coventry. Little is known of Edith's early life, but it must have been turbulent. Her father was exiled in 1055. He returned soon afterwards with an army and raided Hereford before being reinstated to his earldom. In 1058, Elfgar was expelled again. On this occasion, Edith travelled with him, and during the exile, she was married to her father's ally, Gruffydd, King of Wales. This was a political match, and following its celebration, Elfgar returned once again to his earldom with Welsh help. He died around 1062.

Edith bore her husband a daughter, Nest, but no other children are recorded. Gruffydd was considered a major threat to England, and Edward the Confessor was determined to destroy him. In 1063, the brothers, Harold and Tostig Godwin, invaded Wales. They won a major victory over the Welsh, and Gruffydd was killed by his own men on 23 August 1063. Harold had his head brought to him and then sent to King Edward. At some point following Gruffydd's death, Edith returned to her family, bringing her daughter with her.

Edith's brother, Morcar, succeeded their father as Earl of Mercia, and following a rebellion in Northumbria, her second brother, Edwin, became earl there. Edith's brothers were powerful men, and their support was vital for Harold when he became king following the death of Edward the Confessor. Within weeks of his accession, he had married Edith in order to cement the political alliance. It is likely that Edwin and Morcar insisted on a full church marriage ceremony and a consecration for Edith as queen, and she was always referred to as Harold's queen during his reign.

Edith was in London at the time of the Battle of Hastings, and according to Florence of Worcester, as soon as they heard of Harold's death, Edwin and Morcar withdrew from the battle and travelled to London to find her. They hurried her to the safety of Chester, in the heart of Mercia, and it was there, shortly afterwards, that she bore a son named Harold. Edith spent some years at Chester, and during this time, her brothers continued to oppose William the Conqueror, first proclaiming Edward the Confessor's great-nephew, Edgar Ætheling, as king before abandoning him. It is likely that they hoped to set young Harold up as king, but in 1072, Edwin was killed by his own men and Morcar was captured by William.

In 1069–70, William occupied Chester and Edith fled. She left her daughter, Nest, behind, and the Welsh princess married Osbern, son of Richard FitzScrob, a French nobleman living in the Welsh Marches. In 1098, young Harold reappears in the sources as a follower of King Magnus Olafsson of Norway, who accompanied him on expeditions to the Orkneys and Mervanian Isles. Nothing more is known of Edith's son and he never attempted to reclaim his father's throne.

Edith must have spent the remainder of her life in exile. It is possible that she ended her days as a pilgrim in southern France. Sources at the Abbey of La-Chaise-Dieu in the Auvergne region of France record that an English 'Queen Edith' was cured of leprosy by the abbot there. In gratitude, this queen paid for the construction of the monastic dormitory and was annually commemorated by the monks. She was buried there in the 1070s or 1080s. This Queen Edith may have been Edith of Mercia, and it is possible that she was on a pilgrimage to Rome when she stopped at the abbey by chance. Alternatively, the fame of the abbey's founder, St Robert of Turland, or the growing monastic community there may have attracted her in her search for a cure. If the mysterious woman was indeed Edith, it demonstrates that she was able to retain her wealth following her flight from Chester and was free to travel as an independent woman.

Edith of Mercia was the last of the Anglo-Saxon queens of England, and like so many before her, she is a shadowy figure who made little impact on the records of her time. In spite of this, all the Anglo-Saxon queens helped to contribute to the development of the role of the queen in England, and their successors, the Norman queens, actively sought to maintain this. Just as William the Conqueror wanted to portray himself as the legitimate heir to the Anglo-Saxon kings, so his wife and her immediate successors wanted to show that they were the legitimate inheritors of English queenship.

3

The Norman Queens

William, Duke of Normandy, claimed the English crown through an English queen. According to the chronicler William of Poitiers, 'if it be asked what was his hereditary title, let it be answered that a close kinship existed between King Richard and the son of Duke Robert whose paternal aunt, Emma, was the sister of Duke Richard II, the daughter of Duke Richard I and the mother of King Edward himself'. Queens were important to the Norman kings, and the Norman period in England saw a number of prominent queens, culminating in the rivalry between the cousins Matilda of Boulogne and the Empress Matilda. The office of queenship remained remarkably stable, and Matilda of Flanders, the wife of William I, made a conscious effort to present herself as an English queen, in order to emphasise the continuity of her dynasty from what had gone before.

MATILDA OF FLANDERS (c. 1031–83) was the daughter of Baldwin V, Count of Flanders, and his wife, Adela, daughter of Robert II, King of France. On her father's side, she was descended from Alfred the Great. Little evidence survives of Matilda's upbringing, but the chronicler Orderic Vitalis claimed that 'the queen herself was endowed with fairness of face, noble birth, learning, beauty of character, and – what is and ever will be more worthy of praise – strong faith and fervent love of Christ'. William of Malmesbury also noted that Matilda 'was a model of wisdom and exemplar of modesty without parallel in our time'. This suggests that Matilda was educated, and it is likely that she could read and write. Religion was important to her, and she distributed alms to the poor every day, as well as giving extravagant gifts to the church throughout her lifetime.

Matilda had a number of suitors. One story claims that, during her youth, she fell in love with a young English nobleman who had been sent as an ambassador to her father's court. Matilda's passion was unrequited and the young nobleman refused to marry her, returning to England in something of a hurry. Matilda was furious at this rejection and, when she became queen of England years later, used her influence to have her former love imprisoned for life and confiscated his property. This story is almost certainly fanciful and, in reality, most unmarried young noblemen in Europe would have been pleased to marry Matilda.

Matilda's family connections recommended her to William, Duke of Normandy. William was born a few years before Matilda in around 1027. His childhood could not have been more different from the stable upbringing that Matilda received in Flanders because, whilst he was the only acknowledged son of Duke Robert I of Normandy, his mother was merely the duke's mistress, Herleva, the daughter of a tanner of Falaise. William succeeded his father as Duke of Normandy at the age of seven. As a result of his illegitimate birth, he wanted to marry a woman of good lineage, and as early as 1047, his attention focused on Matilda, who he tried to abduct. In around 1049, William made a more formal proposal and Count Baldwin, who, by then, looked more favourably on the young Duke, agreed to the match.

The marriage occurred in around 1050, when Matilda was nineteen and William twenty-three. At first glance, the couple must have appeared somewhat ill-matched, as William was a tall man, approaching six feet in height, and Matilda was unusually short even for the eleventh century, never reaching five feet. In spite of this, the couple fell in love. Matilda's near-contemporary Orderic Vitalis later referred to her as William's 'beloved wife'. Another near-contemporary, William of Malmesbury, wrote that William was devoted to her and that 'he had many children by Matilda, and she, with her willingness to please her husband and her ability to bear him children, kindled a passionate attachment in the spirit of that great man'.

Whilst the marriage brought personal happiness to the couple and, also, provided the young Duke with a boost to his international prestige, their union was not without controversy. When the couple's betrothal had first been announced in 1049, Pope Leo IX called a Church council at Reims in which he expressly forbade the marriage.

The Pope's opposition was on the grounds of consanguinity, as the couple were both descended from Rollo, the first Duke of Normandy. A much closer link had also been provided by the betrothal of Matilda's mother, Adela, to William's uncle, Richard III, Duke of Normandy, which had ended with his death in 1027. This was not an actual blood tie between Matilda and William, but it was enough, from the Church's point of view, for them to be considered to be first cousins. In any event, Pope Leo IX was hostile to William and had no desire to see him make an advantageous marriage.

Both Matilda's father and William were prepared to ignore the hostility of the Church, and the marriage occurred without the required dispensation. This was a very dangerous position for the couple to be in, and William was forced to depose his uncle, Mauger, Archbishop of Rouen, for his opposition to the marriage, as William of Malmesbury explains:

> Some say there was a secret reason for this deposition: Matilda, who William had taken as his wife, was a near relation, and in his zeal for the Christian faith Mauger had found it intolerable that two blood-relations should share the marriage-bed and had aimed the weapons of *excommuni* against his nephew and his nephew's consort.

The threat of excommunication was a terrifying one and would have meant that the couple would no longer be able to participate in the services of the Church. They were forced to wait until the death of Leo IX in 1059 to make their union official, receiving a retrospective dispensation from the new pope, Nicholas II, who was anxious to be on friendlier terms with William. In order to atone for marrying without the Church's sanction, the couple built two religious houses in Caen: William, the monastery of St Stephen's for monks, and Matilda, Holy Trinity for nuns.

It must have been a great relief to Matilda to have her marriage recognised by the Church, as, by 1059, she had already borne William several children. The exact number of children born to the couple is not recorded. Orderic Vitalis believed that it was eight: Robert, Richard, William, Henry, Adelaide, Constance, Cecilia and Adela. Robert was the eldest son and always Matilda's favourite. William's own favourite was their second son, Richard, who, to his parents' grief, was killed in a hunting accident in the New Forest in 1075. The third and fourth sons, William and Henry, would become kings of England. Of their daughters, Constance, who was named after Matilda's grandmother, Constance of Arles, Queen of France, married the Duke of Brittany in 1068, and Adela, the youngest daughter, married the Count of Blois. Cecilia was dedicated in her childhood to Matilda's foundation of Holy Trinity, and Matilda spent a considerable amount of time with her in the abbey over the years. Adelaide, the last daughter named by Orderic Vitalis, also became a nun, and a further daughter, Matilda, who is named in other sources, appears to have died young. In another part of his history, Orderic Vitalis also noted that a daughter of William's, Agatha, had been betrothed to Harold Godwin when he visited Normandy during the reign of Edward the Confessor, and that, following the Battle of Hastings, she was sent to marry the King of Galica. This was a personal tragedy for Agatha, who was surely Matilda's eldest daughter, and 'she had seen and loved the Englishman, but she was terrified of the Spanish husband she had never seen'. Agatha never did see her Spanish husband, as she died on the journey.

Matilda and William were often in each other's company during the early years of their marriage, and their relationship underwent a fundamental change in 1066. William had always asserted that his cousin, Edward the Confessor, had named him as his heir, and given the English king's Norman upbringing and background, this is possible. However, Edward appears to have had second thoughts or, at least, did not specifically name William on his deathbed and, instead, his brother-in-law, Harold Godwin, took the crown. As soon as Harold's accession was known, William began to build an invasion fleet and Matilda played an important role in this, secretly fitting out a ship for William to use as his flagship. The ship was named the 'Mora' and the prow was fitted with a representation of their then-youngest son, William Rufus, with his right hand pointing towards England and his left holding an ivory horn to his mouth. This was an expensive gift, and William was so pleased that, following the conquest, he granted Matilda the revenues from the earldom of Kent.

William trusted Matilda's political judgement, and when he sailed for England, he left her to act as co-regent of Normandy with his friend,

Roger of Montgomery. Matilda did a good job, and William repeated the compliment several times during their marriage. According to Orderic Vitalis, in 1069, for example, 'King William sent his beloved wife Matilda back to Normandy so that she might give up her time to religious devotions in peace, away from the English tumults and together with the boy Robert [her son] could keep the duchy secure.' Matilda spent a great deal of time in Normandy as regent following 1066, whilst William was occupied in England. She also, on occasion, acted as regent of England. When the couple were together in England, William accorded Matilda prominence, and she witnessed a number of charters during the reign. In the foundation charter for the priory at Lewes, for example, Matilda witnessed immediately after the King, taking a place higher than her sons.

Matilda was in Normandy when she heard the news of William's victory at the Battle of Hastings. He was crowned King of England at Christmas that same year, and it was not until March 1067, when William paid a brief visit to Normandy, that the couple were reunited. At Easter 1068, William sent ambassadors to Normandy to summon Matilda to England. She crossed the Channel triumphantly, accompanied by a great retinue of attendants, and upon her arrival in Winchester, she had a no-doubt-emotional reunion with William. William was determined that his wife should be officially recognised as queen, and on Whit Sunday, she was crowned by the Archbishop of York. William's coronation had been a hurried and tense affair, and he used Matilda's coronation as the first great state occasion of the Norman regime in England. William and Matilda quickly re-established the intimacy in their marriage, and Matilda bore her youngest child, Henry, at the end of 1068 or early in 1069.

Although their marriage was a happy one, as their children grew, Robert, the eldest, became a source of concern and disagreement for his parents. He was eager to attain his inheritance and was anxious to secure more authority for himself, placing himself in direct opposition to his father and allying himself with his cousin, Philip I of France. This caused the only known disagreement between Matilda and William as, according to Orderic Vitalis, Matilda was unable to cut all ties with her favourite child as William had done:

Queen Matilda, feeling a mother's affection for her son, often used to send him large sums of silver and gold and other valuables without the king's knowledge. On getting word of it he [William] ordered her, in a passion, never to do such a thing again. When she recklessly renewed her offence, the king exclaimed in anger. 'How very true here and now is the maxim of a certain sage, "A faithless wife brings ruin to the state". After this who in this world shall ever find himself a trustworthy helpmate? The wife of my bosom, whom I love as my own soul, whom I have set over my whole kingdom and entrusted with all authority and riches, this wife, I say, supports the enemies who plot against my life, enriches them with my money, zealously arms and succours and strengthens them to my grave peril.' Whereat she replied, 'O my lord, do not wonder that I love my first-born child with tender affection. By the power of the Most High, if my son Robert were dead and buried seven feet deep in the earth, hid from the eyes of the living, and I could bring him back to life with my own blood, I would shed my life-blood for him and suffer more anguish for his sake than, weak woman that I am, I dare to promise.'

For Matilda, it must have been traumatic to find herself at odds with William, and she was horrified when he ordered that one of her messengers, Samson, should be blinded as a punishment. Samson was forewarned, perhaps by Matilda himself, and managed to flee before the punishment could be carried out, but the disagreement caused Matilda great grief. In spite of this, she was unable to stop herself from doing all she could to aid Robert. At some point after her disagreement with William, she heard of a hermit who lived in Germany and apparently had the gift of prophesy. She sent gifts to him and asked him to pray for both William and Robert. The response that Matilda received was not what she hoped for, as the hermit informed her that Robert would succeed his father in Normandy, but that he would give himself over to lust and indolence and govern poorly. Matilda was, perhaps, less than reassured when the hermit continued by saying that she would never see this, as she would die before William.

As the hermit predicted, Matilda did not survive William. She died suddenly of the plague in Caen in Normandy on 2 November 1083. She and William had become reconciled before her death, and according to William of Malmesbury, William's affection for his wife was clear both in the splendid funeral that he gave her at Holy Trinity in Caen 'and showed by many days of the deepest mourning how much he missed the love of her whom he had lost'. Following her death, William abandoned pleasure of every kind. He never contemplated marrying again, and he died, still grieving for Matilda, just under four years later in September 1087.

Matilda of Flanders was one of the luckier medieval queens of England, as she enjoyed a happy marriage with a man who loved her deeply. The marriage of her daughter-in-law, Matilda of Scotland, proved to be less happy, although Matilda of Flanders' successor as queen was every bit as capable as her mother-in-law.

William I bequeathed the English crown to his next surviving son, William Rufus, rather than his estranged eldest son, Robert. Rufus never married and England had been without a queen for nearly twenty years when, in 1100, the King was killed in a hunting accident in the New Forest. Rufus's younger brother, Henry, who was conveniently close by when the accident occurred, hurried to have himself declared king, and it was Henry who provided England with the second Norman queen of England, MATILDA OF SCOTLAND (1080–1118).

Matilda of Scotland was an immensely important bride for Henry I. In spite of his father's claims to be the heir to Edward the Confessor, in reality, his title was based solely on conquest. At the time of Henry and Matilda's marriage, the *Anglo-Saxon Chronicle* enthused that she was 'of the rightful royal family of England' and the marriage went some way to healing the wounds created by the Conquest less than forty years before. Matilda of Scotland was the daughter of Malcolm Canmore, King of Scotland, who would later be immortalised by Shakespeare in *Macbeth*. It was Matilda's maternal family that was important to both Henry and to the people of England, as her mother was St Margaret, the daughter of Edward the Exile. Matilda was therefore the great-granddaughter of Edmund II and his wife, Aldgyth, and a great-great-niece of Edward the Confessor. St Margaret had been born during her father's exile in Hungary and she returned with the rest of her family to England when they were summoned to the court of Edward the Confessor. Although Edward the Exile died soon after his arrival, Margaret, her sister Christina and brother Edgar

Ætheling were raised at court, and Edgar, as the last direct male-line descendant of Alfred the Great, was proclaimed king by some members of the nobility following the Norman Conquest. This came to nothing, and William the Conqueror tolerated the family for a time, although also viewing them with suspicion. In 1068, the family, headed by Margaret's mother, announced that they were returning to Hungary. Their ship was driven by storms to Scotland, forcing them to land in Lothian. Perhaps, unwilling to entrust their lives to the sea again, they remained in Scotland, and by 1070 or 1071, Margaret had married the Scottish king. Margaret's Anglo-Saxon descent was an important factor in the ambitious Malcolm's selection of her. This can be seen in the fact that their first five children were given royal English names: Edward, Edmund, Ethelred, Edgar and Edith. It was the couple's eldest daughter, Edith, who later took the name Matilda, who would unite the English and Norman royal houses. In spite of the political nature of their marriage, the couple were fond of each other, and the *Life of St Margaret* records that Malcolm was determined to please his wife and 'anything she rejected, he also rejected, and anything she loved, he loved because of his desire for her love. And for this reason, even though he was illiterate, he would hold the books that she used for reading or to assist in her prayers in his hands and look at them'.

Edith, or Matilda, was born in the late summer or early autumn of 1080, the fifth of the eight children born to her parents. Matilda's mother, St Margaret, was an exceptionally pious woman, and according to the *Life of St Margaret*, 'she was a very image of virtues'. Margaret played a major role in the upbringing of her children, and she was determined that they should be a credit to her, as this passage from the *Life* indicates:

> She poured out care to her children not less than to herself, seeing that they were nurtured with all diligence and that they were introduced to honest matters as much as possible. And because she knew the Scripture, 'who spares the rod hates the child', she had ordered her household steward that, whenever the children committed some childish mischief, as young children will, that they should be punished by him with threats and beatings. And because of the religious zeal of their mother, the children's manners

were far better than those of other children older than they. And they never fought amongst themselves, and the younger children always displayed respect to the elder ones. For this reason, during solemn mass, when they followed their parents up to the altar, the younger never tried to outdo the elder but went up by age, oldest first. Margaret had her children brought to her very often, and she taught them about Christ and faith in Christ, using words suitable to their age and understanding. She admonished them diligently: 'Fear the Lord,' she said, 'O my children, because those that fear him will not be in need, and if you delight in him, O my flesh, he returns goodness to you through prosperity in the present life and by giving you a happy afterlife with all the saints.' This was the desire of the mother, these were the admonishments, this was the prayer that she prayed day and night, with tears on behalf of her offspring, so that they might come to know their Creator in faith which works through love, and knowing, that they might worship, worshipping, that they might love him in everything and above all things, loving, that they might arrive at the glory of the heavenly kingdom.

Margaret was literate and loved holy books, and it is likely that she supervised the early education of her daughter.

Matilda did not spend her entire childhood in Scotland. In 1086, her mother's sister, Christina, left Scotland to become a nun at Romsey Abbey in England, taking Matilda and her younger sister Mary with her. Matilda and Mary spent some time at Romsey before moving to the royal nunnery of Wilton to continue their education. Wilton was still famous as a centre of learning and Matilda received an education fitting for a royal princess. It is possible that, in sending her daughters to Romsey with her sister, St Margaret intended that they would both become nuns. This was certainly Christina's hope, and she put considerable pressure on her young nieces to take the veil. According to Matilda's own account, given to Archbishop Anselm, Christina was convinced that the veil was the only way to protect her young charges:

For when I was quite a young girl and went in fear of the rod of my Aunt Christina, whom you knew quite well, she to preserve me from the lust of the Normans which was rampant and at that time ready to assault any woman's honour, used to put a little black hood on my head and, when I threw it off, she would often make me smart with a good slapping and most horrible scolding, as well as treating me at being in disgrace. That hood I did indeed wear in her presence, chafing at it and fearful; but, as soon as I was able to escape out of her sight, I tore it off and threw it on the ground and trampled on it and in that way, although foolishly, I used to vent my rage and the hatred of it which boiled up in me. In that way, and only in that way, I was veiled, as my conscience bears witness.

Whilst it is possible that Margaret hoped that her daughters would follow a religious life, Malcolm had no such intentions for them.

Malcolm Canmore had married Margaret for her grand lineage, and he was anxious to ensure prestigious marriages for his daughters. Orderic Vitalis claimed that Count Alan the Red of Richmond and the Earl of Surrey both asked for Matilda's hand in marriage. The King, William Rufus, was also rumoured to have been her suitor. According to William of Malmesbury, Matilda would wear the veil in order to reject unworthy suitors who came to her at the nunnery and this is borne out by Matilda's own account of one such occasion: in 1093, her father arrived unexpectedly at Wilton with Count Alan, intending that he should marry her. Malcolm, 'when by chance he saw me veiled snatched the veil off and tearing it to pieces invoked the hatred of God upon the person who had put it on me, declaring that he had rather have chosen to marry me to Count Alan than consign me to a house of nuns'. Malcolm was so furious that he took Matilda back to Scotland without taking the time to arrange her marriage.

Matilda did not spend long in Scotland. In November of that same year, her father was killed in a raid on Northumbria and her mother died only three days later following a long illness. To find herself so suddenly an orphan must have been a shock for Matilda and, with older half-brothers from their father's previous marriage, Matilda and her siblings were in a very difficult position. Matilda's uncle, Edgar Ætheling, was concerned about the danger and hurried his sister's younger children south to England immediately upon hearing the news of St Margaret's death. There is no evidence for Matilda's whereabouts between 1093 and 1100, but she may perhaps have returned to either Wilton or Romsey to finish her education.

Although William Rufus had earlier shown an interest in Matilda, he was not eager to embark on matrimony with anyone and was happy to let the matter rest. In 1100, soon after becoming king, Rufus's younger brother, Henry I, proposed marriage to Matilda. Henry had been born and raised in England and he was much more in tune with the political situation in the country than his two predecessors as king. He understood that, given the fact that Edgar Ætheling was unmarried and childless, as far as most people were concerned, the true heirs of Edward the Confessor were the children of St Margaret. The alliance was entirely political on both Matilda's and Henry's parts, and for Matilda, it was a way to ensure that she finally escaped the veil. The couple did at least have some common interests as both were noted for their scholarly pursuits.

The marriage plans did not run entirely smoothly. Many people, including Anselm, Archbishop of Canterbury, believed that Matilda was a nun and the Church forbade the marriage and ordered her to return to the convent. Matilda went personally to Anselm to ask for his help. She vehemently denied that she was a nun and set out the full story of her childhood with her aunt, Christina, and the pressure that had been put upon her. Anselm, to Matilda's relief and gratitude, believed her story and called a Church court at Lambeth, which investigated her claims. Matilda attended the council, and according to the report of Eadmer, a follower of Anselm, she offered to swear that she was free to marry. This was enough for the Archbishop, and he declared that she had never been a nun, allowing the couple to marry a few days later on 11 November 1100. Soon after the ceremony, Anselm consecrated Matilda as queen.

Matilda's contemporary William of Malmesbury characterised her as the ideal medieval consort. According to the chronicler, 'she was a woman of exceptional holiness, and by no means negligible beauty, in piety her mother's rival, and in her own character exempt from all evil influence, outside the royal marriage-bed of unblemished chastity, and untouched even by the breath of suspicion'. Matilda fulfilled her primary role as queen, bearing two children within three years of her marriage: Matilda in 1102 and William in 1103. According to William of Malmesbury, 'the bearing of two children, one of either sex, left her content, and for the future she ceased either to have offspring or desire them, satisfied, when the king was busy elsewhere, to bid the court goodbye herself, and spent many years at Westminster'. Henry acknowledged over twenty illegitimate children, and whilst most were born before his marriage, some were born after 1105. Given the fact that Matilda produced two healthy children so soon after her marriage, and the evidence of her husband's notorious fertility, it seems likely that the couple ceased to have a sexual relationship as soon as Matilda had fulfilled her primary duty and produced a son. William of Malmesbury, a great admirer of Matilda, suggested that this was Matilda's own choice, although it was rumoured that Henry, disgusted by Matilda's habit of kissing the sores of lepers, was unwilling to live too closely to her for fear of infection. Henry always showed respect for Matilda, but it appears that, after 1103, they came to an agreement to share the rule of the kingdom without living as man and wife.

In spite of the failure of the physical side of their marriage, Matilda had a great deal of influence over Henry. She was affectionate to Archbishop Anselm, presumably due to his assistance concerning her marriage. Anselm, following a disagreement with Henry, left England in April 1103. He corresponded with Matilda throughout his two and a half years of exile, and during the period, Matilda witnessed at least one charter as 'Matilda, daughter of Anselm', a clear statement of her allegiance. Matilda worked on Anselm's behalf with Henry, and in one surviving letter to Anselm, she spoke both of her devotion to the archbishop and her efforts to secure his return:

I give unnumbered thanks to your unceasing goodness, which, not unmindful of me, has condescended, by your letters presented to me, to shew forth your mind, though absent. The clouds of sadness in which I was wrapped being expelled, the streamlet of your words had glided through me like a ray of new light. I embrace the little parchment sent to me by you, as I would my father himself: I cherish it in my bosom, I place it as near my heart as I can; I read over and over again the words flowing from the sweet fountain of your goodness; my mind considers them. My heart broods over them; and I hide the pondered treasures in the very secret place of my heart. Yet, while I praise all you have said, at one thing alone I wonder; that is, at what your discreet excellency has said about your nephew. Yet I do not think I can deal otherwise with your friends than my own. I might say with 'mine' than my own, for all who are yours by kindred are mine by love and adoption. Truly the consolation of your writing strengthens my patience, gives and preserves my hopes, raises me when falling, sustains me when sliding, gladdens me when sorrowful, softens me when angry, pacifies me when weeping. Farther, frequent though secret, consultation promises the return of the father to his daughter, of the lord to his handmaiden, of the pastor to his flock. I am encouraged to hope the same thing from the confidence which I have in the prayers of good men, and from the good will which, by skilfully investigating, I find to be in the heart of my lord. His mind is better disposed towards you than many men think; and I, favouring it, and suggesting wherever I can, he will become yet more courteous and reconciled to you. As to what he permits now to be done, in reference to your return, he will permit more and better to be done in future, when, according to time and opportunity, you shall request it. But even though he should persist in being an unjust judge, I entreat the affluence of your piety, that, excluding the bitterness of human rancour, which is not wont to dwell in you, you turn not from him the sweetness of your favour, but ever prove a pious intercessor with God for him and me, our common offspring, and the state of our kingdom. May your holiness ever fare well.

It is clear, in the dispute between Anselm and Henry, where Matilda's sympathies lay and it was not with her husband.

Matilda was very politically influential and issued thirty-three surviving charters, as well as attesting a large number of Henry's. Henry spent much of his reign in Normandy whilst Matilda made only one brief visit there in 1106. It appears that Matilda, who had been largely raised in England, preferred to remain there and Henry made use of this preference, often requiring her to act as regent in his absence. In September 1114, Henry spent ten months in Normandy with Matilda remaining in England as regent. She was called upon to act as regent again in April 1116 and remained as England's ruler until her death in 1118. During her last period as regent, Matilda was assisted by her son, William, and she began to train him for his future role as King of England. She also played a prominent role in justice. In spring 1116, she became involved in the case of Bricstan of Chatteris, an unjustly condemned prisoner. According to reports, Bricstan, who had hoped to take holy vows before being arrested for some unknown offence, repeatedly called upon St Benedict and St Etheldreda for assistance. The saints tore his chains from him before throwing them against the wall with such force that the guards went rushing to the Queen. Matilda sent an investigator and, when convinced that a miracle had indeed occurred, she ordered Bricstan's release, as well as ordering the bells in London to be rung in celebration and special Masses heard.

In spite of her abilities as regent, Matilda is chiefly remembered for her piety and, to her contemporaries, her charity work with the poor and sick led to her being known as 'Good Queen Matilda'. William of Malmesbury tells us that Matilda wore a hair-cloth shift under her royal robes and went barefoot to church in Lent. She had a particular interest in lepers, perhaps seeking to imitate Christ in his own favourable treatment of the marginalised group. She washed and handled the feet of lepers, as well as kissing their hands and feeding them herself. Matilda founded a leper hospital dedicated to St Giles, which was located just outside London and endowed with some of her revenues as queen. She was also a benefactress of the leper hospital at Chichester in West Sussex. Matilda tried to follow her mother's example in her piety, and she worked to improve the lives of her poorest subjects. She patronised the Augustinians and founded a priory in Aldgate in 1107 or 1108. Matilda had an interest in holy men and gave generously to them, in one case meeting with a former knight who had vowed always to wear his mail shirt next to his skin so that he would be armed to fight against Satan. Matilda was so impressed with this man's piety that she asked to feel his mail shirt and, as she did so, slipped a purse of gold inside.

Matilda died during her last regency on 1 May 1118, at the age of thirty-seven. The cause of her death is not recorded, but it may have been unexpected, as Henry did not travel back from Normandy. Matilda's daughter was absent in Germany, where she had married the Holy Roman Emperor, and of her two children, it is likely that it was to her son, William, that Matilda was closest. If this is the case, then she was, at least, spared the news of his drowning, in 1120, in the wreck of the White Ship. This was a calamity for Henry I and was a major catalyst in his decision to take a second wife, Adeliza of Louvain.

ADELIZA OF LOUVAIN (*c.* 1103–51) was the eldest daughter of Godfrey, Count of Louvain, and his first wife, Ida of Namur. She had one of the grandest lineages of any queen of England and was a descendant of Charlemagne on both sides of her family. Adeliza was born in around 1103, and whilst it is unclear whether she received any formal education, she was skilled in embroidery and, during her childhood, produced a standard for her father in silk and gold. She was a great beauty and was nicknamed 'the fair maid of Brabant' by her contemporaries. Another contemporary, John of Worcester, declared that she was 'a maiden of great beauty and modesty'. Adeliza's father was a vassal of the Holy Roman Emperor, Henry V, and it is likely that she would have had some contact with her future stepdaughter, the emperor's wife and King Henry I's daughter, the Empress Matilda. In February 1110, Count Godfrey met the Empress at Liege, when she agreed to intercede for him in relation to a dispute. It is not inconceivable that Adeliza was present. In any event, a common fondness for Germany provided a bond between Matilda and Adeliza in later years.

In December 1120, William, the only son of Henry I, drowned in the wreck of the White Ship whilst on his way home to England from Normandy. Henry I had been a widower for over two years by 1120 and had shown no real inclination to remarry. The loss of his only legitimate son made a new marriage a matter of urgency, and he swiftly began the search for a new bride. Adeliza was chosen in order to strengthen his alliance with the Holy Roman Empire, which had first come into effect with the marriage of his daughter. For Adeliza, it was a prestigious match, and she arrived in England in January 1121.

According to the *Anglo-Saxon Chronicle*, Henry spent Christmas 1120 at Brampton before travelling to Windsor, where he and Adeliza were married on 24 January. The next day, Adeliza was crowned as queen. Both ceremonies were marred by a farcical dispute between the Archbishop of Canterbury and the Bishop of Salisbury, within whose diocese Windsor fell. The aged Archbishop claimed the right to conduct royal ceremonies anywhere in England, and he therefore conducted the marriage ceremony. He was so slow with age that Henry ordered the Bishop of Salisbury to conduct the coronation. The following day, everyone entered the church where the Bishop of Salisbury crowned Henry. Before he could reach Adeliza, the

Archbishop strode in, all his infirmities forgotten in his fury. He promptly removed the crown from Henry's head before crowning him again. He then crowned and anointed Adeliza as Queen of England.

The thirty year age gap between the couple must have seemed large to Adeliza at the time of her marriage. In spite of this, she made attempts to share Henry's interests and affection developed between the couple. Henry had an interest in exotic animals, creating a zoo at Woodstock Palace. Adeliza commissioned the first known French bestiary, a work by Phillippe du Thuan, and this was, perhaps, an attempt to involve herself in pursuits enjoyed by the King. Due to the desperate need for an heir, Adeliza spent most of her marriage with Henry and the couple travelled together, in stark contrast to his first marriage. Surviving charters show that Adeliza was with Henry consistently until 1131. For example, the couple were at Winchester at Easter 1123, Normandy in 1125, England between 1126 and 1127, and Normandy again between 1129 and 1131.

Adeliza stopped travelling with Henry in 1131, and it is likely that it was at that point that the couple accepted that their marriage would produce no child. There is no evidence that Adeliza ever conceived during her marriage to Henry, to her great distress. She is known to have written to the churchman Hildebert of Lavardin for advice and comfort in relation to her childlessness. It is possible that her apparent barrenness also caused Adeliza to take an increasing interest in the traditional queenly pursuits of piety and patronage. She maintained a correspondence with Hildebert of Lavardin and one of his surviving letters granted her request to become a lay daughter of St Vincent's Abbey. He also praised her dedication and support of the monks of St Vincent and her visits there. Adeliza maintained friendly relations with several bishops. She warmly addressed Alexander, Bishop of Lincoln, in one charter, and William, Bishop of Hereford, later donated land in memory of Henry and Adeliza for 'nurturing' him. Adeliza made gifts to Waltham Abbey and Reading Abbey, and whilst her piety attracted less attention than that of her predecessor, Matilda of Scotland, she was devout.

Adeliza played a very limited political role during her time as queen. She was never named as regent, as her predecessor had been, a fact that can be attributed to Henry's need to keep her with him in the hope of conceiving a child. She was allowed some role in government and was present at several councils during Henry's reign. She is known to have been present at the great councils in May 1121 and Easter 1123, and she was present in the council chamber at Christmas 1126 when Henry named his daughter, Matilda, as his heir. She also participated in crown-wearing ceremonies, designed to emphasise the importance of the monarchy.

Adeliza worked to advance her countrymen. When she arrived in England, she brought a number of her compatriots with her, and her first chancellor was a Lotharingian called Godfrey, who was appointed Bishop of Bath by Henry in 1123. Godfrey took several of his countrymen with him to Bath, and a Chamberlain called Rothardus witnessed charters by him in 1135, as well as being present when Adeliza issued charters following Henry's death. Adeliza's second chancellor, Simon, who was also a Lotharingian, became Bishop of Worcester. He remained in contact with Adeliza and witnessed several of her grants. The evidence of her chancellors suggests that Adeliza used her influence with Henry to advance the careers of the Lotharingians who travelled to England with her. She was also accompanied by a number of Lotharingian ladies and helped them make advantageous marriages, with Juliana, the wife of the nobleman Jordan of Auffay, recorded as having arrived in England with the Queen. Adeliza's cousin, Melisende of Rethel made two English marriages, receiving a dowry on her second from Adeliza. Following Henry's death, Adeliza's half-brother, Jocelyn, arrived from Louvain and was prominent in her household.

Henry I died near Rouen in Normandy on 1 December 1135. Although he was in his late sixties, his death was unexpected, and Adeliza was not with him, although she attended his burial at Reading Abbey on Christmas Day. Adeliza and Henry had been married for fifteen years and she grieved for him, giving the manor of Eton in Hertfordshire to Reading Abbey on the first anniversary of Henry's death in exchange for prayers to be said for his soul. She gave one hundred shillings for a lamp to burn perpetually at his tomb. Adeliza continued to style herself as queen in charters, but retired from court, moving to Arundel Castle in Sussex, one of her dower properties.

Adeliza did not entirely shut herself away from the world and, around 1139, she married William d'Aubigny, a royal butler. It is likely that the couple had known each other at court during Henry's lifetime, and there is every reason to assume that it was a love match. William held lands in Norfolk and Suffolk and was made Earl of Lincoln by King Stephen early in 1139, although he later exchanged this earldom for the earldom of Arundel. Although no evidence of the couple's relationship survives, it must have been happy, and in spite of the childlessness of her first marriage, Adeliza bore her second husband at least seven children. William d'Aubigny was a supporter of Stephen throughout the civil war that wracked England following Henry's death, and the impetus for Adeliza's last public role came from her rather than from her husband.

Adeliza had maintained contact with her stepdaughter Matilda following Henry's death. The two were very close in age and, with their shared interest in Germany, had much in common. When Henry's nephew Stephen, the son of his sister Adela, seized the English crown, Matilda was, at first, unable to do anything to assert her claim but, by 1139, she had gained enough strength to take action. Adeliza offered her stepdaughter Arundel as a base from which to establish her claim to the throne, and later that year, Matilda arrived at the castle to stay with her. Adeliza had underestimated just what the backlash to her hospitality would be, and according to William of Malmesbury, she, 'with a woman's fickleness, in despite of the undertakings she had given via the many messengers she had sent to Normandy, broke the faith she had sworn'. In reality, Adeliza was in a very difficult position. She wanted to assist her stepdaughter and knew that Henry would have wanted her to provide Matilda with all the support that she could. However, as soon as Stephen heard of his cousin's arrival, he immediately moved to besiege Arundel, terrifying Adeliza. Rather than betraying Matilda, she took the only steps that she felt were possible and negotiated with Stephen for her stepdaughter to be given a safe-conduct to join her half-brother, Robert, Earl of Gloucester, in Bristol. Whilst Adeliza was not able to offer Matilda a refuge in the long-term, she helped her travel to her supporters in the South West, and she therefore played a role in ensuring that Matilda remained at liberty to pursue her claim.

Adeliza all but disappears from the sources following the events of 1139. It is unclear whether she had any further contact with Matilda, and she certainly played no further role in the civil war. It is likely that she spent most of her time at Arundel, creating her half-brother, Jocelyn, castellan there in the 1140s. She also granted him the honour of Petworth, which formed a substantial part of her income and was intent on furthering his career. Following Adeliza's death, Jocelyn continued to work closely with her husband.

By 1150, Adeliza had retired to the continental monastery of Affligham in Flanders, which had been founded by her father and uncle. Her retirement perhaps signified a decline in her health, and she died there on 24 March 1151. Her body was taken to Reading, where she was buried beside Henry I. At her burial, Jocelyn confirmed gifts to the abbey in her memory, and later, William d'Aubigny made a religious gift for the good of Adeliza's soul.

Adeliza of Louvain seems, for the most part, to have had a happy life. Family was important to her, and she was loved by both her own family and the family she acquired through marriage. In spite of this, she was grieved by her childlessness in her first marriage, and in her last years, she was painfully aware that if she had only provided Henry with a son, the turmoil that engulfed England following his death could have been avoided.

Matilda of Boulogne (*c.* 1103–52), the wife of King Stephen, is one of England's lesser-known queens, and she has always been overshadowed by her more famous cousin and namesake, the Empress Matilda. In spite of this, Matilda of Boulogne was a prominent political figure and one of the few women of her time to conduct a military campaign and lead her own troops as she sought to support her husband's debateable right to the English crown.

Matilda of Boulogne was the only child and heiress of Count Eustace of Boulogne and his wife, Mary, the younger sister of Matilda of Scotland. Matilda of Boulogne was always close to her English family and she was named after her aunt, the queen. She spent her childhood in England and was well known to her English family, including her uncle, Henry I. She is likely to have been educated at Bermondsey Abbey, of which her mother was a major benefactor, and she may have been present when her mother died there suddenly in 1115 during a visit.

Matilda was the heiress to the counties of Boulogne and Lens, as well as to extensive estates in England, making her one of the greatest heiresses in Europe. Henry I had always favoured his nephew, Stephen, the son of his sister, Adela, and, in 1125 he arranged for Stephen to marry Matilda. Stephen was around seven years older than Matilda and, as a younger son, could expect little inheritance of his own. Henry had raised Stephen in England, creating him Count of Mortaine in 1115, and he was described by the *Gesta Stephani* as the dearest of Henry's nephews. This is likely and, certainly, Henry's bestowal of Matilda on Stephen was a mark of great favour. It is also not impossible that the couple already knew and liked each other. Stephen was a kindly and affable man, with the *Gesta Stephani* describing him as 'rich and at the same time unassuming, generous, courteous; moreover, in all the conflicts of war or any siege of his enemies, bold and brave, judicious and patient'. The couple quickly became devoted to each other, and Matilda spent the rest of her life trying to protect her husband and children. Stephen was faithful to his wife, and his only recorded illegitimate child was born before his marriage.

As well as wanting to advance his favourite nephew, it is likely that Henry I had another motive for arranging the marriage. By 1125, he had come to terms with the probability that he would die without a male heir and Stephen, who had already sworn to support the claims of Henry's daughter, the Empress Matilda, may have been advanced as a reward for his compliance. If Henry hoped that the marriage would buy Stephen's support for his daughter, he was to be disappointed. Stephen and Matilda of Boulogne were together in Boulogne in December 1135 when word reached them of Henry's death in Normandy. Matilda must have been aware of her husband's intentions, and it is clear that his actions on his uncle's death had been planned for some time. According to the chronicler Henry of Huntingdon, as soon as word reached Stephen of Henry's death, he left his wife to sail to England:

> For without delay came Stephen, younger brother of Theobald, count of Blois, a man of great resolution and audacity, who, although he had sworn an oath of fealty for the realm of England to the daughter of King Henry, trusting in his strength, shamelessly tempted God and seized the crown of the kingdom. William, archbishop of Canterbury, who had been the first to swear allegiance to the king's daughter, alas! crowned Stephen king, wherefore God visited him with the same judgment which he had inflicted on him

who had stricken Jeremiah, the great priest; namely, that he should not live out the year. Roger, the great bishop of Salisbury, who had been the second to take the aforesaid oath and had ordered all the others to do likewise, contributed everything in his power to secure for him the crown. He, too, by the just judgment of God was afterwards taken captive by him whom he had made king and in dire torments came to a wretched end. But why tarry? All those who had sworn fealty, whether prelates, earls or magnates, offered to accept Stephen and paid homage to him. This indeed was an evil sign, that the whole of England should so suddenly and without delay or struggle, and, as it were, in the twinkling of an eye, submit to Stephen. So, after his coronation at Christmastide, he held his court at London.

In the early twelfth century, the English succession was far from settled, and Henry I himself had always maintained his claim to the kingdom in preference to his eldest brother, Robert, and Robert's son. However, the fact that Stephen, along with much of the English nobility, had sworn an oath to support the Empress as Henry's heiress was uncomfortable for the new king. Matilda of Boulogne never appears to have doubted her husband's title to the throne and she always regarded Stephen as the rightful king, perhaps considering that the crown belonged to its first successful claimant.

Matilda had joined her husband in England by Easter 1136 and she was crowned at Westminster on 22 March of that year before the court moved to Oxford. Matilda used her role as queen to support her husband throughout his reign and their marriage continued to be a happy one, in spite of the difficulties he faced as king. Stephen and Matilda were often described as a partnership in sources, and it appears that their characters complemented each other. Whilst Stephen was kindly and generous, Matilda was described in the *Gesta Stephani* as 'a woman of subtlety and a man's resolution'. Matilda bore Stephen five children and Eustace, William and Mary survived to adulthood. Eustace, the eldest son, was a favourite of his mother, but Matilda loved all her children and her grief at the deaths in infancy of her children Baldwin and Matilda can be seen in the gifts she gave to Holy Trinity, Aldgate, in their memory once she had become queen of England.

Matilda played a major political role during Stephen's reign. Soon after Stephen's coronation in December 1136, David of Scotland, the uncle of both Matilda of Boulogne and the Empress Matilda, invaded England in support of the Empress's claim. Peace was made between the Scottish king and Stephen in February, and it appears that this was linked to Matilda's influence and her imminent coronation. David of Scotland perhaps reflected that he would gain more from favouring Matilda of Boulogne over the Empress at that time, as, in 1136, the Empress was in no position to come to England and claim her crown. The Empress had also been raised in Germany, and David is likely to have had considerably more contact with Matilda of Boulogne over the years and to have been fond of her. Matilda played a significant role in the later peace negotiated between David and Stephen between September 1138 and Easter 1139, and she acted for her husband in the negotiations, being present in person when the terms were ratified at Durham on 9 April 1139. She then personally escorted David's son, Henry, south to London to be invested with the title of Earl of Northumbria by Stephen.

Stephen's reign has been referred to as a period of 'anarchy', and it was certainly a time of turmoil. Although the Empress was initially unable to lay claim to the crown, the threat that she might one day assert her rights hung over both Stephen and Matilda of Boulogne during the last years of the 1130s. With a disputed entitlement to the crown, Stephen found that he could not always rely on the loyalty of his vassals in England, and in 1138, he occupied Hereford in an attempt to assert his authority there. At the same time, Matilda of Boulogne took steps of her own to help secure her husband's crown, and according to Orderic Vitalis,

> The queen besieged Dover with a strong force on the land side, and sent word to her friends and kinsmen and dependants in Boulogne to blockade the foe by sea. The people of Boulogne proved obedient, gladly carried out their lady's commands and, with a great fleet of ships, closed the narrow strait to prevent the garrison receiving any supplies.

Matilda was present at the siege and co-ordinated the attack on the town herself. Faced with attacks on both sides, the castle surrendered, and Matilda entered the town in triumph. In order to ensure that the port remained in Stephen's hands, Matilda appointed her cousin, Pharamus of Boulogne, as castellan of Dover, before hurrying back to join her husband.

The Empress finally arrived in England in September 1139. Matilda of Boulogne immediately began working to secure her husband's grip on the throne, and she used her children's marriages to secure support for the King. It was Matilda who arranged the marriage of her second son, William, to Isabella, the heiress of the Earl of Surrey, a key ally for Stephen. She also personally oversaw the negotiations for the marriage of Eustace to Constance, the sister of Louis VII of France. In February 1140, Matilda and Eustace travelled together to France for the betrothal. At the same time, in return for a large sum of money paid by Matilda, Louis VII invested Eustace as Duke of Normandy. Matilda was too important to Stephen to remain long in France, and in August 1140, she attended a conference at Bath designed to negotiate peace with the Empress. As a mark of his respect for her, Stephen appointed Matilda, along with his brother, the Bishop of Winchester, as his representatives at the conference. Unfortunately, the two opposing parties were unable to agree terms, and both Stephen and Matilda of Boulogne were disappointed as the civil war continued to drag on.

The Empress and Stephen remained fairly evenly matched during the first few years of the civil war, with the Empress controlling the west of England and Stephen the remainder of the country. Early in 1141, however, disaster struck for Stephen at the Battle of Lincoln. According to Henry of Huntingdon, Stephen decided to besiege Lincoln Castle, which belonged to Ranulf, Earl of Chester, an important ally of the Empress. Ranulf was joined by the forces of Robert, Earl of Gloucester, an illegitimate son of Henry I, and the Empress's greatest supporter. On his arrival, it became clear that Stephen would have to give battle, and 'overwhelmed with a flood of cares', he heard Mass before entering into battle with the Empress's army. Early in the battle, the troops on Stephen's flanks fled, leaving him alone with his infantry. According to Henry of Huntingdon, Stephen was encircled and attacked from all sides:

Thenceforth the battle was seen to rage horribly around the royal defences, helmets and swords gleamed as they clashed, and the dreadful noise re-echoed from the hills and the walls of the city. The cavalry, furiously charging the royal column, slew some and trampled down others, while yet others were dragged away captive. No respite, no breathing-space was given, except in the quarter where the most valiant king had taken his stand and the foe recoiled from the incomparable ferocity of his counter-strokes.

Stephen fought bravely, but his forces were inferior to those of the Empress, and by the end of the day, he was a prisoner, being carried as a captive to Bristol in chains. Matilda of Boulogne recognised that Stephen was unlikely to recover his crown, and the *Gesta Stephani* claims she 'sent envoys to the Countess [of Anjou, i.e., the Empress] and made earnest entreaty for her husband's release from his filthy dungeon and the granting of his son's inheritance, though only that to which he was entitled by her father's will'. Unsurprisingly, given the fact that she had been deprived of her own inheritance by Stephen, the Empress was not disposed to grant him his own lands, nor to suffer the release of a known oath-breaker in return for his promise not to challenge her title to the throne. There was no love lost between Matilda of Boulogne and her cousin, the Empress, and the only response she received to her message was abuse in 'harsh and insulting language'. Matilda of Boulogne also petitioned a number of the leading noblemen in England who, according to the chronicler, John of Worcester went to the Empress and 'offered to give her many hostages, castles, and great riches, if the king were to be set free and allowed to recover his liberty, though not his crown'. This approach also failed, and Matilda of Boulogne set about rebuilding the King's forces. According to Henry of Huntingdon, only Matilda of Boulogne and the captain of her troops, William of Ypres, 'continued to fight against the empress with all their might'. Stephen's cause must have looked hopeless to Matilda, as even her brother-in-law, the Bishop of Winchester, submitted to the Empress as the victor of the civil war.

Matilda retained some support in Kent and Surrey following her husband's imprisonment, and she raised an army there in Eustace's name as heir to the throne. In April 1141, at the Council of Winchester, the Empress was declared ruler of England and made her way slowly towards London, where she intended to be crowned. Whilst she was waiting at Westminster for her ceremonial entry to the city, she became on increasingly bad terms with the Londoners, and Matilda of Boulogne moved her army up the Thames to London. There, she set about negotiating with the Londoners and allied herself with them, causing them to expel the Empress from the city on 24 June 1141. This was a major victory for Matilda of Boulogne, and on her triumphant entry to the capital, she 'bore herself with the valour of a man; everywhere by prayer or price she won over invincible allies'.

Stephen's brother, Henry, Bishop of Winchester, had changed his allegiance to the Empress following his brother's capture at Lincoln. The bishop was the most powerful churchman in England, and whatever her personal opinion of the man who had abandoned his own brother, Matilda of Boulogne was determined to win him back to Stephen's cause, going in person to him at Guildford. According to the *Gesta Stephani*, Matilda 'humbly besought the Bishop of Winchester, legate of all England, to take pity on his imprisoned brother and exert himself for his freedom, that uniting all his efforts with hers he might gain her a husband, the people a king, the kingdom a champion'. Matilda's appeal touched the bishop, who was already contemplating returning to his brother's cause, and he wept as he declared that he would assist her. Following the meeting, the bishop returned to his see at Winchester.

The Empress was furious when she heard of the bishop's betrayal, and she took an army to Winchester in an attempt to capture him, besieging him in his castle. The Empress's forces were led by her leading supporters, King David of Scotland and her half-brothers, Robert of Gloucester and Reginald of Cornwall. When Matilda of Boulogne heard of the siege, she moved her army, augmented with almost one thousand Londoners, to besiege the besiegers at Winchester. Matilda of Boulogne's actions took the Empress by surprise, and whilst she was able to flee, her greatest supporter, Robert of Gloucester, was captured and brought to Matilda of Boulogne. Matilda was jubilant at her victory and had Robert imprisoned in Rochester Castle whilst she set about negotiating a prisoner exchange. The Empress knew that her cause was lost without her half-brother, and on 1 November 1141, Stephen was finally released from Bristol Castle, leaving Matilda of Boulogne and Eustace behind as sureties for Robert. Stephen then rode to Rochester, where Robert was released after leaving his son as a surety. Robert rode to Bristol, where Matilda of Boulogne and her son were freed. Finally, Matilda and Eustace travelled to Rochester to secure the release of Robert's son, and it was there that Matilda was finally reunited with Stephen.

No record survives of the reunion between Stephen and Matilda, but it must have been an emotional one. Certainly, Stephen appreciated his wife's efforts on his behalf, and soon after he was released from his imprisonment, he bestowed a number of honours on Eustace, something that was designed to please his son's doting mother. According to the *Gesta Stephani,*

> The king, in the presence of the magnates, ceremonially girded with the belt of knighthood his son Eustace, a young man of noble nature, and after most bountifully endowing him with lands and possessions, and giving him the special distinction of a most splendid retinue of knights, advanced him in rank to the dignity of count [of Boulogne].

Stephen also set about trying to recover his position as king, but whilst, at Christmas, he and Matilda were crowned again by the Archbishop of Canterbury, he was never able to assert his authority over the whole of England. Matilda continued to work for Stephen after his release, and in 1142, she held a court at Lens, which suggests that she was visiting her continental lands in order to recruit foreign mercenaries. She was the driving force behind attempts to have Eustace crowned as king during his father's lifetime in order to further secure his succession. From 1150, Stephen made strenuous efforts to achieve this, even sending the Archbishop of York to Rome to obtain papal support for the coronation. This mission was unsuccessful, but Stephen tried again in April 1152 during a Church council in London, attended by Matilda herself. Once again, the bishops refused to recognise Eustace as heir to the throne, to Matilda's disappointment.

As well as being politically ambitious, Matilda became increasingly devoted to the Church as she aged. It was Stephen and Matilda's patronage that led to the establishment of the Templar movement in England, and in 1137, they jointly founded a monastery at Cressing for the order, endowing it with lands inherited by Matilda in England. The couple founded several other religious houses, including one at

Longvilliers in 1135, Cowley in 1138 or 1139, and Faversham in 1148. In 1148, Stephen and Matilda established the convent at Lillechurch in order to allow their daughter, Mary, who had been dedicated as a nun in childhood, to become its first abbess. In addition to this, Matilda founded the Hospital of St Katherine by the Tower. Genuine piety played a major role in Matilda's activities, but she also used her gifts for political purposes, and Faversham, for example, was intended to be the family's mausoleum and was part of the conscious promotion of their dynasty, which had also prompted the attempts to crown Eustace as king during his father's lifetime.

Matilda was worn down by the continuing struggle to maintain Stephen's throne, and from around 1147, she went into semi-retirement, basing herself away from Stephen at Canterbury. She may also have been in ill health by this time, as she frequently stayed at St Augustine's Abbey in the city. Matilda remained an important figure, and she attended councils in London in 1151 and April 1152. On her way home from the second of these councils, she stopped to visit her friend Euphemia, Countess of Oxford, at Hedingham in Essex. Whilst there, Matilda suddenly became unwell, and she died on 3 May 1152. As she would have wanted, she was buried at her new foundation of Faversham.

Matilda's death caused Stephen great grief, and it was followed, on 10 August 1153, by the death of the couple's favoured eldest son, Eustace, who was buried beside his mother. Eustace's death saw the end of Stephen and Matilda's dynastic hopes, and the King gave up his attempts to retain the English crown for his own offspring, instead coming to terms with Henry of Anjou, the son of the Empress. Stephen died early in 1154. Stephen and Matilda's second son, William, who made no attempt on the English crown and may have been in ill health, inherited Matilda's county of Boulogne on Eustace's death, but died soon afterwards himself. This left only Abbess Mary to continue Stephen and Matilda's line, and with her accession as Countess of Boulogne, she was abducted from her convent and forced to marry the nobleman Matthew of Flanders. Marriage was not something that Mary desired, and after bearing her husband two daughters, she returned to her convent. Matilda of Boulogne was as powerful and dominant a personality as her cousin and rival, the Empress Matilda, but it was the Empress who would ultimately find herself the victor in the civil war.

The EMPRESS MATILDA (1102–67) was England's first potential queen regnant. She was never crowned but was acknowledged as ruler of England between February and November 1141 and ruled the west of the kingdom for a number of years. She was born on 7 February 1102 at Sutton Courtenay, near Abingdon. She was the eldest child of Henry I and Matilda of Scotland, and her birth was followed a year later by that of William, her only legitimate sibling. Matilda, as the King's only daughter, was a great diplomatic asset to him. According to the *Anglo-Saxon Chronicle*, in 1109, Henry I swore at Westminster to marry his daughter to the Holy Roman Emperor, Henry V. This was an extremely prestigious marriage and the initiative came from Henry V, who was in urgent need of funds. Henry I was excited at the prospect of his daughter becoming an empress, and he provided a large dowry of around 10,000 marks in silver. Matilda left for Germany the following year shortly before her eighth birthday. She must have been apprehensive, and she would have been aware that she was unlikely ever to see her homeland again. According to the chronicler Robert of Torigni, the emperor, 'who having won her hand welcomed her, escorted by famous men, bishops and counts acting as envoys, laden with innumerable presents from both her parents, to his realm, where at Utrecht the following Easter they were betrothed. After the betrothal she was crowned on St James' Day at Mainz by the archbishop of Cologne'. Matilda was still too young for a full marriage, and so, after her arrival in February 1110, she was sent away from her husband to learn the German language and customs.

Matilda, at the age of only eight, is unlikely to have had much idea about what to expect from her husband, and he must have seemed a daunting figure. Henry V was then aged twenty-four and had ruled much of modern Germany since 1106. During his lifetime, he had a rather sinister reputation. Whilst Henry V was still a very young child, his elder brother, Conrad, had rebelled against their father, Henry IV. This had led to Henry IV naming his younger son as his heir in 1098, in exchange for 'a solemn vow, specifically that he would never intrude himself either into the royal power or into the lands of his father while he [the father] was living, except, perchance, by his consent'. This oath meant little to Henry V, and by 1106, the younger man was in open rebellion against his father. The account of Henry IV himself discusses this:

All these oaths were cast aside and handed over to oblivion on the advice of treacherous perjurers and of our mortal enemies. So he was separated from us so completely that, wishing in every way to attack us in our holdings as well as in our person, he made it his constant goal from that hour to deprive us of kingship and life.

Through both military strength and treachery, Henry V secured the throne for himself in his father's lifetime, forcing the older man to abdicate. Henry V's reputation, as a usurper, was in no way helped by his father's suspicious death in captivity later in 1106. In spite of this, he always treated Matilda kindly. In 1114, she was deemed old enough for marriage, and the couple were married at Worms. The wedding ceremony was magnificent and was intended to reflect the glory of both the groom and his young bride. Matilda herself was described at the marriage as beautiful and distinguished, and she rapidly became popular in Germany, being remembered long after her death as 'the good Matilda'. She received a second coronation as empress at St Peter's in Rome in 1117.

During her time in Germany, Matilda gained practical experience of government, and her husband trusted her to act as regent for him on a number of occasions. In 1117, for example, Henry V left Matilda to rule over Italy, and she retained this position until summoned to rejoin him in Lotharingia in 1119. In spite of her abilities as regent, Matilda failed in her primary duty as empress. In the eleven years of her marriage, she bore only one child, a baby that died in its infancy and when Henry V died on 23 May 1125, he left Matilda a childless widow at the age of twenty-three.

By the time she was widowed, Matilda had spent over fifteen years in Germany, and the country had become her home. It is unlikely that she had much memory of England, and her wealth and status in the Holy Roman Empire made her the object of interest of a number of German princes who sought her hand in marriage. Following the death of her brother William in 1120, and her father's subsequent childless marriage to Adeliza, Henry I was adamant that Matilda should return home. She was, at first, reluctant to heed her father's summons, but, eventually, she submitted, perhaps reasoning that the position of heir to England and Normandy was preferable to that of a wealthy, but politically powerless, widow in Germany. No details of Matilda's reunion with her father survive, but it must have been satisfactory, and at the Christmas court at Windsor in 1126, Henry made all those present swear an oath to Matilda, recognising her as his successor. Anxious that Matilda should provide him with grandsons, the following spring, Henry opened marriage negotiations for her with Geoffrey, the fifteen-year-old son of the Count of Anjou.

Matilda, who was eleven years older than Geoffrey and had been the wife of the greatest ruler in Europe, was furious when she heard of the proposed marriage. Henry was determined that the marriage would go ahead and locked her in her room until she submitted. Matilda and Geoffrey were married on 17 June 1128 at Le Mans, but it quickly became apparent that the union was not a success, and in July 1129, after only one year of marriage, Matilda returned to her father in Rouen, seeking a divorce. Personally, the couple were entirely incompatible and they loathed each other, with Matilda always refusing to use the title of 'Countess of Anjou'. Henry I was uncertain about just what to do with his daughter, and in 1131, she accompanied him back to England, where a council was held at Northampton to debate her future. The council decided to send Matilda back to Anjou, and she set out once again to join her husband. This time, the couple were determined to make their marriage work, and both perhaps reasoned that they were unlikely to be granted a divorce and needed to make the best of things instead. The reunion was a partial success, and though the couple always disliked each other, their first son, Henry, was born at Le Mans in March 1133. A second son, Geoffrey, was born in Rouen in 1134, and a third son, William, in 1136. Matilda wept throughout the baptism of her eldest son, and his birth finally took away the stigma of her childlessness. Between 1133 and 1135, Matilda spent most of her time with her father and children in Normandy, receiving only occasional visits from Geoffrey. Later, following the birth of their third son, both felt that they had done enough for the succession and permanently separated.

In spring 1135, Henry quarrelled with Geoffrey and Matilda, who, in spite of her dislike of Geoffrey, knew that she was bound to him and took her sons to join him in Anjou. This proved to be a disaster for her cause in England and Normandy, and she was still in Anjou and heavily pregnant with her third son when word reached her in December 1135 of her father's death. On his deathbed, Henry confirmed Matilda as his heir and she took steps to occupy the Norman border castles that comprised her dowry, remaining on the edge of Normandy whilst she awaited the birth of her son. There was little else that Matilda could do, and within three weeks of her father's death, she had heard that her cousin, Stephen of Blois, had usurped the English throne and had had himself crowned. Matilda was in no position to invade England and was forced to bide her time. In September 1136, Geoffrey invaded Normandy on her behalf and Matilda arrived with troops to join him at Le Sap. Geoffrey's invasion was not a success, and it took him nearly nine years to conquer Normandy and restore Matilda's rights there.

Matilda spent four years in Normandy, biding her time. Finally, in 1139, she was joined by her half-brother, Henry I's favourite illegitimate son, Robert, Earl of Gloucester, who offered her his support. Robert had initially acquiesced to Stephen's accession to the throne but was uncomfortable with the King's treatment of his sister and, by 1139, was ready to act. His support was a godsend for Matilda, and she accepted his aid willingly, always relying on him as her greatest councillor. Matilda and Robert sailed to England in October 1139, landing at Portsmouth with a large army. On their landing, Robert travelled to Bristol whilst Matilda journeyed to visit her stepmother, Adeliza, at Arundel. Following Stephen's siege of the castle, Matilda was given a safe-conduct to travel to Bristol, and she joined her brother there, spending two months in the city receiving homage and dispensing laws as the ruler of England. For fifteen months, there was a war of sieges with little gain on either side. Whilst Stephen controlled the bulk of the kingdom, Matilda was the ruler in the west of England, spending most of 1140 at Gloucester. The turning point came in 1141, when Stephen quarrelled with the powerful Earl of Chester and his brother. They immediately turned towards Matilda, swearing fealty to her as queen. On 2 February 1141, they were attacked by Stephen at Lincoln. Stephen was captured in battle and taken to Matilda, who ordered him to be imprisoned in chains in Bristol Castle.

According to John of Worcester, Matilda 'was ecstatic at this turn of events, having now, as she thought, gained possession of the kingdom, which had been promised to her by oath'. Within weeks of Stephen's capture, Matilda had made a pact with his powerful brother, Henry, Bishop of Winchester, as recorded in the *Gesta Stephani*:

> When they had jointly made a pact of peace and concord he came to meet her in cordial fashion and admitted her into the city of Winchester, and after handing over to her disposal the king's castle and the royal crown, which she had always most eagerly desired, and the treasure the king had left there, though it were scanty, he bade the people, at a public meeting in the market-place of the town, salute her as their lady and their queen.

The council at Winchester was the moment of Matilda's greatest triumph, and the following day, 3 March, 'she was received in Winchester cathedral in ceremonial procession, with the bishop who was also legate, escorting her on the right side and Bernard, Bishop of St David's, on the left'. A few days later, whilst she was staying at Wilton, Matilda received a visit from the Archbishop of Canterbury, who recognised her as England's ruler.

At Winchester, the Bishop and other assembled dignitaries, recognised Matilda as the 'Lady of England'. This title was a recognition of Matilda's right to the throne, and it is unclear whether she ever actually used the title of queen. Matilda usually preferred to be addressed as 'Empress' but, on the majority of her charters between 1141 and 1148, she used the title of 'Lady of the English'. There are two extant charters from 1141 in which Matilda apparently referred to herself as Queen of England. However, these are both copies and must be treated with suspicion. There is evidence that Matilda commissioned a seal calling herself Empress of the Romans and Queen of England. It seems likely that Matilda intended to delay declaring herself Queen of England until after her coronation. In spite of this, during 1141, she was the ruler of England and a queen in all but name.

It took Matilda two months to persuade the Londoners to receive her for her coronation. Whilst she was waiting at Oxford, she was visited by her uncle, King David of Scotland, who came to see his niece crowned. According to the admittedly biased *Gesta Stephani*, Matilda began to allow her position to go to her head, and she arbitrarily annulled any grant that had been made by Stephen, as well as receiving Stephen's erstwhile supporters ungraciously. It was not unnatural for Matilda to wish to punish those who had supported the usurper, but it was not the most tactful approach to take. As a woman in what had always been a man's office, she was at a disadvantage and behaviour that would have been seen as kingly in a man was, in Matilda, considered arrogant. The *Gesta Stephani* claims that, when the King of Scotland, Bishop of Winchester and Robert of Gloucester came to Matilda on bended knee, she refused to rise respectfully, instead receiving them sitting down. She apparently 'repeatedly sent them away contumely, rebuffing them by an arrogant answer and refusing to hearken to their words; and by this time she no longer relied on their advice, as she should have, and had promised them, but arranged everything as she herself thought fit and according to her own arbitrary will'. Matilda's behaviour was heavily censured, and she continued to distance people throughout 1141.

Matilda was finally admitted to London in June 1141, arriving at the head of a large army to a rather muted welcome. She made Westminster her base as she prepared for her coronation. Matilda badly misjudged the mood of the Londoners. According to the *Gesta Stephani*, she alienated the Londoners by making demands for large sums of money. When the representatives of the city refused to pay, Matilda, 'with a grim look, her forehead wrinkled into a frown, every trace of a woman's gentleness removed from her face, blazed into unbearable fury. Saying that many times the people of London had made very large contributions to the king, that they had lavished their wealth on strengthening him and weakening her'. Matilda was furious at the Londoners' years of support for Stephen, but her reaction was counterproductive, and the leading men of the city began to correspond with Stephen's queen, Matilda of Boulogne, in Kent. On 24 June, as Matilda was sitting down to dinner, a mob came streaming out of the city, and she was forced to flee to Oxford, leaving her possessions behind. This was the end of Matilda's hopes of securing a coronation and, soon afterwards, with the capture of Robert of Gloucester at Winchester, she was forced to release Stephen from captivity and retreat to her powerbase in the west. Following 1141, the aim of Matilda's campaign changed markedly, and she came to accept that she was never likely to win the crown for herself, instead focusing her efforts on keeping her claim alive for her young son, Henry.

During Lent 1142 Matilda held a council at Devizes with her supporters, and it was agreed that she would have to send to Geoffrey in Normandy for aid. Geoffrey sent a response saying that he would deal only with Robert of Gloucester in person, and Matilda's half-brother crossed the Channel to confer with her husband. This was the opportunity that Stephen had been waiting for, and whilst Matilda was staying in Oxford castle, he moved to besiege her. During the three month siege, supplies ran dangerously low, and this led to one of the most famous incidents of Matilda's career. The *Gesta Stephani* records that, as winter set in and the people in the castle grew increasingly hungry and desperate, Matilda 'left the castle by night, with three knights of ripe judgement to accompany her, and went about six miles on foot, by very great exertions on the part of herself and her companions, through the snow and ice'. Matilda and her companions wore white cloaks as camouflage against the snow as they slipped past the lines of Stephen's soldiers, and it must have been a tense and exhausting journey as they crossed the frozen Thames before reaching Wallingford that night.

Matilda returned to Devizes following her escape from Oxford. Robert of Gloucester, who had returned from Normandy with nothing from Geoffrey but Matilda's nine-year-old son Henry, settled in Bristol with the boy whilst Matilda continued to use Devizes as her base and ruled the west of England from there. Matilda minted coins in her name at Bristol and Cardiff, as well as intermittently at Oxford and Wareham. She controlled the appointments of sheriffs in her Gloucestershire heartland and made grants of royal lands. In spite of this, Matilda knew that she was fighting a cause that she could not win, and finally, in 1148, judging her son old enough to take on her claim, she sailed to Normandy, never to return to England.

Matilda settled in Rouen in Normandy, taking an active interest in the politics of the duchy. In 1151, Geoffrey died suddenly, leaving Matilda a widow for the second time. The couple had learned to tolerate each other, but it is unlikely that she mourned his loss. In November 1153, the civil war finally came to an end with Stephen's recognition of Henry as his heir, and Matilda must have been jubilant: she had spent nearly twenty years working for the recognition of her rights in England, and the succession of her son had finally been secured. When Stephen died early the following year, Matilda did not accompany Henry to England for his coronation, perhaps aware of her controversial reputation there.

Matilda spent the rest of her life in Rouen, acting as Henry's unofficial regent in Normandy. Henry respected his mother's political judgement, and she had a great deal of influence over him. She is known to have dissuaded him from invading Ireland in order to provide his brother William with a kingdom, and in joint charters issued by Henry and Matilda, Henry always allowed his mother to be named first, in recognition of her prior rights to Normandy and England. Matilda was acknowledged as ruler of Normandy in a letter from Louis VII of France in 1164.

As Matilda aged, her influence over Henry began to wane. She advised against Thomas Becket's appointment as Archbishop of Canterbury but was overruled by Henry. She was still known for her power to persuade Henry, and in 1164, when Becket was exiled by the king, he appealed to Matilda to intercede for him. A surviving letter of Matilda's outlines her response to this request, and it is clear that she was no friend of the Archbishop:

My lord Pope sent to me, enjoining me, for the remission of my sins, to interfere to renew peace and concord between you and the king, my son, and to try to reconcile you to him. You, as you well know, have asked the same thing from me; wherefore, with the more goodwill, for the honour of God and the Holy church, I have begun and carefully treated of that affair. But it seems a very hard thing to the king, as well as to his barons and council, seeing he so loved and honoured you, and appointed you lord of his whole kingdom and of all his lands, and raised you to the highest honours in the land, believing he might trust you rather than any other; and especially so, because he declares that you have, as far as you could, roused his whole kingdom against him; nor was it your fault that you did not disinherit him by main force. Therefore I send you my faithful servant, Archdeacon Laurence, that by him I may know your will in these affairs, and what sort of disposition you entertain towards my son, and how you intend to conduct yourself, if it should happen that he fully grants my petition and prayer on your behalf. One thing I plainly tell you, that you cannot recover the king's favour; except by great humility and most evident moderation. However what you intend to do in this matter signify to me by my messenger and your letters.

Matilda, reluctantly, attempted to heal the rift between her son and his erstwhile friend, but she was unsuccessful, and the conflict led ultimately to the Archbishop's murder.

As well as maintaining her political interests, Matilda became increasingly pious in her later years, and most of her charters after 1154 were made in favour of Norman monastic houses. Her main patronage was reserved for the monks of Bec, and she was a great benefactor to them. She died in Rouen on 10 September 1167, having remained active to the end and, in accordance with her last wishes, was buried in the abbey of Bec-Hellouin.

Matilda is remembered as the woman who so nearly won the English crown, and she can be considered, to some extent, England's first queen regnant. She was unable to subvert the usual role accorded to women, and her famous epitaph 'great by birth, greater by marriage, greatest in her offspring, here lies the daughter, wife and mother of Henry' sums up the way that she continued to be viewed in relation to her male kin. Matilda's greatest achievement was in keeping her claim to the English throne alive, and the succession of Henry II and his Plantagenet dynasty in England was due to her persistence. Every reigning monarch of England after 1153 has been a direct descendant of the Empress Matilda and she, and her fellow Norman queens, helped shape the role of queen as it developed into the later medieval period.

4

The Plantagenet Queens

Henry II, the first Plantagenet king, claimed the throne through his mother, the Empress Matilda. She, in turn, was the daughter of Matilda of Scotland, the woman who brought the blood of the Anglo-Saxon kings into the Norman royal family. Henry II and his sons ruled over a territory larger than any other English kings either before or after them: the Angevin Empire. The early Plantagenet kings found themselves constantly drawn into continental wars or otherwise busy on the Continent. As a result of this, the office of queen consort during the period reached the pinnacle of its power, and queens were frequently called upon to rule as regents. Between 1154 and 1399, whilst the Plantagenet kings sat on the throne, there were no English queen regnants, but there were many powerful and prominent queens.

The first Plantagenet queen was one of the most prominent women of the medieval period, and she was easily a match for her husband, Henry II. ELEANOR OF AQUITAINE (1122–1204) was the wife of two kings, the mother of a further two, and an important hereditary ruler in her own right. She was the most famous woman of her day and is still widely known and remembered today.

Eleanor of Aquitaine was the heiress of one of the richest fiefdoms of medieval Europe, the duchy of Aquitaine and the county of Poitou. Eleanor's grandfather, Duke William IX, had created a cultured and literary court, and he dominated Eleanor's early childhood. Some years before Eleanor's birth, he had caused a scandal by abducting the beautiful Viscountess of Châtellerault and installing her as his official mistress, forcing his wife to enter a nunnery. The Viscountess persuaded her lover to marry his son to her daughter and William X and Aénor of Châtellerault were married in 1121. They had three children: Eleanor, born in 1122, followed by Petronilla and William Aigret. In 1130, both Eleanor's mother and her brother died suddenly. These deaths were followed in 1137 by William X, and Eleanor became Duchess of Aquitaine and Countess of Poitou.

On his deathbed, William X placed his daughters under the guardianship of Louis VI of France. This was a great opportunity for Louis, and on 18 June 1137, his sixteen-year-old son, also named Louis, set out with a large escort for Aquitaine to marry Eleanor. Eleanor had no input into the choice of her husband. Politically, the match was a good one, but personally, the couple were ill-suited. Eleanor completely dominated her husband after their marriage on 25 July 1137. Louis had been born a second son and raised for a career in the Church, something that had left him deeply pious, but entirely unprepared for the political world that he was forced to enter on the death of his elder brother. Eleanor was deeply unimpressed with her young husband, although Louis was overawed by his fiery and beautiful wife.

Louis VI died on 1 August 1137, leaving the throne to Eleanor's husband and obliging the couple to travel at once to Paris. Eleanor found Paris a very poor substitute for the opulence that she had known in her childhood, and the royal palace, in particular, was in a bad state of disrepair. She was crowned queen of France at Christmas 1137, although she was given little role in government, appearing only rarely in the charters of Louis's reign.

Whilst she had no defined political role, Eleanor was able to influence Louis. In 1141, for example, he invaded the county of Toulouse on her behalf, a territory claimed by her family. The campaign was a disaster, but it was not the last military exploit that the French king carried out for Eleanor. In 1142, Eleanor's sister, Petronilla, caused a scandal by marrying the nobleman Raoul de Vermandois, who then sent his existing wife, the niece of the Count of Champagne, home to her family in disgrace. The Count of Champagne appealed to the Pope for his niece's reinstatement, and Eleanor, who threw her support behind her sister, persuaded Louis to invade Champagne in January 1143. This campaign proved to be not just a military disaster, but also a personal one for Louis: when his army reached the town of Vitry in Champagne, the church there was accidentally set alight, burning those who had taken shelter inside to death. Following the disaster, Louis's captains found him in a trance-like state. A further breakdown in the summer of 1143 caused him to begin wearing monastic habits and spend hours at prayer. The trouble in Eleanor's marriage dates to this time, and she declared that 'she had married a monk, not a king'.

Eleanor already had reason to feel discontented with her marriage. By 1144, she had become worried by her failure to conceive a child. In June, she met with the churchman Bernard of Clairvaux privately to ask for his assistance in lifting the sentence of excommunication that hung over Petronilla and Raoul de Vermondois. Instead of offering to help, Bernard criticised Eleanor for involving herself in politics, and she promptly burst into tears, saying that she did so only because she had no child. Bernard then offered a deal: if she stopped interfering in politics, he would ask God to send her a child. Eleanor duly did as she was asked, and in 1145, she bore a daughter, Marie. The child's sex was a disappointment, but she was, at least, proof that Eleanor could bear a child. Her difficulties in conceiving appear to have been due more to her husband than to herself with Louis able to consummate his three marriages only rarely, and then often only after pressure from the Church.

Louis's piety increased, and at Easter, the court gathered at Vezelay, where he promised to undertake a crusade. His decision to take the cross was intended to be a great ceremonial occasion, and according to the chronicler Odo of Deuil, Bernard of Clairvaux 'mounted the platform accompanied by the king, who was wearing the cross; and when heaven's instrument [Bernard] poured forth the dew of the divine word, as he was wont, with loud outcry people on every side began to demand crosses'. Eleanor also did her bit for recruitment; as soon as her husband had taken the cross, she and her ladies appeared, dressed as Amazons, and rode through the crowd, encouraging those assembled to join the crusade. The recruitment drive continued right up to the moment of departure, and before the army set out, there was a great ceremony at St Denis at which Louis received a banner and a pilgrim's wallet, accompanied by a personal blessing from the Pope. Eleanor was once again right in the centre of events, and Odo of Deuil tells us that 'the crowds and the king's wife and his mother, who nearly perished because of their tears and the heat could not endure the delay'.

Eleanor's enthusiasm for the crusade was as genuine as Louis's, although, unlike her pious husband, it is likely that she saw it as a means to escape the tedium of her daily life in Paris. It was not unusual for women to accompany their husband's on crusade and the chronicler William of Newburgh believed that the impetus behind Eleanor's participation came from Louis himself:

Initially she had so emmeshed and captivated the heart of the young man with the charm of her beauty and that when he was about to embark on that most celebrated expedition his over-urgent longing for his young wife led him to decide that she should certainly not be left at home, but should set out with him to the wars.

It is difficult to imagine Louis VII having an over-urgent longing for anything other than the Church, and it was also cruelly suggested that he did not trust his wife enough to leave her behind.

Louis and Eleanor followed the route that their ally, the Holy Roman Emperor Conrad, had taken some months before, breaking their journey in Constantinople. Eleanor and the Byzantine Empress Irene corresponded during the journey to Constantinople and, upon their arrival there, Eleanor and Louis were entertained lavishly. They were taken to visit shrines and other sites, as well as invited to banquets in their honour. Eleanor was impressed by the city. Odo of Deuil comments on Constantinople:

In every respect she exceeds moderation; for, just as she surpasses other cities in wealth, so, too, does she surpass them in vice. Also, she possesses many churches unequal to Santa Sophia in size but equal to it in beauty, which are to be marvelled at for their beauty and their many saintly relics. Those who had the opportunity entered these places, some to see the sights and others to worship faithfully.

The presence of an army encamped outside his capital was not entirely to the taste of the Byzantine emperor, and he made it clear that his guests were expected to leave as soon as possible. The French set out in high spirits and were disconcerted to hear, soon after leaving Constantinople, that the German army had been decimated in the Holy Land. In November 1147, the Holy Roman Emperor, fleeing the ruins of his army, joined the French, and Louis and Eleanor had no choice but to continue onwards towards Antioch.

In order to reach Antioch, it was necessary to cross Mount Cadmos, where the Germans had sustained their heavy defeat. Eleanor rode separately from Louis, in the vanguard of her army, which was led by one of her own vassals. On the day of the crossing, the vanguard, which carried little luggage, quickly reached the proposed campsite. Anxious to cross the mountain as quickly as possible, they decided to press on. This proved to be a disaster for the rear of the army, which was led by Louis. His soldiers, arriving at the original campsite only as night was falling, were horrified to find that the vanguard was nowhere in sight. As darkness set in, they were attacked by the Turks, causing heavy losses. The royal guard was killed and Louis, who fought bravely, only escaped because he was not recognised in his simple clothes. He spent the night hiding in a tree, before limping over the mountain to join the vanguard in the morning. Eleanor was later blamed for the ambush, with claims that her luggage hampered the army's progress.

Eleanor was relieved to finally reach Antioch on 19 March 1148 and spent ten days there in luxury. Antioch was ruled by her uncle, Raymond of Aquitaine, her father's younger brother, who had married the heiress to the principality. Raymond, like all the male members of Eleanor's family, was tall and handsome and, unlike Louis, had a reputation as a soldier. Eleanor found him fascinating, spending a great deal of time in his company. This caused comment, and according to one contemporary, John of Salisbury, whilst the French remained in Antioch

to console, heal and revive the survivors from the wreck of the army, the attentions paid by the prince to the queen, and his constant, indeed almost continuous, conversation with her, aroused the king's suspicions. They were greatly strengthened when the queen wished to remain behind, although the king was preparing to leave, and the prince made every effort to keep her, if the king would give him consent. And when the king made haste to tear her away, she mentioned their kinship, saying it was not lawful for them to remain together as man and wife, since they were related in the fourth and fifth degrees.

It is not impossible that Eleanor and her uncle were lovers, and the scandal remained with her throughout her lifetime. However, she stayed in Antioch for only ten days, and it seems more likely that she found a sympathetic confidant in her uncle and finally decided to end her loveless marriage. The consanguinity between Eleanor and Louis had already been mentioned before they left France, and it had been suggested that this could be the reason for their lack of sons. Eleanor, who had no desire to continue following Louis's disastrous crusade, or even remain as his wife, seized upon this as a way of securing a divorce. Louis did not know how to respond to Eleanor's request, but his servants persuaded him that it would shame him if he left Antioch without her, and when it was time to travel to Jerusalem, she was bundled along against her will.

Eleanor remained in disgrace throughout her time in Jerusalem. It is a measure of the estrangement between her and Louis that, when they finally set sail for France, in April 1149, they sailed in separate ships. Louis, faced with Eleanor's coldness towards him, agreed to consider the state of their marriage, and both he and Eleanor broke their journey to visit the Pope at Tusculum. To Eleanor's horror, the Pope dismissed her concerns about the marriage, taking it upon himself to reconcile them. According to John of Salisbury, 'this ruling plainly delighted the king, for he loved the queen passionately, in an almost childish way'. The Pope even went so far as to prepare a special bed in which the couple were to cement their reunion, leading to the birth of a second daughter, Alix, in the summer of 1150. Eleanor was nonplussed by the Pope's enthusiasm for her marriage, but the birth of another daughter did prove something of a blessing to her, as, soon after Alix's birth, even Louis's council began to suggest that he take a new wife who could give him a son.

For Eleanor, the situation in Paris remained unsatisfactory until August 1151 when Geoffrey, Count of Anjou, and his son, Henry FitzEmpress, arrived to perform homage for Normandy. Henry was over ten years younger than Eleanor and he was not handsome, being stocky with a large head and a reddish, freckled, complexion. He compared favourably to Louis though, being an active and energetic ruler, unlike the monkish Louis. It is improbable that Eleanor and Henry had the privacy to commit adultery in Paris, but during the visit, they agreed to marry once Eleanor was free. A contemporary,

Gerald of Wales, commented that Henry 'basely stole Queen Eleanor from his liege lord, Louis, king of the French, and then married her'.

Following Henry's departure from Paris, Eleanor again requested a divorce. After fifteen years of sonless marriage, Louis was prepared to consider the matter, and on 21 March 1152, their marriage was annulled on the grounds of consanguinity. The separation was amicable, with Louis retaining custody of their two daughters. He was entirely oblivious to Eleanor's plans for the future and allowed her to return home to Aquitaine without attempting to assert any control over her lands or freedom.

Henry arrived secretly in Poitiers in mid-May, and he and Eleanor were married. The marriage was not a love match and was solely based on political considerations: Eleanor was the greatest heiress in Europe, and Henry, who had already conquered Normandy, was close to victory in the civil war in England. The marriage was soon successful, and on 17 August 1153, Eleanor gave birth to her first son, William. For Eleanor, at thirty-one, this was a major triumph and further joy followed soon after with the death of King Stephen. Eleanor and William joined Henry in Rouen in June 1154, sailing for England in December. The couple were crowned together at Westminster on 19 December 1154, and in February 1155, Eleanor bore her second son, Henry. Henry II, who was often absent from England, relied on Eleanor to fulfil a political role, leaving her as regent in 1156 when he crossed to Normandy. Eleanor performed the role again in 1158, and Henry had full confidence in her abilities.

Although Eleanor was allowed a defined political role for the first time in her life during her marriage to Henry, her main activity was childbearing. To his parents' grief, William died in 1156, but in June of that year, Eleanor bore a daughter, Matilda. Her birth was followed at Oxford in September 1157 by that of Richard, with Geoffrey being born in September 1158. Daughters, Eleanor and Joanna were born in 1161 and 1165 respectively, and Eleanor's last child, John, was born on Christmas Eve in 1166. After years of childlessness and disappointment, Eleanor was delighted in her children, and of the eight she bore Henry, only William died in infancy. Richard was always Eleanor's favourite and she named him as the heir to Aquitaine at his birth.

In the early years of their marriage, Eleanor and Henry worked together as an effective team in ruling their empire but personal relations between them soured quickly. Henry was unfaithful and began his most long-lasting affair, with Rosamund Clifford, in around 1165. That Christmas was the first of their marriage that Eleanor and Henry spent apart, with Eleanor at Angers and Henry at Oxford. There was something of a reconciliation at Easter 1166, when Eleanor conceived her youngest child. She was again alone at Christmas 1166. There were no further reconciliations between the couple, and from mid-1166, they lived apart.

Eleanor spent 1167 preparing for her daughter Matilda's marriage to the Duke of Saxony, and in September, she escorted her to Dover. That Christmas, Eleanor informed Henry that she had decided to return to Aquitaine, a move that was, in effect, an informal separation. Henry agreed to this and Eleanor departed for Poitiers, accompanied by several of her children. She spent the years 1168 to 1173 ruling Aquitaine personally, and this may have been the happiest time of her life. She was visited by all her children except Alix and John, and even her eldest daughter, Marie, Countess of Champagne, spent time with her mother, with an affection developing between the two women, who were virtual strangers.

In spite of her personal happiness, animosity continued to grow between Eleanor and Henry. In 1170, Henry succeeded in having their eldest son, young Henry, crowned as his heir at Westminster, an event to which Eleanor was not invited. Like Eleanor, Henry was very fond of their children, but he was unable to see that they were growing up and needed their independence. This led to a growing resentment between Henry and his elder three sons, and in April 1173, they rose against him. Eleanor was the ringleader in this revolt, and when Henry summoned her to join him, at Easter 1173, she refused to come. The Archbishop of Rouen threatened Eleanor with excommunication if she persisted in her refusal, but she remained in Aquitaine. By June, the rebellion had spread throughout Henry's French lands. In August, he struck back, and Eleanor found herself cut off from her sons and other allies at Poitiers as Henry marched towards her. A few weeks later, she was captured trying to escape to France dressed as a man. Henry brought Eleanor back to England as a prisoner, ordering that she be kept closely confined at Salisbury castle.

Eleanor's fortunes reached their lowest ebb in 1173, and she spent the rest of Henry's reign as a prisoner: sixteen long years. Though some news reached her in her prison, she was effectively cut off from the world. In 1179, Louis died. Whilst Eleanor is unlikely to have grieved for him, news of his death must have reminded her of her own mortality. A bigger blow came in June 1183 with the death of her eldest surviving son, Henry, the Young King. According to the chronicler Roger de Hoveden, the Young King had remained in rebellion against his father, and in 1183, finding himself short of funds, he stripped the tomb of St Andemar at the monastery of Saint Mary de Roche Andemar and carried away the treasures for his own personal use. The Young King's contemporaries saw his death as the judgement of God, as he fell dangerously ill soon after his attack on the tomb. Aware that he was dying, he sent for his father, but Henry refused to come, understandably fearing treachery. As a sign of his repentance, he confessed his sins and put on a hair shirt before ordering that a cord be tied around his neck. As a final act of penitence, he was laid on a floor strewn with ashes before dying. When Henry heard the news of his son's death, he burst into tears and threw himself on the ground with grief. Eleanor and Henry's grief was further increased in 1186 when their third surviving son, Geoffrey, was killed in a tournament in Paris.

The Young King's last request was that his father show his mother mercy. Henry heeded this, and the conditions of Eleanor's imprisonment eased somewhat as the years went on. In October 1183, for example, Eleanor was brought to Normandy to take possession of certain castles that were disputed by France. Although she remained a prisoner, she was able to spend six months in the company of her daughter, Matilda, and on her return to England, her daughter visited her. At Lent 1185, Eleanor was again summoned to Normandy by Henry in order to receive the surrender of Aquitaine from Richard. Henry, bewildered by the hostility directed at him by his sons, was by then already worn down by the years of struggle, and during the winter of 1188 and 1189, Richard was in open rebellion with Philip Augustus, the young king of France. By July 1189, Henry was finally defeated by his son. He was also in ill health, and when, as part of the terms of his surrender, he received a list of those who had rebelled against him, he was heartbroken to see his youngest, and favourite son, John, at the top of the list. With this revelation, Henry II turned his face to the wall and died.

Eleanor did not mourn Henry, and she welcomed his death for the change that it brought to her circumstances. Her favourite son, Richard, succeeded unchallenged and immediately sent word to England that Eleanor should be set free and appointed to act as regent. Eleanor immediately went on a progress throughout the kingdom, promoting her son's rule, as Roger de Hoveden recounts:

[She] moved her royal court from city to city, and from castle to castle, just as she thought proper; and sending messengers throughout all the counties of England, ordered that all captives should be liberated from prison and confinement, for the good of the soul of Henry, her lord; inasmuch as, in her own person, she had learnt by experience that confinement is distasteful to mankind, and that it is a most delightful refreshment to the spirits to be liberated therefrom.

This was a cause close to Eleanor's heart, and it also made Richard, who was something of an unknown quantity in England, very popular.

Richard landed at Portsmouth on 13 August 1189 and met Eleanor at Winchester. They travelled slowly towards London, where Eleanor had arranged a grand coronation at Westminster Abbey, which was held on 3 September. Richard had little knowledge of England, and he relied upon Eleanor to help govern his new kingdom. He also had no intention of remaining in England for long and quickly set about raising money to fund his plans to go on crusade.

Eleanor's release also saw her reunited with her youngest son, John, whom she had not seen since his infancy. When Richard was ready to leave for the crusade, he obtained an oath from John that he would not enter England for three years. Eleanor was determined that John should not be disadvantaged, and at her express request, Richard agreed that John could be released from his oath. Soon after Richard left for the Holy Land in December 1189, Eleanor set out for Navarre to fetch a bride for Richard. She and the selected bride, Berengaria of Navarre, travelled together to Sicily, where Eleanor left her new daughter-in-law with her son before hurrying back to England, where her presence was badly needed.

Eleanor's appeal for Richard to release John from his oath proved to be a costly mistake, as, soon after Richard left, John began to call himself the king's heir and had himself appointed as the supreme governor of England. Eleanor landed at Portsmouth on 11 February 1192. As soon as he heard of her arrival, John ordered that a ship be prepared so that he could flee to Philip Augustus in France, but Eleanor swiftly prevented him. According to Richard of Devizes,

> His mother, however, fearing that the light-minded youth might be going to attempt something, by the counsels of the French, against his lord and brother, with an anxious mind tried in every way she could to prevent her son's proposed journey. Her maternal heart was moved and pained when she called to mind the condition of her older sons and the premature deaths of both of them because of their sins.

Eleanor continued saying 'with all her strength she wanted to make sure that faith would be kept between her youngest sons, at least, so that their mother might die more happily than had their father, who had gone before them'. She called four great councils, at Windsor, Oxford, London and Winchester and, with tears and pleas to the noblemen assembled, obtained John's promise to remain in England whilst Richard was away.

Eleanor took control of the government on her return to England. She hoped that Richard's absence would only be brief, so the news, in January 1193, that Richard had been captured on his way home from the crusade was devastating. Eleanor dispatched the Abbots of Boxley and Robertsbridge to Germany to find out where Richard was being held, and from them, she learned that he had been handed over to the Holy Roman Emperor, Henry VI. Eleanor called a council at St Albans in June 1193 to discuss the terms of Richard's release and to appoint officers to collect the ransom demanded. She threw herself into securing Richard's release and personally selected hostages from amongst the nobility to be sent to Germany.

Eleanor also directly appealed to the Pope for help. Two of her letters survive, and they show just what a remarkable character the queen was:

To the reverend Father and Lord Celestine, by the Grace of God, the supreme Pontiff, Eleanor; in God's anger, Queen of England, Duchess of Normandy, Countess of Anjou, begs him to show himself to be a father to a pitiable mother. I had decided to remain quiet in case a fullness of heart and a passionate grief might elicit some word against the chief of priests which was somewhat less than cautious, and I was therefore accused of insolence and arrogance. Certainly grief is not that different from insanity while it is inflamed with its own force. It does not recognise a master, is afraid of no ally, it has no regard for anyone, and it does not spare them – not even you.

So no-one should be surprised if the modesty of my words is sharpened by the strength of my grief – I am mourning for a loss that is not private; but my personal grief cannot be comforted – it is set deep in the heart of my spirit. The arrows of the Lord are truly directed against me, and their anger will drain my spirit. Races which have been torn apart, peoples which have been shattered, provinces which have been stripped, in general the whole western church which is worn out with deep sorrow, they are all beseeching you in a spirit which has been ground down and humiliated, you whom God established above the races and kingdoms in the fullness of His power.

Please listen to the cry of the afflicted, for our troubles have multiplied beyond number; and you cannot conceal those troubles in as much as they are a mark of criminality and disgrace, since you are the Vicar of Christ Crucified, Peter's successor, the Priest of Christ, the Lord's Anointed one, even a God over Pharaohs. Father, may your face provide a judgement, may your eyes see impartially, the prayers of the people depend on your decision and on the mercy of your see; unless your hands seize justice more quickly, the complete tragedy of this evil event will rebound on to you.'

Eleanor's first letter continued at length, using allusions from the Bible and from history to demonstrate both her grief and her need for the Pope to intervene and help secure Richard's release. When her first letter failed to have the desired effect, she drafted a second, speaking of the conflict and misfortune that had afflicted her sons:

My insides have been torn out of me, my family has been carried off, it has rolled past me; the Young King and the earl of Brittany [Eleanor's son, Geoffrey] sleep in the dust – their mother is so ill-fated she is forced to live, so that without cure she is tortured by the memory of the dead. As some comfort, I still have two sons, who are alive today, but only to punish me, wretched and condemned. King Richard is detained in chains; his brother John is killing the people of the prisoner's kingdom with his sword, he is ravaging the land with fires.

Eleanor received little help from the Pope, but by 1194, the ransom had been raised and she and the Archbishop of Rouen were summoned by the Emperor to bring the ransom to Speyer. In late January 1194, Richard was released, and Eleanor and her son returned home in triumph. It was around this time that Eleanor also began to feel her age, and content that Richard was secure on his throne, she retired to Fontrevault Abbey in Aquitaine, where she hoped to live quietly in retirement. Eleanor rarely appears in sources between 1194 and 1199, and she lived a secluded and religious life.

Even at the age of seventy-eight, Eleanor did not entirely cut herself off from the world, and in April 1199, when she received word that Richard was lying dangerously wounded at Chalus, she travelled day and night to be with him. He was beyond help when she arrived, and he died in her arms on 6 April 1199, having named John as his successor. This was the biggest blow of Eleanor's life, but she did not allow herself to collapse with grief and, instead, threw herself into securing the throne for John. Eleanor's son, Geoffrey, had left a son, Arthur of Brittany, and Arthur, as the son of the elder brother claimed the throne in preference to his uncle. Eleanor, who supported her youngest son, advised him to go at once to Chinon to secure the royal treasury. John then crossed to England, where he was crowned on 27 May, whilst Eleanor remained on the Continent, making a tour of her lands. In mid-June 1199, she travelled to Tours, where she did homage in person to Philip Augustus for Aquitaine in order to ensure that Arthur could make no claim to her duchy.

Eleanor was deeply involved in the negotiations for a truce between John and Philip Augustus shortly after Christmas 1199. As part of the terms of the truce, it was agreed that John would provide a bride for Philip's son and Eleanor accordingly set out on the long journey to Castile to select one of the daughters of her daughter, Eleanor, the Queen of Castile. This was an arduous journey for a woman approaching her eightieth birthday, but she was at least able to spend some months in Castile meeting her grandchildren and reacquainting herself with her daughter. Eleanor selected her youngest granddaughter, Blanche, and the pair set off towards Normandy. Age finally caught up with Eleanor, and whilst she had hoped to escort her granddaughter all the way to Normandy for her marriage, she was forced to admit defeat, leaving Blanche with her escorts and travelling instead to Fontrevault for some much needed rest.

Eleanor's story did not end with her return to Fontrevault. Whilst John had secured his throne through his alliance with Philip, Arthur of Brittany remained a threat. In May 1202, Eleanor decided to travel to Poitiers to aid John in his war against his nephew. When Arthur learned that his grandmother had left Fontrevault, he pursued her, and Eleanor found herself besieged in the flimsy Castle of Mirebeau. By the time John reached Mirebeau, Eleanor and her retinue were trapped in the keep with the rest of the castle occupied by Arthur and his men. John swept into Mirebeau, capturing Arthur and winning what was to be his only victory on the Continent. Eleanor was relieved to see her son, and they had a conference together before she gladly returned to Fontrevault. Given Arthur's attack on her, it is unlikely that she was sympathetic about his fate. He disappeared into John's dungeon and was probably murdered soon afterwards.

Eleanor never emerged from her third period of retirement at Fontrevault, and at some point in 1204, she slipped quietly into a coma, dying on 1 April 1204 at the age of eighty-two. She was one of the longest-lived and most active of all the English queens, and she became a legend in her own lifetime. She entirely overshadowed her daughter-in-law, Berengaria of Navarre.

With the exception of Sophia Dorothea of Celle, who was never recognised as queen, BERENGARIA OF NAVARRE (*c.* 1165/70–1230) was the only English queen never to actually visit England. Though she was the wife of Richard I 'the Lionheart', her marriage, which began with such great promise, was a failure. Berengaria was the eldest daughter of King Sancho VI of Navarre, a kingdom that lay to the south of Aquitaine, and his wife, Sanchia of Castile. Her date of birth is nowhere recorded, but an analysis of her skeleton suggested a date of around 1165–1170. Berengaria was educated and was good at languages, speaking Castilian, Basque and Latin. Following her mother's death in 1179, Berengaria took on something of the queen's role at court, and this may account for the fact that no marriage was, at first, arranged for her. In recognition of this, in 1185, Berengaria's father gave her independent standing at court with the grant of a fiefdom.

Richard I succeeded his father as king of England in 1189. He had been betrothed since childhood to Alais of France, but both he and his mother, Eleanor of Aquitaine, were determined not to allow the marriage. Contemporary sources suggest that Richard was suspicious of Alais's virtue, and there were rumours that she had been his father's mistress. Whatever the truth of this, Richard had no intention of marrying Alais, and it fell to his mother to organise an alternative marriage. Eleanor's choice of Berengaria made sound political sense, guaranteeing a friendly neighbour to Aquitaine during Richard's absence on crusade. There were also links between the two families. Richard was a good friend of Berengaria's brother, and her father had been entertained by Henry II at Limoges in 1172.

Berengaria's father was flattered at the suggestion of the match, and he entertained Eleanor lavishly when she arrived in Navarre in September 1190. Eleanor was in a hurry to supply Richard with a bride before he sailed for the Holy Land, and after only a short visit, she and Berengaria set out to join him. Berengaria's thoughts on the betrothal do not survive, but she must have been in awe of her famous mother-in-law, and she was never able to move out of Eleanor's shadow. The *Gesta Regis Ricardi* states that Richard 'was attracted by her graceful manner and high birth, he had desired her very much for a long time – since he was count of Poitou'. Richard competed in a tournament in Navarre before he became king, and the couple may have met then. According to legend, Richard was captivated by Berengaria but was unable to marry her at the time due to his engagement to Alais. Given the later disinterest shown by Richard towards Berengaria, a love affair seems unlikely, and Berengaria was apparently no beauty, with one contemporary, Richard of Devizes, commenting that she was 'a maiden more prudent than pretty'. Richard was probably bisexual, with a preference for male partners, and Berengaria was never able to capture his interest.

After leaving Navarre, the party set out across the Alps and travelled through Italy towards Sicily. They arrived in Brindisi in March 1191, where Richard sent ships to bring his mother and fiancée to Reggio. Richard travelled in person to meet them and escorted them to Messina. He was satisfied with Berengaria, and his mother left soon afterwards, leaving Berengaria under the chaperonage of Richard's widowed sister, Joanna, Queen of Sicily. Since Berengaria's arrival coincided with Lent, it was decided that the marriage would occur after Easter, when the couple had reached the Holy Land.

Richard was eager to set out for the Holy Land, and on 10 April 1191, his two-hundred-strong fleet set sail. According to Richard of Devizes, in the first rank of the fleet sailed three ships, 'in one of which were the queen of Sicily and the Navarrese maiden, perhaps still a virgin'. The crossing was an ordeal and a number of ships were driven by storms onto the coast of Cyprus. Berengaria's own ship, which was driven into the port of Limassol, cast anchor and waited for Richard, with everyone on board uncertain as to whether it was safe to land. The *Gesta Regis Ricardi* explains that they 'had not dared to go on shore because they did not know the state of the country and they were afraid of the cruelty and treachery of the emperor'. They were right to be concerned. News of their presence reached the Emperor of Cyprus, who resolved to seize the ship and take the occupants captive. The emperor sent a message to the two queens, telling them that they could come to shore in safety and sending them presents of food and wine in an attempt to tempt them to land. Joanna and Berengaria were troubled and 'they began to waver, anxious that if they submitted to the emperor's persuasions they would be taken captive. On the other hand, they were afraid that he would attack them in their refusals'. Finally, on the third day, the two women sent a message to the emperor saying that they would disembark the next day, in order to buy themselves some time. Their ruse paid off and 'on that same Sunday, while they were gloomily discussing and bewailing their situation to each other and gazing out across the sea, two ships appeared in the distance'. They were overjoyed when gradually more ships appeared and they realised that it was the royal fleet. In anger at the emperor's treatment of his ships, Richard attacked the island and conquered it.

Berengaria was widely considered an excellent choice of a bride for

Richard, and the *Gesta Regis Ricardi* commented that she was 'very wise and of good character'. Due to the delay occasioned by Richard's conquest of Cyprus, the couple were finally married at Limassol on 12 May 1191, with Berengaria being crowned Queen of England at the same time. Richard was reported to have been very merry at the ceremony, and whilst no record of Berengaria's demeanour or dress survives, Richard arrived for his marriage splendidly dressed. For Berengaria, her marriage was perhaps the happiest moment of her life, and it was as a bride that she was portrayed in her tomb effigy many years later. Within a month of the wedding, Richard set sail for the Holy Land with Berengaria and Joanna, who had been joined by a captured Cypriot princess, travelling together in their own ship.

Berengaria played no part in the military campaigns of the crusade. Soon after her arrival, the crusaders secured the fall of Acre, and Richard had the royal palace there fitted out for his wife and sister. Whilst Berengaria lived in some luxury during the crusade, she was not sheltered from all its horrors, and it is likely that she witnessed the slaughter of prisoners ordered by her husband before he left Acre. In August, Richard headed south with his army, leaving Berengaria, Joanna, and the Cypriot princess under a protective guard in Acre. The three royal women spent an isolated month in the palace before Richard returned and instructed them to follow him to the newly captured city of Jaffa. Richard then moved on towards Jerusalem and Berengaria and Joanna joined him for Christmas at his camp. They spent the rest of the crusade in various strongholds, then sailed for home from Acre on 29 September 1192. Richard sailed separately the following month.

Berengaria and Richard spent little time together during the crusade, and it appears that they quickly found themselves to be incompatible. There is no evidence that Berengaria ever conceived a child. and there have been suggestions that the marriage was never consummated. This is possible, but it seems unlikely, as Richard's need for an heir was the main reason behind his marriage. Once it became clear that there would be no child, the King had little use for his marriage or for Berengaria.

The years between 1192 and 1199 are the most obscure of Berengaria's life. She and Joanna arrived in Rome after leaving the crusade and spent six months there. It was there that they learned of

Richard's capture in Austria, and Berengaria appealed to the Pope for aid in securing her husband's release. A romantic legend claims that it was Berengaria herself who first raised the alarm about Richard's capture. According to the story, she was shopping in the market when she saw a jewelled belt for sale that she recognised as belonging to Richard. This story is merely part of the legend that has built up around the capture of the famous king, but it is clear that Berengaria was distressed by her husband's imprisonment. Berengaria and Joanna left Rome in June 1193 and Berengaria played no further part in securing Richard's release. She remained quietly on the Continent, perhaps waiting for a summons, but on his return to England in 1194, Richard made no attempt to send for his wife. It was his mother, Eleanor of Aquitaine, who was present at his ceremonial second coronation, not Berengaria.

In 1195, Berengaria and Richard were finally reconciled. The sources differ as to the reason for the reconciliation, although it was Richard who took the initiative. One story claimed that Richard met a hermit whilst out hunting who admonished him for his sexual sins. Richard ignored this warning but fell ill soon afterwards and, seeing this as God's anger at his conduct, sent for Berengaria. Another version holds that the famous Bishop Hugh of Lincoln rebuked Richard, saying that 'concerning you, indeed, and I speak in sorrow, it is generally reported that you are not faithful in your marriage bed, and do not keep inviolate the privileges of the church, especially in the matter of the appointment or election of Bishops'. Bishop Hugh had little respect for Richard and his siblings, claiming, on his deathbed, that it was better to die than to see how the English Church would fare under Angevin rule, claiming,

The words of the Bible must inevitably be fulfilled in the case of the descendants of King Henry. 'Bastard shoots will not have deep roots' and 'the offspring of an adulterous union shall be destroyed'. The present king of the French will avenge his pious father Louis on the sons of the adulteress [Eleanor of Aquitaine] who forsook her lawful husband shamelessly for his rival.

Bishop Hugh publicly censured the King for his abandonment of his wife, and chastened, Richard recalled Berengaria. Berengaria was

Above left: 7. Queen Bertha in stained glass at Canterbury Cathedral. Bertha has been credited with bringing Christianity to England, and her family insisted that she be granted the freedom to practise her faith in Kent.

Above right: 8. Queen Bertha from Canterbury Cathedral. The Frankish princess founded the first Anglo-Saxon Christian church in England.

Right: 9. A folio from the manuscript by the early British chronicler Nennius (*Historia Brittonum*) and the earliest mention of King Arthur, who was a real historical figure, unlike his queen, Guinevere, who was purely mythical.

In illo tempore saxones invalescebant in multitudine & crescebant in brittannia. Mortuo aute hengisto octha fili' ei' transivit de sinistrali parte brittanniae ad regnum cantoru & de ipso orti sr reges cantie. Tunc arthur pugnabat contra illos in illis dieb; cu regibz brecconu f ipse dux erat bellorum. Primu bellu fuit in ostiu fluminis quod dicit glein sctm & tciu & qrtu & quintu sup aliud flumen quod dicit dubglas & in regione linnuis. Sextu bellum sup flumen quod vocat bassas. Septimu fuit bellu in silua celidonis idt cat coit celidon. Octauum fuit bellu in castello guinnion. In quo arthur portauit imagine sce marie ppetue uirginis sup humeros suos & pagani uersi sr in fugam in illo die. & cedes magna fuit sup illos p uirtutem dni nri ihu xpi & p uirtute sce mariae uirginis genitricis ei. Nonu bellu gestu in urbe legionis. Decimu gessit bellu in litore f flaminis quod vocat tribruit. Undecimu factu bellu in monte qui dicit agned. Duodecimu fuit bellu in monte badonis. in quo corruer in uno die nongenti sexaginta uiri de uno impetu arthur.

Above left: 10. Offa's Dyke. The great barrier built between England and Wales stands today as a testament to King Offa's power.

Above right: 11. Silver penny of Cynethryth. Cynethryth was the most notorious of the early queens. The wife of King Offa of Mercia, Cynethryth (died after 798) is the only Anglo-Saxon queen to have minted her own coins.

12. Offa from a thirteenth-century English manuscript.

Above left: 13. A statue of King Alfred at Winchester. Alfred is remembered as having been one of the greatest kings England ever had, and most of the later kings and queens of England were his descendants. *Above right:* 14. Winchester Cathedral. Winchester was the capital of the Anglo-Saxon kingdom of Wessex, and a number of early queens are associated with the cathedral and monasteries there. Alfred the Great's wife, Queen Ealswitha, is buried here in the New Minster beside her husband. It was rare for Anglo-Saxon queens to be buried with their husbands, and this is a further indication that Ealswitha enjoyed a happy life and a long and contented marriage. *Below:* 15. The ruins of St Oswald's Minster, Gloucester. The original church was built on the orders of Ethelfleda of Mercia, the daughter of King Alfred and an important Anglo-Saxon ruler in her own right.

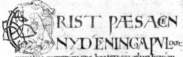

Above left: 16. The *Anglo-Saxon Chronicle*. The *Anglo-Saxon Chronicle* mentions Ethelfleda of Damerham as Edmund I's queen.

Above right: 17. The coronation of King Edgar at Bath Abbey. Unusually for the Anglo-Saxon period, Elfrida, Edgar's queen, shared his coronation.

Left: 18. Queen Emma's Mortuary Chest at Winchester Cathedral. The Queen shares her grave with her second husband, King Cnut, and son, King Harthacnut.

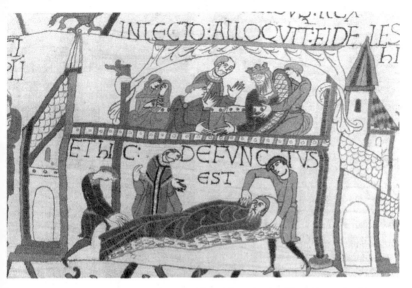

19. Queen Edith at King Edward the Confessor's deathbed from the Bayeux Tapestry.

20. A page from a gospel book belonging to St Margaret, a descendant of the Anglo-Saxon royal dynasty and the mother of Matilda of Scotland.

Above left: 21. The coat of arms of Matilda of Flanders, the first Norman queen of England, from Lincoln Cathedral. Matilda's descent from the English royal family and close relationship with the kings of France was a deciding factor in William the Conqueror's choice of her as a bride.

Above right: 22. The coat of arms of Matilda of Boulogne, the wife of King Stephen, from Lincoln Cathedral. Stephen relied on his wife to aid him in his war with his cousin, the Empress Matilda, and Matilda of Boulogne proved herself to be an effective military commander.

Left: 23. A depiction of St Catherine in a stained-glass window from the church at Deerhurst in Gloucestershire. The saint is depicted in the dress of a medieval queen.

24. Isabella of Angoulême from her tomb at Fontrevaud.

25. Eleanor of Aquitaine from her tomb at Fontrevaud Abbey. The abbey became the mausoleum of the early Plantagenet kings and queens and was the place of both Eleanor of Aquitaine and Isabella of Angoulême's retirement and death.

26. Coat of arms of Isabella of Angoulême, wife of King John, Lincoln Cathedral.

27. A medieval king and queen embracing from an thirteenth-century English manuscrpt.

Above left: 28. The Eleanor Cross at Geddington. Only three of the monuments to Queen Eleanor of Castile now survive.

Above right & below: 29. and 30. The Eleanor Cross at Hardinstone. The Eleanor Crosses provided a lasting testament to Edward I's devotion to his wife, Eleanor of Castile.

31. The Eleanor Cross at Waltham Cross. During her lifetime, Eleanor of Castile's reputation was poor, but the crosses served to create a posthumous reputation for queenly virtue.

32. Eleanor of Castile, effigy on monument, Lincoln Cathedral.

33. Berkeley Castle. Edward II was imprisoned and murdered in the castle on the orders of his wife, Isabella of France, and her love, Roger Mortimer.

34. Actual portraits of Richard II and Anne of Bohemia, though the results may be affected to some extent by their conformity to the type of features from which artists found it difficult to escape. From *Liber Regalis* (Coronation Book of Richard II) executed in 1377 or 1378.

Above left: 35. The tomb of Joan of Navarre at Canterbury Cathedral. Joan and Henry IV made a love match, but Joan's time in England was far from easy, and she was the only queen to be punished for witchcraft.

Above right: 36. The coronation of Joan of Navarre, Westminster Abbey February 1403.

Left: 37. Joan of Navarre at a joust on the occasion of her marriage to Henry IV in 1403.

Above left: 38. Catherine of Valois, Henry V's queen, giving birth to Henry VI.

Above right: 39. The marriage of Catherine of Valois to Henry V in the parish church of St John, Troyes, 2 June 1420, a direct result of the Treaty of Troyes ratifed less than a fortnight earlier on 21 May.

Right: 40. A queen depicted in a window in Fromond's Chantry, Winchester College. Work on the building was carried out during Catherine of Valois' time as queen and queen dowager. It is possible that the queen with her blond wavy hair was based upon Catherine, who was often depicted in a similar manner.

Above left: 41. Elizabeth Woodville.

Above right: 42. Richard III. The last Yorkist king married Anne Neville, the widow of the Lancastrian Prince of Wales, in order to secure a share of the great Warwick inheritance.

43. Warwick Castle. One of the residences of Anne Neville, the wife of Richard III.

Right: 44. Margaret Beaufort from Christ's College, Cambridge. Margaret Beaufort passed her claim to the throne to her son, Henry Tudor, who took the crown as Henry VII.

Below: 45. Anne Neville (centre), her first husband Prince Edward of Lancaster (left) and her second husband, Richard III (right). Anne and Richard are depicted with crowns and sceptres.

Above left: 46. Henry VII. The first Tudor king was always sensitive to claims that he wore the crown in right of his wife.

Above right: 47. Elizabeth of York was the daughter, sister, niece, wife and mother of kings of England, and it was through her that the Tudor dynasty gained its legitimacy.

Left: 48. This richly illuminated psalter belonged in turn to Elizabeth of York, then Catherine of Aragon. It notes the birth of Henry VII and Elizabeth of York's eldest son, Arthur. Marked in the psalter are the precious statements: 'Thys boke ys myn Elisabeth ye quene' and 'Thys boke ys myn Katherina the quene'.

given a more public role after 1195, and she was present at Joanna's second marriage in 1196. In 1199, she also gave judgement with Eleanor of Aquitaine and Richard's brother, John, in a dispute concerning the see of St David. She was not invited to visit the kingdom of which she was queen, however, and she still spent little time with Richard. She was not summoned to his deathbed in April 1199.

Berengaria was at Beaufort Castle in Anjou when word reached her of Richard's death. There is no evidence that she ever contemplated a new marriage, and this, and the fact that her funeral effigy was that of a bride, may suggest that she grieved for her husband, in spite of their estrangement. A few days after Richard's death, she visited Fontrevault Abbey, where Richard's body had been taken for burial, before travelling on to Chartres in order to escort her sister, Blanche, to her wedding with the Count of Champagne. Almost immediately after Richard's death, Berengaria displayed the strong streak of independence that she would demonstrate throughout her widowhood, entering into a dispute with Richard's successor, King John, over her dower rights, which were her only source of income. In 1200, she was driven by poverty to seek refuge with her sister in Champagne.

John had no desire to make the payments that Berengaria was entitled to as part of her dower. As a consequence of this, Berengaria spent over twenty years battling first with King John and then with the minority council of his son, Henry III. She was able to enlist the support of Pope Innocent III, who, along with her sister, was her greatest supporter. A number of papal letters survive concerning Berengaria's dower. The first, dated March 1200, shows that Berengaria was denied her dower soon after Richard's death. In that same month, the Pope also sent two letters offering to relax the Interdict he had imposed on John if he would do justice to Berengaria. In a letter to John in 1204, Innocent again threatened the King with papal censure if he would not carry out his obligations towards Berengaria, and in September 1207, the King was ordered to appear personally before the Pope to answer to the Queen. The Pope's continuing interest was maintained by Berengaria's repeated appeals. By January 1204, she was in desperate straits, once again being compelled to seek aid from her sister. John was already in dispute with the Pope on other matters and had little regard for the threats made by Innocent. Finally, on 25

September 1215, he agreed to pay Berengaria a settlement, but her joy was short-lived, as, in 1216, her brother-in-law wrote to inform her that he could not, in fact, afford to pay her any money at all.

John died in 1216, and his successor, Henry III, proved to be more amenable to papal pressure. In spite of this, Berengaria still found herself without funds, and in 1220, she wrote to the Bishop of Winchester to ask for his assistance in the matter:

> We send to you our well-beloved Friar Walter, of the Cistercian order, the bearer of these presents, beseeching you humbly and devotedly with all the humility that we can, that, in reference as well to this present feast of All Saints as to other terms now past, you will cause us to be satisfied about the money due to us according to the composition of our dower, which, by your mediation, we made with our brother John, of happy memory, formerly king of England.

Henry III finally agreed to settle the debt owed to Berengaria in 1225–26. She still had to fight for the payment, writing personally to Henry III in 1225:

> We requested you by our letters patent, sent to you by Brother Walter de Persona, our chaplain of the Cistercian order, that you would send to us by the said Brother Walter and Master Simon, our clerks, 1,000 marks sterling, which you owe us at this feast of All Saints, according to the composition of our dower solemnly drawn out between us and you. But since the said Master Simon, being detained by sickness, cannot come to you, we send in his stead our servant Martin, the bearer of these presents, earnestly requesting you to send us the thousand marks by the said Brother Walter, and by this Martin, or by one of them, if by any chance impediment both cannot come to you.

It must have been a relief to Berengaria, after years of fighting for her funds, that she finally received them. In the intervening years, however, when the English royal family had effectively washed its hands of her, she had been forced to rely on the French royal family for support.

In 1204, the French king, Philip Augustus, had taken Normandy from John. Later that same year, he granted Berengaria the city of Le Mans and 1,000 marks in exchange for the renunciation of her dower rights in Normandy. Since Berengaria had never actually received her dower, this was an excellent exchange, giving her financial security for the first time since Richard's death. Berengaria moved her household to Le Mans and she came to love the city, staying there for the rest of her life. She had a reputation for good works there and gave money to the Abbey of La Couture and the hospital of Coeffort. Berengaria also gave land in 1215 to the Franciscans to build a convent. She always wanted to build her own religious foundation, and in recognition of this, in 1228, Richard's great-nephew, Louis IX of France, granted her land at L'Epau near Le Mans. Berengaria spent the last years of her life engaged in the foundation of the abbey, with the monks arriving in May 1230. She died in Le Mans in December 1230 and was buried in her new foundation, one month before it was consecrated.

The marriage of Richard and Berengaria was not a success, and Berengaria was allowed no role in politics or even the opportunity to assert herself a queen. During her long widowhood, she showed that she had the strength and tenacity to take on the English crown and enlist papal support, and once she had the funds to support herself, she lived a life of great independence. John's first wife, Isabella of Gloucester, was not so lucky.

ISABELLA OF GLOUCESTER (*c.* 1160–1217), the first wife of King John, was never acknowledged as queen. She is often mistakenly called Hawise or Avice, which is probably the result of sources confusing her with her mother. It is as Isabella that John's first wife described herself in charters. She was the third and youngest daughter of William, Earl of Gloucester, and his wife Hawise, the daughter of Robert, Earl of Leicester. Isabella's father was the first cousin of Henry II as the son of the Empress Matilda's illegitimate half-brother, Robert of Gloucester, and Isabella was therefore the great-granddaughter of Henry I. Isabella's father was a magnate of some standing, but at her birth in around 1160, she must have seemed of little importance and nothing of her childhood is recorded. In 1166, her only brother died, leaving Isabella and her sisters as co-heiresses to their father's estates.

Whilst, in the medieval period, the eldest son would inherit the entire patrimony, where a landowner left only daughters, his estates were split equally between them rather than passing only to the eldest. Isabella's father was anxious to keep his estates together in order to maintain the power of his earldom and his house. In 1176, he entered into an agreement with Henry II. Henry II had been looking to provide his youngest son, John, with an inheritance for some time, and it was agreed that John should marry a daughter of Earl William in exchange for being named as the earl's heir. Isabella's two elder sisters, Mabel and Amica, were already married, and so it was decided that Isabella would become her father's sole heiress. Isabella's sisters were compensated with an income of £100 whilst John, through Isabella, succeeded to the titles and lands.

Isabella's father died on 23 November 1183. Instead of pressing for the marriage, Henry II took Isabella into his wardship and appropriated the Gloucester income for himself. Henry, who had endured years of rebellion from his elder sons, wanted the funds from Isabella's estates and, in spite of his fondness for John, was not prepared to simply hand over such a rich revenue stream to him. John, who had been born at the end of 1166, was some years younger than Isabella, and Henry may also have felt that his son was not yet ready for marriage. He had felt no such compunction about marrying his eldest son, young Henry, in his infancy, however, so it is likely that he was motivated by financial considerations.

Henry II died in July 1189 and was succeeded by his son, Richard I. On 13 August 1189, Richard arrived in England and was soon joined by John. The royal party moved on to Marlborough, where, on 29 August, John and Isabella were finally married. At the same time, Richard created John Count of Mortaine, endowing him with rich lands in England. For Isabella, the marriage represented a release from royal wardship, which, for a woman of nearly thirty, must have been irksome.

Due to the fact that both John and Isabella were the great-grandchildren of Henry I, a dispensation from the Pope was required in order to authorise the marriage. John did not bother to wait for this, marrying Isabella without papal sanction. This was to prove to be the first of John's many disputes with the Church and papacy, and Archbishop Baldwin of Canterbury summoned him to account for the marriage. John failed to appear before the Archbishop, and an interdict was laid over John and Isabella's lands, banning church services and other ceremonies there. This was a serious penalty and one that could not be ignored, leading John to appeal to the papal legate. To John and Isabella's relief, the legate cancelled the interdict following assurances from John that he would apply for a dispensation. There is some confusion over the result of John's application. It has been claimed that a dispensation was awarded with the bizarre condition that, whilst the couple were legally married, they could no longer have sexual relations with each other. The childlessness of the marriage has been given as evidence of this condition and is portrayed as the reason for John's divorce once he became king and needed an heir. However, it would be an extremely odd condition for the Pope to impose on a married couple, and dispensations for consanguinity were easy to obtain at the time. It, therefore, seems more likely that no dispensation actually arrived, perhaps because it became unnecessary when John and Isabella ceased to co-habit in their loveless marriage. Equally, John, who was never a friend of the Church, may simply not have bothered to apply for one.

Little evidence survives concerning John and Isabella's marriage. Charters issued by the couple suggest that they made at least one progress to Normandy together. By 1193, they appear to have become estranged from each other, with Isabella presumably retiring to live on her estates. The reason behind the estrangement is not clear and it may be that the couple simply found themselves to be incompatible.

During Richard I's absence on crusade, John set up a court of his own in England. He also made an alliance with Philip Augustus, King of France, around that time, promising to marry Philip's sister, Alais, in return for Richard's French lands. John was about to sail to France to carry out the terms of the alliance when his mother, Eleanor of Aquitaine, arrived, and he was forced to remain in England. In 1193, when news reached England of Richard's imprisonment, John travelled to Paris to do homage for Richard's French possessions and once again promised to marry Alais. The fact that John entered into negotiations for another marriage implies that he did not consider himself bound to Isabella. Divorce in 1193 was averted only by Richard's impending return. On his return, Richard held a council at Nottingham in March 1194 at which, as a punishment, John's lands were confiscated. These included Isabella's own lands, and she must have resented deeply her husband's actions. John behaved more loyally to his brother for the remainder of the reign and, in 1195, he was restored to the honour of Gloucester and his own county of Mortaine.

John was on the Continent when word reached him of Richard's death, and he returned to England in May 1199 to be crowned king at Westminster Abbey. Isabella did not share his coronation, and there was no suggestion that she would do so. Within months of his accession John had begun to look around for another bride, and in the summer of 1199, he sent envoys to the King of Portugal regarding his daughters. Due to the lack of a dispensation, it was an easy matter for John to annul his marriage, and he achieved this shortly after his accession. It is possible that Isabella objected to this, as, throughout her life, she continued to use a seal calling herself Countess of Gloucester and Mortaine.

Divorce failed to free Isabella from John, as he took her into his custody in order to prevent her from making a new marriage and bestowing her lands on her second husband. John already had other plans for Isabella's lands. In October 1199, he entered into a treaty with Philip Augustus, which included the marriage of his niece, Blanche of Castile, to Philip's son. Blanche's dowry included the rich city of Evreux, which belonged to Isabella's nephew, Amaury, Count of Evreux. In compensation, John granted to Amaury Isabella's earldom of Gloucester, and he issued a number of charters as earl until his death in 1213. Isabella deeply resented the loss of her lands, but as John's prisoner, there was nothing she could do. She spent her imprisonment in a number of places, including Sherborne Castle in Dorset, where she made her Will in 1213.

Isabella resigned herself to a life in captivity and the fact that she made her Will suggests that she was in ill health. In 1214, her fortunes changed again. In late 1213, John found himself in need of funds for an expedition to Poitou, part of the duchy of Aquitaine that he had inherited from his mother. He returned the earldom of Gloucester to Isabella before selling her, with her lands and titles, to Geoffrey de Mandeville, Earl of Essex. For the honour of marrying Isabella, Geoffrey paid 20,000 marks, the highest known sum paid for an English medieval heiress. Geoffrey and Isabella were married in January 1214, and whilst Isabella was undoubtedly forced to make her second marriage, it also meant a release for her. Isabella and Geoffrey acted jointly together during their marriage, which implies that they spent time together. The couple made a gift of land to Bassaleg Priory, for example.

The price agreed for Isabella was apparently too high even for the wealthy Earl of Essex, and he missed the first instalment of the money promised to John in early 1215. John responded in February 1215 by confiscating the Gloucester estates. This action drove Geoffrey towards the baronial opponents of King John and he was prominent at Runnymede when John was forced to sign the Magna Carta, setting down in writing the rights of the English nobility for the first time in history. It is not impossible that Isabella encouraged Geoffrey's participation in the rebellion, as there is unlikely to have been any love lost between her and her former husband. The success of the rebellion led to Geoffrey's reinstatement to the Gloucester lands in June 1215.

On 23 February 1216, Geoffrey died from wounds received in a tournament in London. The death ushered in the only period of independence that Isabella ever knew and, as a statement of her relief at finally being granted her freedom, she issued charters during the period with the words 'in my free widowhood'. Isabella had little time to enjoy her freedom. John died later in 1216 and was succeeded by his nine-year-old son, Henry III. In September 1217, Hubert de Burgh, one of the regents of the young king became Isabella's third husband. Once again, her wealth and status were the motivating factors and she had no choice in the matter. The marriage was destined to be brief, as Isabella died on 14 October 1217. She was buried at Christ Church, Canterbury, and was succeeded to her earldom by her sister Amica, Countess of Hertford.

Isabella of Gloucester has one of the unhappiest stories of any queen of England or king's wife. Her successor as John's wife, Isabella of Angoulême, enjoyed an equally turbulent and unhappy relationship with the King, but she at least was able to escape this with John's death and assert her own independence in later life as an autonomous European ruler.

ISABELLA OF ANGOULÊME (c. 1188/92–1246) was the only child and heiress of Aymer, Count of Angoulême, and his wife, Alice de Courtenay, a cousin of Philip Augustus of France. Her mother had been married twice before, and her parents cannot have been married before 1184. They are first recorded as married in 1191, and it is likely that Isabella was very young at the time of her marriage to John in 1200. She was frequently described as twelve years old in 1200, but this may have been because this was the legal earliest age for marriage, and she may have only been around eight or nine years old.

Isabella's father technically held Angoulême as a vassal of the duchy of Aquitaine, but, in reality, he had a great deal of independence. He had caused trouble during Richard I's reign by paying homage directly to Philip Augustus. Count Aymer entered into a more formal alliance with the French king soon after John's accession to the throne. As part of this agreement, he abandoned his claims to the neighbouring county of Le Marche in favour of his rival, Hugh de Lusignan. In early 1200, Isabella was betrothed to Hugh de Lusignan, a man more than old enough to be her father, and sent to live in his household until she was ready for marriage. A marriage between Isabella and Hugh posed a serious political threat to John, and the merger of their lands would have split the duchy of Aquitaine in half. It was very much in John's political interest to stop the marriage.

In the summer of 1200, John set out on a progress through Poitou. During this progress, he visited the Lusignans at Le Marche, meeting Isabella there for the first time. Soon afterwards, he spoke to Count Aymer discreetly about the match. Aymer, keen to see his daughter become a queen, agreed to recall her. John then sent Hugh to England on official business before returning secretly to Angoulême. On 23 August 1200, Isabella was informed by her parents that she was to marry John the next day. Some sources suggest that she wept and protested at the thought of marrying John, but others claim that she wished to become a queen. Whatever her personal feelings, Isabella and John were married the following day at Bordeaux.

Following their marriage, the couple made a leisurely progress through Normandy. They then crossed the Channel and were crowned together at Westminster Abbey on 8 October 1200. They spent the winter travelling around England, spending Christmas at Guildford. Isabella was never given any political role, and whilst this initially may have been due to her age, it is possible that John also did not trust his wife. John was not faithful to Isabella and had a number of illegitimate children. In 1214, he abducted and raped a noblewoman, Matilda FitzWalter, something that must have both been humiliating for Isabella and increased hostility towards John from the nobility.

Isabella bore John five children during their marriage, and the couple did, at least, continue to live together as husband and wife. There is, however, some evidence that Isabella took lovers of her own, with the chronicler Matthew Paris claiming that Isabella was guilty of adultery, sorcery and incest. Whatever the truth of this, the marriage was not a close one, and John did not bother to mention Isabella in his Will.

Politically, John also appears to have come to regret his marriage, in spite of the fact that he obtained possession of Angoulême in 1202 on the death of Isabella's father. The Lusignans initially accepted Isabella's marriage, but in 1201, trouble broke out in Poitou, and John accused the family of treason. In response to this, they turned to Philip Augustus for support, and in 1202, the French king declared that John had forfeited Aquitaine, Poitou and Anjou and bestowed them upon his nephew, Arthur of Brittany. John blamed Isabella for this, telling her so in 1205. Isabella was also popularly held partly responsible for the loss of Normandy, which fell to the French in 1204, with one source claiming that, following their marriage, the couple lay in bed together all morning rather than attending to business.

The last few years of John's reign were racked by civil war in England. It has been suggested that Isabella was imprisoned by John during these years, but references to her being under guard are more likely to have been for her own protection, as she was as deeply unpopular as John. Isabella was constantly on the move throughout her marriage, spending most of her time in the west of England. In early 1216, John's relations with his barons took a turn for the worst and they held a council in which it was decided to elect the French Dauphin, Louis, as king. Louis landed at Thanet on 20 May 1216 and quickly took Rochester castle. He was received with joy in London and, by the autumn, controlled most of southern England. In the midst of this turmoil, John died suddenly at Newark on 18 October 1216 and was buried at Worcester.

Isabella was in Bristol when word reached her of John's death. She travelled to Gloucester, where her nine-year-old son had been brought and had him hastily crowned on 28 October as Henry III. It is an indication of the impromptu nature of the ceremony that there was no crown available for the coronation, and Henry had to be crowned with one of Isabella's gold collars. In spite of this decisive action, Isabella was not permitted any role in the regency. She also had difficulty in securing her own property and this, and her lack of political power, lay behind her decision to return to Angoulême in June 1217, leaving her children in England.

On her return to Angoulême, Isabella was finally able to assert her own independence, and she established her authority in the county, even winning back control of the Cognac region, which had been lost to Angoulême in the 1180s. She still maintained contact with her son in England and wrote to him in around 1218 or 1219, requesting aid both in securing her position in Angoulême against hostile neighbours and in obtaining her English dower:

> Your Grace knows how often we have begged you that you should give us help and advice in our affairs, but so far you have done nothing. Therefore we attentively ask you again to despatch your advice quickly to us, but do not just gratify us with words. You can see that without your help and advice, we cannot rule over or defend our land. And if the truces made with the king of France were to be broken, this part of the country has much to fear. Even if we had nothing to fear from the king himself, we do indeed have such neighbours who are as much to be feared as the said king of France. So without delay you must formulate such a plan which will benefit this part of the country which is yours and ours; it is necessary that you do this to ensure that neither you nor we should lose our land through your failure to give any advice or help. We even beg you to act on our behalf, that we can have for the time being some part of those lands which our husband, your father, bequeathed to us. You know truly how much we owe him, but even if our husband had bequeathed nothing to us, you ought by right to give us aid from your resources, so that we can defend our land, on this your honour and advantage depend.

This is the first indication that the relationship between Isabella and her eldest son was troubled, although, after being granted no role in his upbringing by John, it is hardly surprising that the pair were not close. The English minority council expected Isabella to govern Angoulême for Henry's benefit, and it caused consternation in England when Isabella once again demonstrated her independence, surprising everyone in 1220 by marrying Hugh de Lusignan, the son of her former fiancé.

Isabella knew that news of her marriage would be greeted with hostility in England, particularly as her new husband was, at that time, betrothed to her own daughter Joanna, who was living in his household. Isabella sought to limit any retaliation by writing swiftly to Henry III, setting out her motives for the marriage:

We hereby signify to you that when the Counts of March and Eu departed this life, the lord Hugh de Lusignan remained alone and without heirs in Poitou, and his friends would not permit that our daughter should be united with him in marriage, because her age is so tender, but counselled him to take a wife from whom he might speedily hope for an heir; and it was proposed that he should take a wife in France, which if he had done, all your land in Poitou and Gascony would be lost. We, therefore, seeing the great peril that might accrue if that marriage should take place, when our counsellors could give us no advice, we ourselves married the said Hugh, count of March; and God knows that we did this rather for your benefit than our own. Wherefore we entreat you, as our dear son, that this thing may be pleasing to you, seeing it conduces greatly to the profit of you and yours; and we earnestly pray you that you will restore to him his lawful right, that is, Niort, the castles of Exeter and Rockingham, and 3,500 marks, which your father, our former husband, bequeathed to us; and so, if it please you, deal with him, who is so powerful, that he may not remain against you, since he can serve you well – for he is well-disposed to serve you faithfully with all his power; and we are certain and undertake that he shall serve you well if you restore to him his rights, and, therefore, we advise that you take opportune counsel on these matters; and when it shall please you, you may send for our daughter, your sister, by a trusty messenger and your letters patent, and we will send her to you.

Isabella sought to explain her actions as being in her son's best interests, but in reality, she married for her own advancement, intent on creating the very political crisis that John had sought to avert in 1200. Isabella and Hugh's combined lands split the duchy of Angoulême in half.

Isabella's attempts to put a positive spin on her marriage fooled nobody in England, and Henry III's minority council confiscated her dower. Isabella retaliated by refusing to release her daughter until her rights were reinstated. The dispute dragged on until October 1220, when Henry finally agreed to pay Isabella the sums outstanding to her. In return, Hugh escorted Joanna to La Rochelle, where she was taken back into English custody. Isabella always had a troubled and manipulative relationship with her English children. In 1225, she and Hugh defected to the French, abandoning Henry's interests in return for a pension from the French king. In 1230, Isabella entered into another agreement with France at Henry's expense, in order to increase the size of her pension. Her actions infuriated Henry and his council, and from 1228, the English government was actively petitioning the Pope to annul her second marriage.

Isabella enjoyed a more equal relationship with Hugh than she had with John, and the couple were close in age. She was able to influence her second husband politically, and when, in June 1241, Hugh swore allegiance to Louis IX's brother as Count of Poitou without consulting her, Isabella packed up her household and left her husband. Hugh followed Isabella to Angoulême, begging forgiveness, and when she finally agreed to see him, she attacked him for supporting an alternative Count of Poitou to her own son. The couple were soon reconciled, and at Christmas 1241, Hugh declared against the French and persuaded Henry to join him on an expedition to Poitou.

The English army, led by Henry III and his brother, Richard, sailed on 9 May 1242. No evidence survives of Isabella's reunion with her two English sons, but it is likely to have been tense, as she had not seen them for twenty-five years. Relations between the three became frostier during the campaign, and Hugh almost immediately abandoned Henry for the French. The English campaign was a disaster, and Henry barely escaped with his life. Isabella then decided to take matters into her own hands, hiring assassins in 1244 to poison the French king. The assassins were discovered in the royal kitchens and confessed to Isabella's involvement. Aware that she was doomed if the King of France captured her, Isabella fled to Fontrevault Abbey to claim sanctuary, dying there on 4 June 1246.

Isabella was little lamented in England, and Henry ordered only a brief display of mourning for his distant and unreliable mother.

He did extend a warm welcome to Isabella's children by Hugh, who arrived in England in 1247. The eight children that Isabella bore her second husband proved to be a major source of tension in England during the reign of their half-brother, and they caused particular difficulties for Isabella's successor as queen, Eleanor of Provence.

ELEANOR OF PROVENCE (1223–91) was the second of four daughters born to Raymond Berengar, Count of Provence, and his wife, Beatrice of Savoy. All four sisters were famed for their beauty, and all eventually became queens. This reputation and the marriage of Eleanor's eldest sister, Margaret, to Louis IX of France greatly improved Eleanor's chances of making a grand marriage. Eleanor was born in 1223 and little is known about her childhood, but the close relationship that she had with all her family in adulthood suggests that it was happy.

Henry III had great difficulty in finding a bride and spent ten years in futile negotiations. He succeeded in becoming betrothed to one lady, Jeanne of Ponthieu, only for her to marry Ferdinand III of Castile instead. A legend has built up around the betrothal of Henry and Eleanor, and it has been claimed that Eleanor composed an epic poem about a Cornish hero and sent it to Richard, Earl of Cornwall, as a compliment. Richard was impressed and recommended Eleanor to his elder brother, Henry III. This story is unlikely to be true and it is more likely that Henry selected Eleanor due to her relationship to the Queen of France.

Eleanor and Henry were betrothed on 23 November 1235 when Eleanor was twelve. Henry was twenty-eight, and Eleanor must have been nervous as she set out for England accompanied by her uncle, William of Savoy, and an escort of 3,000 horsemen. She landed at Dover in January 1236 and journeyed to Canterbury, where Henry was waiting. The couple were married on 14 January before setting out for London, where Eleanor was crowned six days later. The couple quickly became close, and a letter written by Eleanor to Henry a decade after their marriage shows her devotion to him, with Eleanor writing that 'we inform your lordship that by the grace of God we and our children are safe and well, which we lovingly hope you are also with our heart and soul'.

Eleanor brought a large train with her to England and many of her attendants chose to stay, hoping to receive rewards from

Henry. Eleanor's uncle, William of Savoy, became one of Henry's chief counsellors and attempts were made to make him Bishop of Winchester, although he was eventually forced to settle for the see of Liege instead. Eleanor's mother came from a large family, and Eleanor had eight maternal uncles with limited resources of their own. At least 170 Savoyards visited England as a consequence of Eleanor's marriage and seventy chose to settle. Henry provided pensions for Eleanor's mother and her uncles Thomas and Amadeus of Savoy in the 1240s. A further uncle, Boniface of Savoy, was appointed as Archbishop of Canterbury in 1244. Eleanor's favourite uncle, Peter of Savoy, was created Earl of Richmond at Eleanor's request. Peter and Eleanor collaborated throughout her marriage, and together they led the Savoyard faction at court. The influx of foreigners greatly damaged Eleanor's reputation in England, especially as she and Peter pursued a policy of marrying their relatives to rich lords and heiresses in England.

Despite Eleanor's unpopularity, personally, she was very happy and bore five children. The eldest, Edward, was born at Westminster on 16 June 1239, and his birth was followed by those of Margaret in 1240, Beatrice in 1242, Edmund in 1244, and Catherine in 1253. Eleanor and Henry were fond parents. The couple's youngest child, Catherine, was born with an unspecified disability, and her parents were deeply distressed by her condition. Henry had an image of Catherine placed on the shrine of Edward the Confessor in the hope that she would be healed, and he also richly rewarded a messenger from Eleanor when she brought him news of an improvement in Catherine's condition. Catherine died young, and her parents grieved deeply for her, commissioning a fine tomb.

Whilst the happy family atmosphere created by Eleanor and Henry was beneficial to their children in their childhoods, in adulthood, they occasionally found it cloying. The couple were unwilling to let go of their children, and when their eldest daughter, Margaret, married Alexander III of Scotland, Eleanor and Henry continued to actively involve themselves in her welfare. In 1255, for example, when they received word that she was being mistreated by the Scottish regents, they set off north with an army, taking Margaret south to stay in Northumberland with Eleanor whilst Henry dealt with the political situation. When Henry went on campaign to Gascony in 1253, he wrote to Alexander asking that Margaret be allowed to come to England to keep her mother company. Margaret came south in 1260 in order to give birth to her first child under her mother's supervision at Windsor. Eleanor also played a significant role in the life of her second daughter, Beatrice, following her marriage to the Duke of Brittany, and she was entrusted with the couple's children when they went on crusade.

Eleanor and Henry desperately wanted to provide for their second son, Edmund, a policy which only served to increase their unpopularity. In early 1254, the Pope offered the crown of Sicily to Edmund on the condition that Henry conquered the island. Henry accepted the offer, agreeing to the enormous financial conditions imposed by the Pope, and the couple became deeply committed to what became known as the 'Sicilian Business', placing the negotiations in the hands of Eleanor's Savoyard uncles. The huge cost of the scheme made it deeply unpopular in England, and it ultimately ended in disaster when Eleanor's uncle, Thomas of Savoy, was captured and imprisoned in Turin. Eleanor was upset by the loss of Sicily, and she was also concerned about her uncle's imprisonment, jointly raising the ransom with Peter of Savoy.

The Sicilian business was not Eleanor's first foray into politics, and throughout her lifetime, she was a political force to be reckoned with. Formal recognition of her political role came in 1253, when she was made joint regent with her brother-in-law, Richard of Cornwall, whilst Henry campaigned in Gascony. Eleanor spent her time as regent raising men and money for Henry, and she had an excellent grasp of affairs in England. One surviving letter written jointly by Eleanor and Richard to Henry shows that they were firmly in control of matters:

We had been treating with your prelates and the magnates of your kingdom of England before the advent of the said Earl and John, on the quinzaines of St Hilary last past [27 January] about your subsidy, and after the arrival of the said earl and John, with certain of the aforesaid prelates and magnates, the archbishops and bishops answered us that if the King of Castile should come against you in Gascony each of them would assist you from his own property, so that you would be under perpetual obligations to them; but with regard to granting you aid from their clergy, they could do nothing without the assent of the said clergy; nor do they believe that their clergy can be induced to give you any help. Unless the tenth of clerical goods granted to you for the first year of the crusade, which should begin in the present year, might be relaxed at once by your letters patent, and the collection of the said tenth for the said crusade, for the two following years, might be put in respite up to the term of two years before your passage to the Holy Land; and they will give diligence and treat with the clergy submitted before them, to induce them to assist you according to that form with a tenth of their benefices, in case the King of Castile should attack you in Gascony; but at the departure of the bearer of these presents no subsidy had yet been granted by the aforesaid clergy.

Eleanor's measures as regent proved to be effective, but they were not popular, and she further damaged her relationship with the Londoners by rigidly enforcing a tax on boats unloading at Queenhithe. She also had two sheriffs of London imprisoned for failing to co-operate with her demands, and the Lord Mayor was punished for refusing the provide aid for Henry. In April 1254, Henry sent for Eleanor to join him in Gascony, and she resigned her regency to Richard of Cornwall.

Eleanor sailed to Gascony in the company of her two sons before journeying to Castile with her eldest son, Edward, for his marriage to Eleanor of Castile. After the wedding, Eleanor rejoined Henry and the couple travelled to visit the French court. To Eleanor's joy, her mother and sisters were present in Paris and Henry and Louis IX formed a firm friendship. It was a pleasant break for Eleanor and Henry before they returned to England, in December 1254, to face increasing baronial hostility.

Eleanor's Savoyard faction was not the only politically influential group of foreigners in England. In 1247, Henry's half-brothers Guy de Lusignan, William of Valence, the cleric Æthelmar, and his half-sister Alesia arrived in England. Henry received his mother's children joyfully and, in 1250, attempted to make Æthelmar Bishop of Winchester. The Savoyards resented the arrival of a competing group seeking patronage from the King. There was rivalry between the two groups from the first, and the Lusignans were always actively hostile to Eleanor.

The Savoyards were not the only party hostile to the Lusignans, and at parliaments in April and June 1258 at Oxford, the barons, led by the King's brother-in-law, Simon de Montford, forced a number of provisions on Henry III, including the acceptance of a council appointed by the barons and the exile of the Lusignans. Both Eleanor and Henry were alarmed by the Provisions of Oxford and the limits that they placed on royal authority. In spite of this, Eleanor did allow herself some triumph at the expulsion of her rivals, the Lusignans, and when they sought safe conduct from Louis IX to journey to France during their exile, this was refused, as the French king was 'exasperated by a complaint made against these Poitevins by the queen of France to the effect that they had shamefully scandalised and defamed her sister, the queen of England'. The triumph Eleanor felt at the expulsion of the Lusignans was short-lived, as she and Henry were forced to take oaths to uphold the Provisions of Oxford. Matters remained tense for the next few years, but by 1261, Henry finally felt strong enough to move against the barons and dismissed his council.

England erupted into civil war in 1263, when Henry refused to renew his commitment to the Provisions of Oxford. Eleanor and the Savoyards were a particular focus for attack, and in June, the Savoyard Bishop of Hereford was captured by the barons and imprisoned. Eleanor's lands were ravaged, and Henry and Eleanor withdrew to the Tower for their own protection. Frustrated by Henry's lack of positive action, Eleanor felt drawn towards her more proactive son, Edward. According to the *Annals of Dunstable*, Henry and Eleanor in the Tower and Edward, who was at Clerkenwell, were all in dire financial straits:

As they were all short of money and there was no one in London who would give them a halfpennyworth of credit, the lord Edward, not wishing to be disgraced, went on the feast of the apostles Peter and Paul, along with Robert Walerand and many others to the New Temple when the gates were closed; and when at his request he was given the keys, he said he wished to see the jewels of his mother, the queen, and summoning the keeper, he by this deceit entered with his men the Temple treasury and there, breaking open with iron hammers that they had brought with them the chests of certain people, he took and had carried away a large sum of money to the amount of a thousand pounds.

Edward's actions caused outrage, but Eleanor approved. She and Henry quarrelled over the best approach to take, and shortly afterwards, Eleanor resolved to leave the Tower and join Edward at Windsor. This proved to be nearly disastrous for her. According to the *Annals of Dunstable*,

> The same year, on St Mildred's day, the queen left the Tower by the Thames on her way to Windsor by boat and came to London Bridge; when the Londoners assailed her and her men shamefully with foul and base words and even casting stones; so that freed with difficulty by the mayor of London and driven by necessity she went back to the Tower. The king would not let her enter, but she was conducted by the mayor of London safely to St Paul's and lodged in the house of the bishop.

This was a terrifying experience for Eleanor, and she would have fared considerably worse if she had not managed to escape from under the bridge. She and Henry were soon reconciled, and Eleanor rejoined her husband, abandoning her plans to go to her son.

Eleanor was with Henry when he surrendered to Simon de Montford on 16 July 1263 and handed over the government to him. This was humiliating, and Eleanor was soon plotting to restore Henry to power. It is likely that it was she who persuaded her brother-in-law, Louis IX, to mediate in the matter, and in October, Henry, Eleanor and their sons, along with Simon de Montford and his own party, crossed the Channel for a meeting with the French king. There they underwent mediation, and when, in January 1264, Louis found for Henry, civil war once more flared up in England. Henry, Edward, and De Montford returned to England before Louis gave his judgement, but Eleanor and her younger son remained in France, refusing to return.

Eleanor had no intention of returning to England whilst civil war raged and, instead, travelled to Paris to take control of Henry's treasury there. She set about raising money by any means possible, including pawning the English crown jewels. Whilst in France, she received the devastating news that Henry and Edward had been defeated at the Battle of Lewes in May 1264 and that both had been captured. In spite of her grief, this spurred Eleanor on, and both she and Peter of Savoy stepped up their efforts to obtain funds.

By the summer of 1264, Eleanor and Peter were ready with an army on the French coast. Eleanor's force was formidable, and the English barons, fearing her arrival, had already fortified the coast of England. Bad weather prevented Eleanor's army from sailing, and by October, her army had dispersed. This was a major blow to Eleanor, but she continued to work for her husband, jointly petitioning the Pope with her sister, the Queen of France, for a new papal legate to be sent to England. By February 1265, Eleanor had taken possession of Gascony, and she was there in May 1265, when she heard that Edward had escaped from captivity. On 4 August, Edward won a decisive victory against the barons at Evesham, killing Simon de Montford and restoring his father to power. Eleanor was jubilant and immediately made preparations to rejoin her family, landing in England on 1 November.

Eleanor returned to an England very different from the country she had left, and her Savoyard faction was never able to re-establish itself as the power that it had been. Eleanor occupied herself with several interests. She is known to have loved gardens and had a number of them laid out near her apartments at various royal palaces. In 1245, a new walled garden was made for her at Clarendon, and at Guildford, her wardrobe was situated above the garden steps so that she was able to access her outside space easily. Eleanor also had gardens at Kempton and Windsor, which she used for recreation in fine weather. She enjoyed reading and a work on the life of Edward the Confessor was dedicated to her. Like most of her predecessors as queen, she was pious, and both she and Henry were devoted to the cult of his canonised predecessor, Edward the Confessor. Eleanor and Henry gave very generously to the Franciscans, and during her widowhood, Eleanor founded a house for the Dominicans in memory of her grandson.

Eleanor remained influential in England, and when Henry died, on 16 November 1272, whilst Edward was away on crusade, she was instrumental in having her eldest son proclaimed king. Eleanor and Henry had been married for over thirty-five years and were devoted to each other. Eleanor, grieving deeply for her husband, focused all her attention on her children and grandchildren. In August 1274, she took Edward's children to Canterbury to meet their parents on their return from the Holy Land. Edward's coronation was a source of great pride for her, but she faced further grief when her eldest daughter, Margaret, died in February 1275, with her younger daughter, Beatrice, following her elder sister to the grave the following month.

Eleanor retired from court during her widowhood, but she remained in touch with affairs. Although, by the time of his accession, Edward was a mature man, Eleanor was unable to let him go, and her letters were filled with personal news and advice for her son:

> Know, dear sire, that we are most desirous to have good news of your health and how things have been with you since you left us. We are letting you know that we are in good health, thanks be to God. We have left Gillingham sooner than we expected, because of the noisomeness of the air, and the thick clouds of smoke which rise in the evenings and have come to Marlborough, arriving on the Friday after Michaelmas. Thanks be to God we are in good health, and we greatly desire to know the same of you.

Edward always treated his mother kindly, although, in spite of her best efforts, he allowed her no role in political affairs in England.

Eleanor became increasingly religious in her old age, and she developed an attachment to Amesbury Abbey, dedicating her granddaughters, Eleanor of Brittany and Mary of England, as nuns there. The two girls were placed in the abbey in order to provide company for their grandmother, and on 7 July 1286, Eleanor herself took the veil, always referring to herself from then onwards as 'Eleanor, humble nun of the order of Fontrevault of the Convent of Amesbury'. She did not entirely follow the life of a nun and retained an interest in the outside world, as well as securing a papal dispensation that allowed her to retain her dower. She continued to advise and cajole Edward, writing to him at one point to ask that he safeguard her Abbey's interests in France from the greed of her brother-in-law, the King of Sicily. More poignantly, she wrote to her son on behalf of one Margaret de Nevile:

> Sweetest son, we know well how great is the desire that a mother has to see her child when she has been long away from him, and that dame Margaret de Nevile, companion of Master John Giffard, has not seen for a long time past her child, who is in the keeping

of dame Margaret de Weyland, and has a great desire to see him. We pray you, sweetest son, that you will command and pray the aforesaid Margaret de Weyland, that she will suffer that the mother may have the solace of her child for some time, after her desire.

Eleanor placed a great deal of importance on family, and it is easy to imagine the sympathy that she felt when the mother presented her petition to her. It may also have been a veiled hint that she would like a visit from her own son, Edward I.

Eleanor spent the rest of her life at Amesbury, and she died there on 24 June 1291. At her request, her heart was buried with her daughter, Beatrice, with the rest of her body interred at Amesbury. Eleanor of Provence lived in turbulent times, and she was, perhaps, the most unpopular queen of England. Her daughter-in-law and successor as queen, Eleanor of Castile, was to find that she too was deeply unpopular.

ELEANOR OF CASTILE (1241–90) enjoyed as contented a marriage as her mother-in-law, Eleanor of Provence. She was born in 1241, the daughter of Ferdinand III of Castile and his second wife, Jeanne of Ponthieu. Jeanne was an indomitable figure and had experience of English kings. She was the daughter of Richard I's discarded fiancé, Alais of France, and had herself abandoned her betrothal to Henry III to marry Ferdinand. As the heiress to the county of Ponthieu, Jeanne was an important political figure in her own right, and she was largely responsible for Eleanor's upbringing. Eleanor was the only daughter in a family of seven half-brothers and four full brothers, and she was a valuable asset to her family. Very little is known of her childhood. She appears to have been present at her father's deathbed in Seville in May 1252 and remained in the city with her mother until shortly before her marriage in 1254. She was educated and fond of reading.

The death of Eleanor's father in 1252 had a profound effect on her childhood. Her eldest half-brother, Alfonso X, who succeeded their father as king of Castile, was a considerably more martial ruler. Castile had laid claim to English-held Gascony since the marriage of Alfonso VIII to Eleanor, the daughter of Henry II and Eleanor of Aquitaine. The claim had lain dormant for several years, but following his accession, Alfonso X invaded Gascony in order to claim it for Castile. Unlike his Castilian counterpart, Henry III of England had no taste for war, and he was eager to come to an agreement, opening negotiations for his eldest son, Edward, to marry Eleanor. Arrangements for the marriage were concluded in March 1254.

Eleanor may have been glad to escape a tense situation at home, as, shortly before her marriage, her mother left Castile for Ponthieu following the discovery of her involvement in a rebellion led by her stepson, Henry. The absence of her mother did not delay the arrangements for Eleanor's marriage, and in late 1254, she travelled with Alfonso to Burgos to meet Edward and his mother. Even at fifteen, Edward was strong and handsome, and he caused a stir by competing in a tournament before being knighted by Eleanor's half-brother. Edward and Eleanor were married at the convent of Las Huelgas near Burgos on 1 November 1254 before travelling to Gascony, which had been made over to Edward at Alfonso's insistence.

Edward and Eleanor always enjoyed a close marriage, and Eleanor bore a daughter at Bordeaux in May 1255 who died soon after birth, demonstrating that the marriage was very rapidly consummated. Even in the thirteenth century, fourteen was young to be a mother, and it is possible that Edward's parents kept the couple separate following the death of their first child, in order to ensure that Eleanor did not bear a second child until she was older and physically better able to cope with childbirth. Certainly, it was some years before her second pregnancy.

In late 1255, Eleanor travelled to England for the first time. Henry III had taken care to ensure that she would be comfortable in England's cold climate, fitting out rooms for her with glazed windows, a raised hearth and a wardrobe. The floors were also carpeted, a feature unknown in England at the time. Eleanor appreciated this thoughtfulness, but it was seen in England as further evidence of the King's favouritism towards foreigners. There was a real fear in England that Eleanor would bring a wave of followers with her as her mother-in-law had done, and the tensions surrounding her arrival did not help the troubled situation faced by the King.

Eleanor was, on the whole, careful to avoid the problems that her mother-in-law had faced, and she was discreet in the advancement of her family. She was young when she came to England, but whilst she had no political role, it was impossible for her to be sheltered from the political turmoil faced by Henry III. On 17 June 1264, following Henry and Edward's capture at the Battle of Lewes, she was ordered to leave Windsor with her baby daughter, Catherine, to join her father-in-law in London. The year that Eleanor spent as the barons' prisoner must have been bleak: her daughter died in September 1264 and a further daughter, Joan, who was born in January 1265, also soon died.

Eleanor's spirits were lifted by news of Edward's escape in May 1265, and in August of that year, following his victory over the barons at the Battle of Evesham, the couple were finally reunited. Eleanor bore her first son, John, in July 1266. His birth was followed by a second son, Henry, in May 1268, and a daughter, Eleanor, in June 1269.

Even before she became queen, Eleanor kept a close eye on her own property, and the acquisitive streak that would make her deeply unpopular during Edward's reign was already apparent in 1265 when she wrote to one of her officers, John of London:

Know that our lord the king gave us the other day the manor of Berewic with its appurtenances, at the solicitation of Sir Roger de Leyburn, and because it is appurtenant to the guardianship of Cantilupe, my lord has given it to another, so that nothing of it is remitted to us, but there is another manor close by in the county of Somerset, which is at the town of Heselbere, which belonged to Sir William the Marshal, who is dead and held it of the king in chief. Wherefore we would desire that you should ask of Sir John de Kyrkbi if the guardianship of that manor is granted, and if it is not then that you should pray Sir Roger de Leyburn and the Bishop of Bath on our behalf that they should procure from our lord the king that he grant us the manor until the coming of age of the heir of Sir William. And, if it is given, there is another manor in the county of Dorset which is called Gerente, which belonged to Sir William de Keenes, who is dead, and he held it in chief of the king, wherefore we would that if we cannot have the other, you should pray them on our behalf that these should apply to the king to allow us this one; the manor of Heselbere is worth less. And if neither, pray Sir Roger in this way. Tell him that the manor of Berewic that the king gave us at his suggestion has been taken from us, for this will tend to make us seem less covetous; and say the same to the bishop of Bath. And if the letters which you have concerning it can profit nothing for this affair, give them to the bearer of this letter, for he will carry them to Walter of Kent, our clerk. Be careful to dispatch this affair, for it will be to our profit, and so suitably procure the affair that they shall not set it down to covetousness.

Eleanor had carried out detailed research to ensure that she received adequate compensation for the loss of the manor. She was right to be wary of appearing to be covetous, and this was how the majority of people in England later came to view her.

Henry III lived to a venerable age for his time, and he is still one of England's longest reigning monarchs. This longevity had its cost, and though Edward was undoubtedly fond of his father, he felt that there was little role for him in England whilst his father was alive. In 1270, Edward decided to join the crusade led by his uncle, Louis IX of France. Like her namesake and predecessor, Eleanor of Aquitaine, Eleanor of Castile insisted on accompanying her husband, declaring that a married couple should not be parted and that Syria was as close to Heaven as England or Castile. Eleanor's words were persuasive, and she and Edward set out for the Holy Land in 1270. On the way, they learned that Louis IX had died at Tunis, but they decided to continue, with Edward's army capturing Nazareth.

The crusade was not a success and disease took its toll on the crusaders. Daily life must have been hard for Eleanor, and she bore two daughters in Palestine, although only the second, Joan of Acre, survived. Eleanor was involved in one of the most dramatic events of the crusade, when an intruder attempted to assassinate Edward in his tent. Edward was stabbed twice before he managed to wrestle the knife away from his attacker, killing him. The attack left Edward gravely ill, and it was generally believed that he would die. A romantic legend survives of Eleanor's reaction when she discovered her husband's grave condition, recorded by the chronicler William Camden:

When her husband was treacherously wounded by a Moor with a poyson'd sword, and rather grew worse than receiv'd any ease by what the Physician apply'd to it, she found out a remedy, as new and unheard of, as full of love and endearment. For by reason of the malignity of the poison, her husband's wounds could not possibly be clos'd: but she lick'd them dayly with her own tongue, and suck'd out the venomous humour, thinking it a most delicious liquor. By the power whereof, or rather by the virtue of a wife's tenderness, she so drew out the poisonous matter, that he was entirely cur'd of his wound, and she escaped without catching any harm.

This story shows great love and devotion. Sadly, it is unlikely to be true, and sources more contemporary to Eleanor claimed that Edward's life was saved by his surgeon and that Eleanor had to be carried, weeping, from his room. In spite of this, Eleanor probably did help to nurse Edward and in that way contributed to his recovery.

The assassination attempt dulled Edward's enthusiasm for the crusade, and he and Eleanor set out for home as soon as he was well enough. Edward's recovery took a considerable amount of time and they made slow progress on their journey home, sailing for Italy in late September 1272 and stopping to visit Edward's uncle, Charles of Anjou, King of Sicily, in his kingdom. During the visit, Eleanor and Edward received news that both their eldest son, John, and Henry III were dead. Charles was amazed by Edward's grief for his father compared to the philosophical way in which he took the news of his son's death and questioned his nephew on it. Edward replied that it was easy to beget sons, but that he would never have another father. It seems doubtful that Eleanor, who, after bearing at least eight children, had only one living son, felt the same way.

Edward and Eleanor were in no hurry to return to England, and in February 1273, after passing through Rome, stopped to visit the Pope at Orvieto. By the summer of 1273, they had reached Gascony, where Eleanor bore her third son, Alfonso. In November, she was visited in Gascony by her half-brother, Alfonso X, who stood as godfather to the prince, and she and Edward then travelled to Ponthieu to visit Eleanor's mother. As a mark of her affection for her mother, Eleanor left her youngest daughter, Joan, in Ponthieu to be raised by Jeanne. The couple then finally crossed to England to be welcomed as king and queen. They were crowned together in August 1274.

Life for Eleanor went on very much as before upon her return to England. Edward, conscious of the dominance that his mother had exerted over his father, was determined to keep his own wife in the background, and Eleanor never obtained a political role. In a Will made by Edward in 1272, for example, Eleanor was to be left wealthy, but she was not appointed as either regent or as guardian of her children. In March 1279, on the death of her mother, Eleanor became Countess of Ponthieu. Whilst this role meant that she was involved in some administration work and diplomacy, she was never responsible for actually ruling Ponthieu, and she never used her title in England. She appears to have been happy with this state of affairs, and her time was almost completely occupied in childbearing and in her land acquisitions.

It is unclear exactly how many children Eleanor bore during her lifetime, although there must have been at least eleven daughters and four or five sons. Neither Edward nor Eleanor had much contact with their children whilst they were young, and this has been interpreted as evidence of a lack of affection for them. Certainly, it does appear callous that neither Edward nor Eleanor visited their dying son Henry at Guildford in October 1274 when they were nearby in London. It was also left to the boy's grandmother, Eleanor of Provence, rather than his parents, to commemorate him. Edward and Eleanor commissioned no memorial Masses for their heir, Alfonso, when he died in 1284, a fact unusual for the time.

There is no doubt that Eleanor and Edward were distant parents, but it is possible that, having lost all but six of her children in infancy or childhood, Eleanor was unwilling to commit herself emotionally to children who were unlikely to survive. There is also evidence of affection towards her children, and Eleanor objected to her daughter, Mary, becoming a nun at Eleanor of Provence's request, arguing that her daughter was too young to be committed in this way. On another occasion, Eleanor worked with her mother-in-law to convince Edward that their thirteen-year-old daughter was too young for marriage and that the ceremony should be delayed for eighteen months. This was obviously based on Eleanor's own experience of early marriage and shows a concern for her daughter. Eleanor's accounts for 1290 show that her eldest surviving daughters, Eleanor, Joan and Margaret, travelled with her for much of the time, and that at Easter, all her children were with her at Woodstock.

Eleanor's greatest interest was land acquisition, and she was perceived by her contemporaries to be hungry for land, making her deeply unpopular during her lifetime. She purchased some land legitimately, but she was also involved in a number of more controversial acquisitions. In 1275, Edward granted her the right to take over the debts owed to Jewish moneylenders. Eleanor would take over a debt and then appropriate the land that had been given as surety. Her association with the hated moneylenders badly damaged her reputation, and the Archbishop of Canterbury wrote to her to warn her that Edward's harsh policies were being blamed squarely on her influence, and that by dealing in debts, she was committing the mortal sin of usury. This did not deter Eleanor, and her accounts from the last year of her life show that she continued to acquire land.

Taking over debts was not the only underhand means that Eleanor employed to gain more land. In 1283, she acquired one manor and promptly ordered her bailiffs to dispute the boundaries, taking 100 acres from neighbouring land. Eleanor's bailiffs and other officials were notoriously corrupt, and Eleanor did nothing to stop them. It is likely that she was not directly responsible for some of their excesses, such as the eviction of a couple from their house, their subsequent imprisonment, and the dumping of their baby in its cradle in the middle of the road. She was, however, aware of what was going on, and she did not punish her officials for their actions. On her deathbed, she requested that compensation be paid for wrongs that had been committed in her name.

Eleanor had a reputation for having a quick temper, and she was not a woman to cross. She liked to involve herself in marriages within her household and, on one occasion, reacted angrily when her wardrobe-buyer's daughter refused to marry the son of Edward's physician at her command. Eleanor felt slighted and, in revenge, confiscated money belonging to the girl. In 1283, Eleanor pursued the Bishop of Worcester for a debt that she claimed was owed to her. The bishop denied that such a debt existed, but Edward's chancellor advised him to pay it rather than anger Eleanor. Such behaviour did not make Eleanor popular, and a contemporary rhyme shows the depth of public feeling against her: 'The king he wants our gold, the queen would like our lands to hold.'

Eleanor's greed and acquisitiveness was not the only side to her character, and both she and Edward were visible presences in their subjects' lives, travelling around the country constantly. Eleanor's accounts show that ordinary people felt able to approach her personally, and she was often given gifts of food by poor women.

Eleanor involved herself in the lives of the poor, and between 1289 and 1290, she gave meals to over 9,000 of her poorest subjects. She widely patronised the Dominicans and founded priories for them in London and Chichester. As well as these charitable interests, Eleanor had an interest in learning, and she commissioned a book on a legendary Count of Ponthieu. She was a patron of both Oxford and Cambridge universities and left money to poor scholars in her Will.

Eleanor and Edward were frequently together, and the couple were devoted to each other, with Eleanor often accompanying her husband on his military campaigns. She was in Wales on campaign when she bore both her daughter Elizabeth in 1282 and her youngest child, Edward, in 1284. Eleanor travelled with Edward to Gascony in 1286, and the couple spent three years there whilst Edward administered his continental lands. Whilst she was in Gascony, Eleanor contracted malaria, and from 1287, she was frequently unwell. In November 1290, she and Edward set out from Clipston for Lincoln, a journey of only fifteen miles. They made little progress, only reaching Harby, still some distance from Lincoln, after nine days on 20 November. Harby was a tiny village with few facilities, and the stay was occasioned by a rapid deterioration in Eleanor's health. She died there in the evening of 28 November 1290.

Edward was grief-stricken at Eleanor's death, and he was determined that she should be commemorated. He ordered that her body be embalmed and placed in a litter for the journey to London. She was given a grand funeral cortege, which took twelve days to reach London. In memory of his beloved wife, Edward ordered that a stone cross be erected at every place that Eleanor's body stopped, with the first at Lincoln and the last at Charing Cross in London, which is a corruption of the French for 'dear queen'. Eleanor was given two fine tombs: one in Lincoln, where her bowels and other internal organs were buried, and the other at Westminster, where her body was interred. No other English queen received as extravagant a memorial as Eleanor, and Edward's actions on her death had a profound effect on her reputation. In the seventeenth century, William Camden wrote of the cross at Charing Cross that 'there stands a monument which King Edward I erected in memory of Queen Eleanor, the dearest husband to the most loving wife, whose tender affection will stand upon record for all posterity'. Posthumously, Eleanor was able to obtain a reputation for queenly virtue purely based on her husband's devotion to her. Edward I, in spite of his harsh military reputation, was a man who liked being married, and nine years after Eleanor's death, he took a second wife, Margaret of France.

MARGARET OF FRANCE (*c*. 1279–1318) is little remembered today and was, even in her own time, overshadowed by her more famous predecessor as Edward's wife, and by her successor as queen, the notorious Isabella of France. She played an important role in keeping the royal family together, and her life appears, in the main, to have been a happy one. She was the youngest child of Philip III of France and his wife, Marie of Brabant, and was born around 1279. In 1285, her father died, and she was raised under the guardianship of her brother, Philip IV.

In 1296, Philip invaded Gascony and took control of the duchy. Edward I was already committed to his war in Scotland and was unable to defend both areas. He had already made one marriage in order to safeguard Gascony from foreign attack, and he was therefore eager, in 1298, to adopt the Pope's suggestion of a marriage between himself and a sister of Philip IV, and for his eldest surviving son, Edward, to marry Philip's daughter, Isabella. At first, it was suggested that Edward marry Margaret's elder sister, Blanche, who was a renowned beauty. At some stage in the negotiations, Margaret's name was substituted for Blanche's. Margaret came from a good-looking family, and her brother was always known as 'Philip the Fair'. Whilst Margaret was always rather overshadowed by her brother and elder sister, she was an attractive woman in her own right, and according to the chronicler Peter Langcroft, she was 'the Lady Margaret, in whose least finger there is more goodness and beauty, whoever looks at her, than in the fair Idione whom Adamas loved'. Edward had no reason to feel short-changed by the substitution of Margaret in place of the fair Blanche.

Margaret must have been apprehensive, as she was, at most, twenty at the time of her marriage whilst Edward was sixty. She arrived at Dover in September 1299 and was taken straight to Canterbury, where she and Edward were married on 8 September. No record of the couple's first meeting survives, but Edward was apparently delighted with his young bride, and the couple, against expectations, became close. Margaret was presented to the people as a peacemaker for her role in ending the conflict in Gascony, and this made her popular, with the contemporary *Song of the Scottish Wars* commenting of the marriage that 'next the king returns, that he may marry Queen Margaret, the flower of the French; through her the kingdoms receive a more complete peace. Anger begets slaughter, concord nourishes love – when love buds between great princes, it drives away bitter sobs from their subjects'. Unusually, Margaret was not crowned, and instead, shortly after the wedding, Edward returned to his campaign in Scotland.

It must have been daunting for Margaret to meet her new husband only for him to rush away, but she continued to make a good impression in England, spending three weeks at the monastery at St Albans shortly after her wedding, where she gave generous charitable gifts. Margaret also joined the fraternity of the monastery. Religion was important to Margaret, and she often chose to stay in monasteries when she travelled.

Margaret regularly accompanied her husband on his campaigns, just as his first wife had done. She quickly fell pregnant following her marriage, and both she and Edward found they missed each other, in spite of the brief time that they had been together. According to the chronicler Peter Langcroft, soon after Easter 1300,

> Queen Margaret, by command of her lord the king, proceeds towards the North; she was advanced in pregnancy; by will of God Almighty at Brotherton on the wharf she is safely delivered of a son who is named Thomas at his baptism. King Edward receives information of it, prepares quickly to visit the lady, like a falcon before the wind. After her purification made solemnly the king resumes his road towards Scotland; the queen with her son waits at Cawood, on the River Ouse, much at her ease.

Given that Margaret had only arrived in England in September 1299 and her first son was born on 1 June 1300, coupled with the fact that Brotherton contained no royal residence, it is clear that Margaret's first child was premature. In spite of this, her son was healthy and as soon as she was well enough to travel she moved to Cawood which had been prepared for her lying-in. Margaret's other deliveries went more smoothly, and she bore Edward two further children: Edmund at Woodstock in August 1301, and Eleanor at Winchester in May 1306. It is a testament to Margaret's good nature that her only daughter was named after her predecessor as Edward's wife.

Like Eleanor of Castile, Margaret spent most of her time travelling with Edward, and she was a distant mother to her children. She did involve herself in their upbringing as much as possible, however, and whilst they had their own household, she is known to have personally selected Thomas's wet nurse. She gave her two sons the gift of an iron birdcage and grieved for her daughter when she died young. Edward was also interested in his children, and a letter survives from him to the steward of his sons' household, telling him to ensure that they attended Mass at Canterbury Cathedral and asking for a report on their conduct during the service. Edward asked for them to be brought to St Radegunds in September 1302 so that he could visit them. In a further letter to the children's household after the birth of Margaret's daughter, Edward asked for details of what the baby was like. It is obvious that both Margaret and Edward attempted to stay involved in their children's lives, and Edward treated the children of his second family with more indulgence than the strict upbringings imposed on his first.

Margaret made an effort to be on good terms with Edward's children from his first marriage. She had considerable contact with the future Edward II, and even though she was only a few years older than him, she filled the role of a mother to him. In 1305, the young Edward and some other youths invaded the estates of the Bishop of Chester, pulling down fences and allowing his game to escape. Edward I was furious with his son and sent him to Windsor, where he spent six months in disgrace. He was only released through a reconciliation engineered by Margaret when she convinced her husband not to punish his son further.

Edward I was faithful to both his queens, and he and Margaret enjoyed a loving relationship. There is evidence that he was anxious about Margaret's health and happiness, as a series of surviving letters show. Margaret was diagnosed with measles in 1305, and Edward was very concerned for her health, cancelling arrangements that had been made for her to travel to see him. In a letter to her physician, Edward told him not to let her travel until she was fully recovered or he would suffer for it.

In a letter written in May 1305 to Margaret's confessor, Brother Henry, Edward showed a desire to spare Margaret's feelings, albeit in a rather tactless way. Edward wrote to instruct Brother Henry to break the news to Margaret of her sister Blanche's death. He suggested that, to comfort her, the confessor might like to point out that she should not grieve too much for her sister, since Blanche had been as good as dead to her anyway since the elder sister had left her family in France for her marriage in Austria. It has been suggested that this callousness was due to a personal grudge against Blanche, as he had wanted to marry her. It seems more likely that Edward was simply trying to think of ways to console his wife.

Margaret was an exemplary queen, and her only recorded vice was a failure to control her finances. She was very extravagant, and by 1302, Edward had had to give her £4,000 out of wardships and marriages so that she could pay her debts. In 1305, her lands had to be increased by £500 a year, again in order to service her debts. Margaret spent the money on luxuries: in 1302, she owed £1,000 to an Italian merchant for fine clothes and other extravagant goods. She was left richly provided for in Edward's Will but died heavily in debt.

In spite of these debts, Margaret was a kind-hearted woman, and she interceded with Edward on a number of occasions on behalf of people who petitioned her. She saved the life of a Godfrey de Cogners, who had unwisely fashioned the crown with which Robert the Bruce was crowned in Scotland. Margaret was kind-hearted even to her opponents. In 1303 or 1304, she issued a writ against two men for trespass in her park in Camel in Somerset. Since both of the accused were in Scotland when the writ was issued, she agreed to postpone her action against them so that they would not be prejudiced by their absence. In a letter to Edward's chancellor, Margaret wrote,

> Because we have granted, at the request of our dear cousin, Sir Aymer de Valence, that the exigence [writ] which is running upon Sir Alexander Cheverel and Roger Parker (who remain in the service of our said lord the king in Scotland) in the county of Somerset by the order delivered to the sheriff of the same place by our said cousin, Sir Hugh le Despenser and Sir Henry le Spigurnel, justices assigned to hear and determine the trespass which was committed against our said lord the king and against ourself in our

park of Camel, should be adjourned until the feast of St Hilary next coming, we command and request you that you hereupon make the said Sir Alexander and Roger have our lord the king's writ to the aforesaid sheriff in due manner, so that they in the meantime do not incur damage or danger by it for this reason.

In any event, at least in relation to one of the trespassers, Margaret did not have to wait too long for justice, writing again to the chancellor within a month to inform him that

because Roger le Parker, who has recently done right concerning the trespass committed in our park of Camel, has paid to us into our Wardrobe his fine which he made for us, for this reason we request and command you that you hereupon cause him to have writs of our said lord the King to the sheriff of Somerset, that he should suffer him to be quit of all manner of exigencies and other demands that he made against him by reason of the before mentioned trespass.

Margaret was less dangerous in her protection of her lands and revenue than her predecessor, Eleanor of Castile, had been.

Margaret was not with Edward when he died on 7 July 1307 at Burgh-by-Sands on his way to yet another campaign in Scotland. Edward's death was unexpected, and Margaret grieved for him deeply, never contemplating a second marriage, in spite of being only in her late twenties at the time. She did not contemplate retiring from public life and, on 22 January 1308, sailed to Boulogne with her stepson, Edward II, for his marriage to her niece, Isabella of France. It had been nearly ten years since Margaret had last seen her homeland and family, and she quickly established a close relationship with her niece.

The royal party returned to England soon after the wedding for Edward and Isabella's coronation. Margaret's brothers, the Counts of Valois and Evreux publicly voiced their disapproval at the prominence given to Edward II's favourite, Piers Gaveston, at the ceremony, and it is likely that Margaret also disapproved. Certainly, she retired from court soon after the coronation. She may also have voiced her concerns to her brother, Philip IV, and in May 1308, it was reported that both Philip and Margaret had sent funds to the Earls of Lincoln and Pembroke to finance their campaign to oust Gaveston from power. She had reason to dislike Gaveston, as, at Easter 1308, Edward took Berkhamstead Castle from her and bestowed it on his favourite. Margaret played only a small role in the campaign against Gaveston, and it was the only foray into politics that she ever made.

Margaret's last public appearance was as a witness to the birth of the future Edward III at Windsor in 1312. She joined her niece, Isabella, two months before the birth and stayed until after the christening before returning to her own estates. She lived quietly for the rest of her widowhood and died at Marlborough Castle in February 1318 of some unspecified illness. At her request, she was buried at Greyfriars church in London, next to the altar in the choir that she had built. In spite of her brief life and even briefer marriage, Margaret of France appears to have been content, and she enjoyed a happier marriage than her niece and successor as queen, Isabella of France.

ISABELLA OF FRANCE (*c.* 1295–1358) is one of the most famous queens of England. She also had one of the most prestigious backgrounds and, with the exception of the later Catherine of Aragon, was the only English queen to be the daughter of two reigning sovereigns. She was the only daughter of Philip IV of France and his wife, Jeanne, Queen of Navarre. Her mother died when she was around ten years old, but she was thoroughly spoiled by her adoring father. Isabella was first betrothed to the future Edward II in her infancy, at the same time that her aunt, Margaret, married Edward's father. Isabella, as the only daughter of the powerful King of France, was the most eligible princess of her generation, and according to the chronicler Froissart, she was also 'one of the feyrest ladyes of the worlde'. She was a member of a very good-looking family, and throughout her lifetime, she was known as 'Isabella the Fair'.

Edward I died in 1307, and Edward II decided to delay his coronation until he could share it with Isabella. Shortly after his accession, Edward crossed to France in the company of his stepmother, Margaret of France. He was met at Boulogne by Isabella and her father, Philip, as well as by other members of her family and the French nobility. Philip had provided Isabella with a magnificent trousseau, including seventy-two headdresses and two gold crowns. Edward and Isabella were married with great ceremony at Boulogne on 25 January 1308. Isabella is likely to have been pleased with Edward when she met him, as he was, by all accounts, a handsome and charming man. It is unlikely that, at first, she noticed anything unusual in his behaviour towards her, although the fact that he sent his wedding presents to his favourite, Piers Gaveston, in England, did not go unnoticed by Isabella's relatives.

Piers Gaveston had been a member of Edward's household since 1300. The relationship had caused Edward I much concern, and in February 1307, he had banished Gaveston, only for Edward II to immediately recall him on his accession. Edward II had an illegitimate son who was born before 1307, and so he clearly did have some attraction to women. They were not his primary interest, however, and several contemporary sources hint at an intimate relationship with Gaveston. Edward II is commonly believed to have been homosexual, and he is very likely to have had sexual relationships with both Gaveston and a later favourite, Hugh Despenser the Younger. Gaveston was also Edward's closest friend and confidant, and he was left as regent by the devoted King when he journeyed to France for his marriage.

Edward and Isabella sailed for England shortly after their marriage, in the company of Isabella's two uncles, the Counts of Valois and Evreux. Both Isabella and her uncles were shocked when, as soon as the ship docked, Edward flew to embrace Gaveston, who was waiting at the harbour. Isabella's uncles wrote indignantly to Philip in France, and Edward's conduct over the next few weeks made them increasingly concerned. The royal couple travelled to London and were crowned together at Westminster in a grand ceremony planned by Gaveston. He had ensured that he played a prominent role in the ceremony, and he caused indignation amongst the assembled English and French nobility by carrying the royal crown before the King. Edward also chose to sit beside Gaveston at the coronation banquet, relegating Isabella to an inferior seat. For Isabella, the daughter of two sovereigns, this rankled, and it was around this time that she noticed Gaveston wearing the jewels that her father had given to Edward as a wedding present.

Soon after the coronation, Isabella's two uncles returned to France bringing their own reports of Isabella's reception and the King's relationship with Gaveston. Edward also faced opposition in England for his conduct, as recorded by the *Chronicle of Lanercost*:

The people of the country and the leading men complained loudly at his [Edward's] coronation against the aforesaid Piers, and unanimously wished that he should be deprived of his earldom; but this the king obstinately refused. The rumours increased from day to day, and engrossed the lips and ears of all men, nor was there one who had a good word either for the king or for Piers. The chief men agreed unanimously in strongly demanding that Piers should be sent back into exile, foremost among them being the noble Earl of Lincoln and the young Earl of Gloucester, whose sister, however, Piers had received in marriage by the king's gift.

Edward had given his niece, Margaret de Clare, the daughter of his sister, Joan of Acre, in marriage to Piers, and this proved to be the final straw for much of the nobility. By June 1308, the King had been compelled to send Gaveston into exile.

Isabella spent more time with Edward during Gaveston's absence, with the couple spending Christmas together at Windsor. The time that they were able to spend together alone led to the couple coming to an understanding with each other, and even after Gaveston's return, they spent time together, with Isabella securing some political influence for herself. In an early letter to Edward, she wrote,

My very dear and dread lord, I commend myself to you as humbly as I can. My dear lord, you have heard how our seneschal and our controller for Ponthieu have come from Ponthieu concerning our affairs; the letters they had to bring can remain in the state they are at present until the parliament – except one which concerns you inheritance in Ponthieu and the Count of Dreux, which should be acted upon immediately in order to keep and maintain your inheritance. I beg you, my gentle lord, that by this message it may please you to request your chancellor by letter that he summon those of your council to him and take steps speedily in this matter according to what he and your said council see what is best to do for your honour and profit. For if action is not speedily taken, this will do you great harm and be of much benefit to the said count your enemy, as I have truly heard by my council. May the Holy Spirit keep you, my very dear and dread lord.

Isabella played an increasingly prominent role as queen, and by 1311, she controlled a household of over 200 people. She also developed an intimate relationship with Edward, and by early 1312, she was pregnant.

Although Edward was able to recall Gaveston to England, his presence was still deeply resented by the English nobility. By 1312, the barons, led by the Earls of Lancaster and Leicester, were actively working against the favourite. The two earls were the maternal half-brothers of Isabella's mother, and it has been suggested that they acted as their niece's champion in their actions against Gaveston. Whilst they certainly resented the slights done to Isabella by Gaveston in the early days of her marriage, by 1312, Isabella was on reasonable terms with the favourite, and she was not actively working against him.

Edward, Gaveston, and Isabella set out north in the early summer of 1312, aware of the hostility that was building towards Gaveston. Whilst they were staying at York, they heard that Lancaster had begun to march north with an army, intent on the favourite's destruction. Terrified, the three fled to Newcastle. Edward and Gaveston then sailed to Scarborough, leaving Isabella to travel to Tynemouth Castle to await the outcome of events. Soon after their voyage to Scarborough, Edward and Gaveston separated. They never saw each other again. Gaveston was captured by Lancaster and turned over to the custody of the Earl of Pembroke. On 19 July 1312, he was taken out to the crossroads at Blacklow Hill, near Warwick, and beheaded by the barons without trial. Edward was furious at the death of his favourite but powerless to take any immediate action in revenge. Isabella's feelings on the favourite's death are not recorded, but it is likely that she was not displeased by Gaveston's removal from Edward's side. Some time after the murder, she travelled slowly south towards Windsor to await the birth of her child.

Isabella bore her first child, a son, on 13 November 1312. According to the chronicler John Capgrave, there was some controversy over the choice of name for the new heir to the throne, and 'many Frensch lordis, that were aboute hir, wold a clepid him Philippea, aftir the kyng of Frans: the Englisch lords wold have him Edward. The king had so grete joy of this child new born, that his heavinesse for Petir [Gaveston] cesed some'. The King won the day, naming his son after himself rather than Isabella's father. Isabella and Edward's personal relationship continued to improve in the years following young Edward's birth, and between 1315 and 1321, Isabella bore a further three children. Whilst the frequency of these births does not suggest regular intimacy, it is obvious that the couple attempted to make their marriage work. Edward placed his trust in Isabella during the period, and the couple travelled to Paris together in 1313. The following February Isabella returned to France alone to negotiate a treaty with her father.

Isabella was probably always aware that there was a danger of Edward acquiring a new favourite to overshadow her. By the time of the birth of her youngest child, Joan, in 1321, Edward was noticeably fond of a father and a son, both called Hugh Despenser. Once again, surviving sources hint at the homosexual nature of the relationship between Edward and the younger Despenser, and Isabella, who would tellingly later have the younger Despenser castrated, was convinced that he and her husband were lovers. According to the chronicler Froissart, Edward was fully in thrall to the younger Despenser, and 'the sayd kyng governed right diversly his realme by the exortatcion of Sir Hewe Spencer, who had been norisshed with hym syth the begynnyng of his yougth; the which Sir Hewe had so enticed the kyng, that his father and he were the greatest maisters in all the realme, and by envy thought to surmount all other barons in Ingland'.

Whilst Isabella had been able to come to terms with Gaveston and tolerate his relationship with her husband, she and the Despensers were always implacably opposed. Froissart claims that 'the sayd sir Hewe Spencer achieved great hate in all the realme, and specially of the quene, and of the erle of Cane [Kent], brother to the kyng. And whan he perceived the displeasure of the quene, by his subtile wytte he set great discord bitwene the kyng and the quene, so that the kyng wold nat se the quene, nor come in her company; the whiche discord endured a long space'. The two Despensers were determined to crush any influence that Isabella had over Edward, and they showed their contempt for her in a number of ways. In 1320, for example, the elder Despenser refused to pay Isabella sums owed to her from her manor of Lechlade, and in 1321, the younger Despenser failed to pay the Queen rents that he owed her from the city of Bristol. When

Isabella complained of this to Edward, she found that he supported his favourites over her.

In late 1321, Isabella decided to go on a pilgrimage to Canterbury, and on 2 October, she went to spend the night at Leeds Castle, one of her dower properties. As she approached the castle, her stewards were denied entry, and when they persisted, the castle guards opened fire, killing a number of Isabella's attendants. The castellan supported the barons who had once again risen to attack Edward due to the rise of the Despensers, and it is probable that Isabella's visit to Leeds was intended by Edward to trigger an attack on his opponents. As soon as Edward received word of what had happened at Leeds, he set out towards the castle with an army of Londoners, rapidly bringing it to submission. Edward then marched north to meet the barons in battle and achieved a great victory at Boroughbridge, ordering Isabella's uncle, Thomas of Lancaster, to be executed in the same manner in which Gaveston had died. Isabella's feelings are likely to have been mixed, but both she and her brother-in-law and cousin, Edmund of Kent were anxious at the power of the Despensers and, shortly after Lancaster's death, 'it was shewed to the quene secretly, and to the earl of Cane [Kent], that withoute they toke good hede to them selfe, they were likely to be destroyed; for sir Hewe Spencer was about to purchase moch trouble to theym'.

Isabella had reason to complain of her treatment in the years following her uncle's death, and with growing hostilities between England and France, she found that she was under increasing suspicion from Edward and the Despensers. In 1324, Isabella's uncle, Charles of Valois, invaded Gascony, and Edward retaliated by seizing Isabella's lands and those of foreign monasteries. Isabella's allowance was cut and her children removed from her custody. She was actively spied upon, and the younger Despenser's wife was 'appointed as it were, guardian of the queen, and carried her seal; nor could the queen write to anybody without her knowledge: whereat my lady the queen was equally indignant and distressed, and therefore wished to visit her brother in France to seek a remedy'. For Isabella, the opportunity to free herself from this scrutiny came in March 1325, when Edward, unwisely, agreed to send her to France to act on his behalf in peace negotiations with her brother, Charles IV, who had succeeded Isabella's father and then her two eldest brothers as king of France.

Edward and the Despensers were eager to get Isabella away from England, and they do not appear to have considered that she could be capable of taking independent action against them. According to the *Chronicle of Lanercost*, whilst Isabella was in France, the younger Despenser sent agents to the Pope to attempt to procure a divorce for Edward, and it is possible that it was intended that Isabella should not return. Isabella landed at Boulogne and immediately made her way towards Paris. According to Froissart, at her very first meeting with her brother, Isabella poured out her heart to him:

> She answered hym right sagely, and lamentably recounted to hym all the felonyes and injuries done to her by syr Hewe Spencer, and required hym of his ayde and comfort. Whan the noble kyng Charles of Fraunce had harde his suster's lamentation, who wepyngly had shewed hym all her need and besynesse, he sayd to her, Fayre suster appease your selfe, for by the faith I owe to God and to saynt Denyce, I shall right well purvey for you some remedy. The quene than kneled downed, whether the kyng wold or nat, and sayd, Y right dere lord and fayre brother, I pray God reward you.

Charles agreed to support Isabella in her dispute with Edward and the Despensers. Edward still suspected nothing, and shortly after her arrival, Isabella persuaded him to allow their eldest son to join her in Paris so that he could do homage for Gascony. Isabella was overjoyed to see her son and knew that, with him in her possession, she had a powerful bargaining counter to use against her husband. The possession of her son caused a number of the English nobility who were hostile to Edward and the Despensers to look towards her as their leader, and several English exiles joined her in Paris, including Edmund, Earl of Kent, and Roger Mortimer, a nobleman who had escaped from imprisonment in the Tower of London some years before.

Once she had secured her son's arrival and her brother's aid, Isabella finally declared her intentions and refused to return to England when summoned. The news of the Queen's defiance spread, and there were 'contradictory rumours in England about the queen, some declaring that she was the betrayer of the king and kingdom, others that she was acting for peace and the common welfare of the kingdom, and for the removal of the evil counsellors from the king'. The younger Despenser was concerned about the threat posed by Isabella, and he sent bribes of gold, silver and jewels to Isabella's brother in an attempt to persuade him to expel her from France. Edward petitioned the Pope, asking him to order Isabella to return to England.

Isabella did have plans to return to England, but not to her role as Edward's wife, and within months of her arrival in Paris, her brother was actively seeking to distance himself from her and her conduct. During their time together in Paris, Isabella and Roger Mortimer became lovers. Isabella remained devoted to Mortimer for the rest of his life, and it is clear that she was in love with him. Mortimer's feelings are less obvious, and certainly, a relationship with the Queen was to his advantage. However, the couple do appear to have had a passionate attachment to each other, to the horror of Isabella's family in France. Finally, embarrassed by all that was happening, Charles asked Isabella to leave, and she, Mortimer, young Edward and their supporters travelled to Hainault, where Isabella's cousin was countess. The exiles were given a warm welcome, and Isabella agreed a treaty, betrothing her eldest son to one of the count's daughters in exchange for ships and men for her invasion of England.

Isabella set sail from Hainault with a large fleet of ships and landed at Harwich on 24 September 1326. Aware of the danger of being perceived as foreign invaders, Isabella, her brother-in-law, Kent, and her son issued a proclamation when they arrived at Wallingford, determined to set out the righteousness of their cause:

Whereas it is well known that the state of the Holy Church and the Kingdom of England is in many respects much tarnished and degraded by the bad advice and conspiracy of Hugh le Despenser; whereas, through pride and greed to have power and dominion over all other people, he has usurped royal power against law and justice and his true allegiance, and through the bad advice of Robert de Baldock and others of his supporters, he has acted in such a way that the Holy Church is robbed of its goods against God and Right and in many ways insulted and dishonoured, and the Crown of England brought low in many respects, through the disinheritance of our lord the king and of his heirs; the magnates of the kingdom, through the envy and wicked cruelty of the said Hugh have been delivered to a shameful death, many of them blamelessly and without cause; others have been disinherited, imprisoned, banished or exiled; widows and orphans have been unlawfully deprived of their rights, and the people of this land much hurt by many taxes and held to ransom by frequent unjust demands for money and by divers other oppressions without any mercy, by virtue of which misdeeds the said Hugh shows himself to be a clear tyrant and enemy of God and the Holy Church, of our very dear lord the king and the whole kingdom.

Edward had made himself very unpopular in England, and Isabella was joined by her uncle Henry, Earl of Leicester, who, on his brother's death, had taken the title of Earl of Lancaster, and other members of the nobility. Isabella moved towards London with her forces and was glad to hear on her approach that the city had risen to support her. She stayed for only a few days in London before setting out in pursuit of Edward and the Despensers, who had fled.

Edward had left the elder Despenser in command at Bristol, and Isabella went there first, winning the town after a short siege. The elder Despenser must have known that he was doomed, and Isabella ordered him to be executed in front of Bristol Castle. Mortimer and Henry of Lancaster then set off in pursuit of Edward and the younger Despenser, who had fled towards Wales. The pair were soon captured and Edward was sent as a prisoner to Kenilworth Castle. Whilst Isabella may not at that point have decided just what to do with Edward, she was determined to have her revenge on the younger Despenser, and he was brought before her at Hereford. According to Froissart, Isabella sentenced her rival to a deeply unpleasant death:

Fyrst to be drawen on an hyrdell with trumpes and trumpettis through all the cite of Herford, and after, to be brought into the market place, where as all the people were assembled, and there to be tyed on high upon a ladder that every man might se hym: and in the same place ther to be made a great fier, and ther his privy members cut from hym, because they reputed hym as an heretyk, and sodomite, and so to be brent in the fyre before his face: and than his hart to be drawen out of his body, and cast into the fyre, bycause he was a false traytour of hart, and that by hys traytours counsel and extorcion, the kyng had shamed his realme, and brought it to great mischief, for he had caused to be behedded the greatest lords of his realme, by whom the realme ought to have been susteyned and defended: and he had so enducd the kyng, that he wolde nat se the quene his wife, nor Edwarde his eldest son, and caused hym to chace them out of the realme for fere of theyr lyves: and than his heed to be stryken of and sent to London. And accordiyng to this judgement, he was executed.

The circumstances of the younger Despenser's death were particularly horrible, and it is a mark of Isabella's belief in his relationship with her husband that she ordered him to be castrated as a sodomite.

Isabella and Mortimer spent Christmas at Wallingford, and in January 1327, they arrived in London, where Isabella called a parliament. As she hoped, parliament agreed that Edward II should abdicate in favour of his son, and that Isabella 'for the great anxiety and anguish she had suffered' should be granted the title of queen for life.

Due to Edward III's youth, the real power behind the throne remained Isabella and Mortimer, something that the young king keenly resented. When Edward II had been asked to abdicate, he had wept and begged to receive visits from his wife and children. Isabella had no wish to see her estranged husband, and when he requested that she visit, she refused, saying that the lords would not allow her to see him. She did send him presents and clothes, although this is more likely to have been to ensure that she maintained the appearance of a dutiful wife rather than because she felt any fondness for her husband. For Isabella and Mortimer, Edward's continued existence was a threat, and he did not long survive his deposition. Late in 1327, he was taken as a prisoner to Berkeley Castle in Gloucestershire, and he died on the night of 1 September. The exact cause of death was not recorded, but it has been rumoured that he was killed by a red-hot spit inserted into his rectum. There is no contemporary evidence for this, but it is certain that Edward was murdered and that Isabella, even if she did not give the order herself, was complicit in the death of her husband. Whilst Mortimer was the dominant force in his relationship with Isabella, it is impossible that he would have acted without her authority.

The rumours surrounding Edward II's death reflected badly on Isabella, and she and Mortimer made themselves unpopular in other ways, too. Edward III and much of the nobility disapproved of their policies, such as the decision to make peace with Scotland. Isabella also caused anger by assigning herself the largest dower ever known for a queen of England, ensuring that she had access to a vast revenue source. Mortimer became increasingly domineering, and in 1329, the couple took steps to neutralise Edmund of Kent when he began to waver in his support for them. Kent was wracked with guilt at his involvement in the deposition of his half-brother, and in 1329, he was informed secretly that his brother was still alive. It is possible that this rumour was spread by Mortimer in order to test Kent's loyalty or to incriminate him, and when Kent responded by sending a friar to enquire into his brother's whereabouts, Mortimer struck. At a parliament later in the year, Kent was accused of plotting to restore Edward II and sentenced to death, with the sentence being carried out against the wishes of his nephew, Edward III. The execution of the son of a king shocked the nobility and undermined any vestige of support for Isabella and Mortimer's rule.

By 1330, Edward III was approaching eighteen, and he resented the dominance of his mother and her lover. He also resented the rumours about Isabella and Mortimer's relationship that were prevalent in England, and Froissart, for example, recorded in his chronicle that Isabella was believed to be pregnant by Mortimer. This rumour was untrue, but it angered the King, and there were also claims that Mortimer wished to depose him and become king himself. In 1330, Mortimer and Isabella called a parliament at Nottingham, and Edward decided to act, entering Nottingham Castle one night with a group of attendants through a secret tunnel. According to the Chronicle of Geoffrey Le Baker,

> Having rushed out of the underground passage and subterranean route, the king's friends advanced with drawn sword to the queen's bedroom, the king waited, armed, outside the chamber of their foes, lest he should be seen by his mother. As the conspirators charged in, they killed Hugh de Turpinton, knight, as he tried to resist them, Lord John de Neville of Hornby directing the blow. Then they found the queen mother almost ready for bed, and the Earl of

March [Mortimer] whom they wanted. They led him captive into the hall, while the queen cried 'fair son, fair son, have pity on gentle Mortimer'; for she suspected that her son was there, even though she had not seen him.

Edward had no intention of showing mercy towards Mortimer, and he was executed. Isabella's life was never in danger, but immediately after his coup, Edward placed her under strict house arrest and seized her lands and goods. Isabella spent two years confined at Castle Rising in Norfolk, grieving for Mortimer and her lost liberty.

Edward retained affection for Isabella, and he gradually allowed her to be rehabilitated back into the royal family. She was never given any political role, however, and Edward never learned to trust her again. She spent the rest of her life quietly, mainly living at Castle Rising. She fell ill on 22 August 1358, apparently due to taking an overdose of medicine, and died later the same day. Edward III gave his mother a royal funeral, which he attended himself, and according to legend, Isabella was buried in her wedding dress, clutching Edward II's heart in a silver casket. This may suggest that she felt remorse for the murder of her husband, but it is more telling that she asked to be buried at Greyfriars in London, the burial place of her true love, Mortimer.

Isabella of France is the most notorious of any post-conquest queen of England, and she is remembered today as the 'She-Wolf of France', thanks to a reference to her role in Edward's murder in a poem by Thomas Grey:

The shrieks of death, thro' Berkeley's roofs that ring,
Shrieks of an agonising king!
She-wolf of France, with unrelenting fangs,
That tear'st the bowels of thy mangled mate,
From thee be born, who o'er thy country hangs
The scourge of Heav'n what terrors round him wait!'

Isabella sought to extend her power as queen beyond the death of her husband and the marriage of her son, and for the first few years of Edward III's marriage to Philippa of Hainault, she refused to yield any power or status to her young daughter-in-law.

PHILIPPA OF HAINAULT (1310–69) was the daughter of William III Count of Hainault and his wife, Jeanne of Valois. She was born in 1310 and was one of a family of four daughters and one son. In December 1325, Philippa's grandfather, the Count of Valois, died, and her mother travelled to Paris for the funeral. It is uncertain whether she brought any of her daughters with her to meet her French kin, but certainly, whilst in Paris, Jeanne met with her cousin, Isabella of France, and suggested a marriage alliance between one of her daughters and Isabella's eldest son. By late 1325, Isabella was badly in need of allies, and it was to Hainault that she and her supporters travelled in July 1326 when they were forced to leave France.

Isabella and her son, Edward, journeyed to Valenciennes in Hainault, where they were warmly received by the townspeople. According to Froissart, Philippa's parents were anxious for such a prestigious match for one of their daughters.

> [Isabella] was brought before the erle Guyllaume of Heynaulte, who receyved her with great joye, and in lyke wyse dyd the countesse his wife, and feasted her ryght nobly. And as than this erle hadde foure fayre daughters, Margaret, Philyppe, Jane, and Isabell; amonge whome the yong Edwarde sette moost his love and company on Phylyppe; and also the yong lady in al honour was more conversaunt with hym than any of her susters.

Isabella and Edward remained with Philippa's family for eight days, and during that time, Edward was given the opportunity to select which of the four sisters he would prefer as a wife. His preference for Philippa soon became clear, and whilst she was no beauty, Edward was pleased with the devotion that she showed towards him. Whilst the choice of bride had not been finalised by the time Edward and his mother left Valenciennes, it was clear that it would be Philippa, and as she said goodbye to her English cousin, she burst into tears.

On 27 August 1326, Isabella and Count William agreed a marriage treaty between Edward and one of the count's daughters. It was agreed that the marriage would take place within two years, and that, in return, William would supply a dowry of troops, ships and money in advance of the wedding. Given the fact that Isabella and Philippa's mother were first cousins, it took some time to secure the necessary dispensation from the Pope, but finally, on 3 September 1327, it was granted, with the document naming Philippa as the intended bride for the first time.

In December 1327, Philippa's uncle, John of Hainault, arrived from England to fetch her for her marriage. Philippa landed in England on 23 December and made her state entry to London the following day. She was lodged at Ely Palace and spent the Christmas period there, feasting and dancing. After Christmas, she set out north to join Edward, who was busy campaigning against the Scots, and they met at York, where they were married on 30 January. The marriage was conducted in the freezing cold, but it was a lavish ceremony and Philippa and Edward found their feelings for each other unchanged after so many months apart. In spite of this, Philippa cannot have failed to notice the prominence of Isabella of France in the young king's affairs, and she may have felt uneasy about the precedence that Isabella enjoyed over her. Unusually, Philippa was granted no dower or independent household at her wedding, and Isabella, anxious to be the only anointed queen in England, refused to allow her daughter-in-law to be crowned.

The first few years of Edward's reign were dominated by Isabella and her lover, Roger Mortimer. Edward keenly resented this and the forced subordination of Philippa, and he had hoped that his marriage would be the occasion at which he was able to assert his authority as an adult. Philippa's lack of a coronation rankled with Edward, especially as by late 1329 she was pregnant. It was unthinkable that an heir to the throne should be born without his mother being crowned, and Isabella finally consented to the ceremony taking place on 4 March 1330. Shortly afterwards, Philippa bore her first son, Edward, who would later be known as the Black Prince. Philippa had no involvement in the coup against Mortimer and Isabella, but she benefited from Isabella's forced retirement and was finally able to take up her position as queen of England.

Philippa and Edward's long marriage proved to be extremely close, and Edward was very protective of her. On 21 September 1331, Philippa and her ladies assembled to watch Edward take part in a tournament at Cheapside. As the tournament began, the wooden stand on which Philippa and her ladies sat collapsed, causing Edward to be thrown from his horse and knocking all the ladies to the ground. No one was badly hurt, but Edward, in a rage, swore that the carpenters who built the stand would be put to death. Philippa, although still shaken from her fall, threw herself on her knees before Edward and begged that the workmen's lives be spared. This appeal softened Edward's mood, and he agreed to her request. This is the first incident of many during their marriage where Philippa calmed her husband and protected those who angered him.

Another indication of the close relationship between Edward and Philippa is their large family. Philippa gave birth to seven sons and five daughters during her marriage, five of whom outlived her. This was a large number of children even in the medieval period, and few queens have equalled Philippa's record. Edward and Philippa were indulgent parents. This can be seen in their treatment of their eldest daughter, Isabella, who went through a number of broken betrothals before finally, in 1350, being sent to France to marry. A few days before the wedding, Isabella changed her mind and promptly sailed for home. Edward and Philippa accepted her decision and she remained unmarried with a generous annual income until 1365 when she eloped with a French hostage imprisoned in London. Again, Edward and Philippa accepted their daughter's choice, and they remained on excellent terms with her. They also allowed their eldest son, Edward, the Black Prince, to make a love match with his cousin, the divorced Joan of Kent, and Philippa was present at their wedding at Windsor on 10 October 1361.

The preoccupation of Edward's life was his invasion of France. Edward's uncle, Charles IV of France, had died in 1328 and was succeeded by his cousin (and Philippa's uncle), Philip V. Edward, as the grandson of Philip IV, believed that he had a better claim to the French throne than his grandfather's nephew and he decided to press his claim through force. He hoped to build an alliance through his and Philippa's family connections, and in August 1336, he banned the export of English wool to the Low Countries in order to persuade them to join with him. English wool was essential to the cloth industries there, and the export ban soon had an effect. This policy damaged Hainault's economy, and Philippa took steps to mitigate the suffering of her countrymen, encouraging foreign weavers to settle in England and using her influence with Edward to assist them in establishing themselves.

By late 1337, Edward's export ban had had an effect, and on 7 October, he felt strong enough to declare himself king of France. He and Philippa sailed on 16 July 1338 to meet with their allies and discuss the proposed invasion. They spent Christmas at Antwerp, where Philippa had given birth to her second surviving son, Lionel, in November. Edward's preparations continued throughout the next year, and in early 1340, he returned to England to raise further funds, leaving Philippa, her daughter Isabella and son Lionel as surety for his good faith to his allies in Ghent. This must have been a lonely few months for Philippa, and it is notable as one of the few occasions when the couple were apart during their marriage. She bore a third surviving son during her stay in Ghent, John of Gaunt. By June 1340, Edward had the money he needed and rejoined Philippa. Given the conflict of interest that Edward's war with her uncle placed her in, she may also have been secretly relieved when her mother, the sister of the French king, negotiated a truce between England and France, allowing Philippa and Edward to return home to England.

The next few years may have been the happiest of Philippa's life. She was extravagant and loved finery and luxuries. For example, in 1335, she ordered a bed of green velvet embroidered with gold, and a velvet robe costing £700, a vast sum. In 1344, Edward founded the Order of the Garter, which entailed an annual celebration on St George's Day at Windsor. According to Froissart, Philippa played a prominent role in the first celebration, appearing richly dressed and attended by 300 ladies.

Whilst Philippa was happiest in England, the peace with France did not last long, and in 1346, Edward left England to invade France, taking his eldest son with him. Philippa remained in England as co-regent with her young son Lionel. Philippa's time as regent was not without drama, as King David of Scotland invaded the country and burned the suburbs of York. According to Froissart, Philippa responded quickly:

[She] got together all the forces she was able, and marching to Newcastle, gave the Scots battle at a place called Neville's Cross, where she took King David prisoner. The capture of the king gave the queen of England a decided superiority over her enemies; they retired and when she had sufficiently provided for the defence of the cities of York and Durham, as well as for the borders generally, she herself set out for London; and shortly after, having confined her royal prisoner in the Tower, joined the king, her husband, at Calais.

Although Philippa did not personally lead her army, she was present in the area throughout the campaign and issued personal instructions to her commanders. Her great victory confirmed Edward's trust in making her regent, although she missed her husband too much to continue with the role and travelled to join him at Calais.

Edward had begun a siege of Calais soon after winning a great victory at the Battle of Crecy in September 1346. According to Froissart, the siege took longer than Edward had planned, and he grew increasingly impatient. Finally, the six principal citizens of Calais came out to meet him wearing ropes around their necks to symbolise their submission and carrying the keys to the castle and the town. Edward was in no mood to be merciful:

[He] loked felly on theym, for greatly he hated the people of Calys, for the gret damages and displeasures they had done hym on the see before. Than he commaunded their heedes to be stryken of. Than every man requyred the kyng for mercy, but he wolde here no man in that behalfe. Than sir Gaultier of Manny sayd, A noble kyng, for Goddessake, refrayne your courage; ye have the name of soverayne nobles. Therefore nowe do nat a thing that shulde blemysshe your renome, nor to gyve cause to some to speke of you villainy; every man woll say it is a great cruelty to put to deth suche honest persons, who by their owne wylles putte themselfe into your grace to save their company. Than the kyng wryed away fro hym, and commanded to sende for the hangman, and sayd, They of Calys had caused many of my men to be slayne, wherefore these shall dye in likewyse. Than the quene beynge great with chylde, kneled downe and sore wepyng, sayd, A gentyll sir, syth I passed the see in great parell, I have desired nothing of you; therefore nowe I humbly require you, in the honour of the Son of the Virgyn Mary and for the love of me that ye woll take mercy of these six burgesses. The kyng behelde the quene and stode styll in a study of space, and than sayd, A dame, I wold ye had ben as nowe in some

49. Queen Philippa (left) and her headstrong eldest daughter, Princess Isabella. Drawings of scenes depicted in tapestries made during the reign of Edward III and which hung in St Stephen's Chapel, Westminster, until they were destroyed when the old Palace of Westminster burned down.

other place, ye make suche request to me that I can nat deny you; wherefore I gyve them to you, to do your pleasure with theym. Than the quene caused them to be brought into her chamber, and made the halters to be taken fro their neckes, and caused them to be newe clothed, and gave them their dyner at their leser; and than she gave ech of them six nobles and made them to be brough out of thoost in savegard and set at their lyberte.

Only Philippa had the influence over Edward to save the six men, and he trusted and relied on her judgement. Soon after the fall of Calais, Philippa bore a daughter, Margaret, before returning home to England with Edward and the infant.

The advent of the Black Death in the late 1340s led to a truce between England and France, as neither country had the men to field an army. The plague touched Philippa and Edward personally, as their daughter Joan, who was on her way to marry the King of Castile, caught the plague at Bordeaux and died within a few hours. For a fond mother like Philippa, this was devastating. She may, however, have found some consolation in her remaining children, and she continued to bear children for several years after Joan's death. Philippa's youngest child, Thomas, was born at Woodstock in 1355, when she was in her mid-forties.

Philippa's interests mainly focused on her family and her enjoyment of fine clothes and entertainments. She was also a patron of learning and is remembered as the foundress of Queen's College, Oxford. She provided the majority of the funds for her college and, in 1342, obtained a confirmation of the foundation from the Pope. She continued to show an interest in her foundation, granting an annual sum for the sustenance and aid of the provost and scholars of the college in July 1347. Philippa was the first queen to found or patronise a college, although most later medieval queens followed her example. She was also the patron of the chronicler Jean Froissart, and he personally handed her a copy of his chronicle when it was completed.

The sources are largely silent on Philippa's whereabouts during the last years of her life, and it is likely that she lived quietly, accompanying Edward on his travels and devoting herself to her family. In the summer of 1369, she fell ill at Windsor, as documented by Froissart:

> Whanne she knewe and perceyved that there was with her no remedy but dethe, she desyred to speke with the kynge her husbande, and whan he was before her, she put out of her bedde her right hande, and toke the kynge by his right hande, who was right sorrowfull at his hert; than she said, Sir, we have in peace, joye, and great prosperyte, used all oure tyme toguyder: Sir, nowe I pray you at our departing, that ye wyll graunt me thre desires. The kynge, ryght sorowfully wepyng, sayd, Madame, desire what ye wyll, I graunt it.

Philippa first asked Edward to pay her debts. She then requested that he honour any promises that she had made to the Church. Finally, and touchingly, she said, 'Thirdely, sir, I requyre you that it may please you to take none other sepulture, whan soever it shall please God to call you out of this transytorie lyfe, but beside me in Westmynster.' Edward agreed to Philippa's requests, and she made the sign of the cross before commending her youngest son, Thomas, who sat weeping at her side, to her husband. Philippa of Hainault then 'yelded up the spiryte, the whiche I believe surely the holy angels received with great joy up in heven, for in all her lyfe she dyd neyther in thought nor dede thing, wherby to lese her soule, as ferr as any creature coulde knowe'.

Edward was devastated by Philippa's death and the whole country grieved for a woman who had been queen for thirty-nine years and who had never been touched by scandal or accusation of wrongdoing. Philippa was a quiet, happy woman who was devoted to her husband and children, and Edward relied on her. With her third request, that Edward should share her tomb, Philippa appears to have feared that Edward might remarry and forget her. She was aware that the King had been discreetly unfaithful to her throughout their marriage and that he was involved in an affair with one of her maids, Alice Perrers. Following Philippa's death, Perrers came to dominate the King, helping to decide policy and controlling access to him. In 1376, the Black Prince died, leaving his young son as heir to England. The following year, Edward III also died, and his body was stripped of its jewels by Alice Perrers before he was even cold. Philippa of Hainault's death left a void in England, and the office of queen was left vacant for nearly twenty years until the arrival of Anne of Bohemia, the first wife of Richard II.

ANNE OF BOHEMIA (1366–94) had great influence over her devoted husband, Richard II, and she was also an important figure in the early religious reform movement. Whilst most of the Plantagenet kings drew their wives from France, Anne of Bohemia's origins were exotic and she was born in Prague in May 1366, the eldest daughter of the Holy Roman Emperor, Charles IV, and his fourth wife, Elizabeth of Pomerania. Anne was very well educated and could speak several languages. Whilst she was still young, her father died and was succeeded by his son, Wenzel. It was Wenzel who negotiated Anne's marriage to Richard II.

Richard II would probably have looked for a bride in France if it had not been for the Great Schism in the Church. In 1376, Urban VI was elected as pope by a conclave in Rome. This appointment was controversial, and shortly afterwards, a further group of cardinals elected a second man as pope. France, Spain, Naples and Savoy supported the second pope, Clement, whilst England and the Holy Roman Empire supported Urban. On the death of Edward III in 1377, his ten-year-old grandson succeeded to the throne as Richard II, and almost immediately, the King's guardians began to search for a suitable bride for him. There appears to have been something of a shortage of eligible ladies, as Froissart comments:

> Ther was great counsaile in Englande amonge the kynges uncles and the prelates and barons of the realme, for to mary ther yonge kyng Richarde of England. And thenglysshmen wolde gladly have had hym to ben maryed in Heynalt, for love of the good lady queen Philyp, wife to kyng Edwarde the Thirde, who was so good and so gracyous a lady, for all the realme large and honourable, who was come out of Heynaulte; but as than the duke Aubert had no daughters to mary. The duke of Lancastre wolde have hadde the king his nephew to have hadde his eldest doughter, my lady Blanche of Lancastre, to his wife: but the realme wolde in no wyse consent therto, for two reasons: the first, bycause the lady was his cosyn germayne, the whiche was to nere of blode to mary toguyder; the other cause was, they wolde the kynge shulde marry without the realme, to have therby more alyaunce.

The council settled on a daughter of the Duke of Milan, and later that year, envoys were sent to Italy to negotiate the match. Pope Urban, anxious to bind his allies more closely together, summoned the English envoys to Rome where he proposed a marriage between Richard and Anne. English interest was pricked and one of the King's advisors, Sir Simon Burley, was sent to negotiate with Anne's brother. Wenzel was eager for the marriage, and Anne's mother, who commissioned a report to discover whether England was a suitable home for her daughter, also gave her consent.

By late 1381, negotiations were complete and Anne was ready to set out for England. Although the marriage had been favourably received in both England and the Holy Roman Empire, it was not treated so positively amongst the supporters of Pope Clement. Anne set out for England accompanied by a great train of ladies and gentlemen, travelling overland to Brussels, which was ruled by her uncle, the Duke of Brabant. According to Froissart, Anne was forced to spend a month in Brussels waiting to continue her journey to England:

> It was shewed her that ther was on the see a xii. Vessels of Normayns bytwene Caleys and Hollande, and they robbed and pylled on the see, they cared nat who. And so they kepte the boundes of the see about Flaunders and Zelande, abyding the coming of this yonge lady. For the French kyng wolde gladly have broken that maryage, for he greatlye douted the alyaunce bytwene Englande and Almayne.

Whilst it was 'nat honourable to take ladyes in warre', the French were determined to capture Anne. Anne's uncle, the Duke of Brabant, took the initiative himself, sending messengers to the King of France and insisting that a safe-conduct be granted. Anxious to remain on friendly terms with the duke, the French king relented, and Anne continued her journey, travelling overland through Flanders and on to Calais, where she was welcomed by a deputation of English noblemen. Anne spent only a short time in the English-held town before sailing to Dover.

Even Anne's sea crossing did not go smoothly, and according to the sixteenth-century historian John Hayward, 'she had no sooner set foote within this land but such a tempest did forthwith arise as had not bene seene many yeares before, whereby divers ships within the haven were quashed to peeces, but especially, and first of all, the ship wherin the quene was carried'. Anne was met at Dover by the King's uncle, John of Gaunt, and taken to Leeds Castle to celebrate Christmas. She then journeyed to Westminster, where she met her future husband for the first time. The couple were very close in age, with Richard only a year younger than Anne, and they rapidly became close, suggesting that their first impressions of each other were favourable.

Anne and Richard were married in the chapel at Westminster Palace on 14 January 1382. The wedding was a small, intimate occasion with the major ceremony being reserved for Anne's coronation. On 18 January, Anne rode on horseback to Westminster. Several days of festivities followed and she was crowned on 22 January. Large crowds turned out to see her, although, according to the Westminster chronicler, she was not received wholly favourably and 'to those with an eye for the facts it seemed that she represented a purchase rather than a gift, since the English king laid out no small sum to secure this tiny scrap of humanity'. Richard himself was never displeased with the bargain he had made for Anne, in spite of the fact that her brother offered no dowry. Soon after their marriage, the couple went on progresses together to the West Country and East Anglia. They fell in love and were inseparable throughout their marriage.

Anne travelled almost constantly with Richard but had little interest in politics. Instead, she became a leader of fashion and is attributed with having introduced both the side-saddle and the high-peaked horn headdress into England. She and Richard loved luxury and enjoyed attending the theatre and pageants. The couple fitted a bath with taps for hot and cold water at their favourite palace of Sheen, and at Eltham, another palace of which they were fond, Richard had a garden laid out and a bathhouse built. In 1390, he held a grand tournament and feasts in London, and Anne and her ladies attended to select the winners and award the prizes. Both Richard and Anne were determined to enjoy themselves, and the couple had many similar interests.

Anne also had a more serious side, and she was devoted to learning. She took a keen interest in Queen's College, Oxford, and wrote a letter on the subject of education. Anne was very well educated and brought copies of the New Testament in Latin, Czech and German with her to England. Soon after she arrived in England, she ordered an English translation of the Gospels: something that was both an attempt to learn English and which demonstrates her interest in religious reform. The Archbishop of Canterbury spoke of her Biblical study in her funeral oration and William Wycliffe, the first person to translate the Bible into English, mentioned Anne's gospels in his writings. Anne's interest in the Bible helped to publicise Wycliffe's translation, and the English Bible was a major focus of the religious reform movement of the sixteenth century. Anne brought a number of Bohemian book illustrators with her to England, and English manuscripts from the period show their distinctive style.

Anne and Richard went on another progress together in 1383, making a pilgrimage to the shrine at Walsingham during their journey.

This pilgrimage may have been intended to seek divine intervention for their childlessness. The couple spent time at Ely during their progress, and there, according to the *Westminster Chronicle,* a royal favourite, Sir James Berners, was struck by lightning and blinded. Anne and Richard witnessed him being healed at the tomb of St Etheldreda in the town, and this merely served to reinforce their own deeply pious beliefs. The progress continued north to Nottingham and York before returning to London again.

In spite of his happy domestic life with Anne, Richard's reign was troubled. Anne had brought a large train with her from Bohemia, and Richard made himself unpopular by arranging marriages between Anne's countrywomen and noblemen in England. The biggest scandal of the reign centred on one of Anne's Bohemian ladies. Richard II's most prominent favourite was Robert de Vere, Duke of Ireland. According to John Hayward, 'Robert Duke of Ireland forsooke the companie of his lawfull wife, whose mother, Lady Isabel, was daughter of King Edward the third, and in steede of her he tooke unto him a base Bohemian, a taverner's daughter. The king little regarded this indignitie done unto his cosin'. Richard and Anne supported de Vere, and Anne went so far as to write to the Pope on his behalf, seeking his divorce. This brought the couple into direct conflict with Richard's uncles, who were angry at the treatment meted out to their discarded niece.

Richard's uncles were a thorn in his side. In 1385, his most senior uncle, the domineering John of Gaunt, left England in order to press his claims to the throne of Castile. Richard was, initially, glad to see the back of him, but he came to regret his absence. In 1386, a hostile parliament assembled and forced Richard to dismiss his chancellor. At the parliament, it became clear that Richard's youngest uncle, Thomas, Duke of Gloucester, was in open opposition to his nephew. By 1387, Gloucester controlled London, and he and the Earls of Warwick and Arundel, who were collectively known as the Lords Appellant, accused Richard's friends of treason at Westminster in November 1387. They were joined in their rebellion by the Earl of Derby (the future Henry IV) and the Earl of Nottingham, who defeated the King's army, led by de Vere, in December.

It is probable that Gloucester had designs on the throne, and this period was one of intense worry for Richard and Anne. The couple were present in February 1388 when the 'Merciless Parliament' was assembled by the Lords Appellant and Richard was forced to dismiss his remaining supporters. Sir Simon Burley was arrested and Anne, who was fond of the man who had negotiated her marriage, threw herself on her knees before Gloucester to beg for his life. This did not have the desired effect, and Gloucester merely told her curtly to pray for her husband and herself. Burley was executed a few months later. The Appellants remained in power throughout 1388, although their popularity began to wane. Finally, on 3 May 1389, Richard confronted them at a council meeting and wrested power back from his opponents.

Anne's intercession on behalf of Sir Simon Burley was not her only attempt to obtain mercy for accused and convicted people in England, and like her predecessor as queen, Philippa of Hainault, she was famed for her good works as a mediator. Intercession was always an important part of medieval queenship, and Anne fulfilled the role to perfection, becoming known as 'Good Queen Anne'. At her request, a general pardon was granted at her coronation, and she interceded successfully for a convicted felon in 1384 by throwing herself at Richard's feet.

Anne's most famous intercession was on behalf of the city of London. In July 1392, Richard called representatives of London to him at Windsor in order to extract a loan from them. When they refused, he swore revenge on the city, to the Londoners' terror. According to the *Westminster Chronicle*, this revenge never occurred:

At length through the intercession, on behalf of the Londoners, of friends, conspicuous among them the queen (who more than once, indeed on many occasions, both at Windsor and at Nottingham, prostrated herself at the king's feet in earnest and tireless entreaty for the city, and the welfare of its citizens that he would cease to direct his anger against them and would not let so famous a city and its teeming masses perish without due consideration simply because of the burning passion of its enemies), the king's mild and kindly nature was moved by pity, and persuaded by the queen and by others among his nobles and prominent men he forgave the Londoners all their offences against him on condition that within the next ten years they paid him or his unquestionable attorneys

£40,000 in real terms of jewels or species and that on the day appointed for his progress, which was 21 August they should come out to meet him and receive him at Wandsworth with appropriate pomp.

On the day of their entry into London, the couple set out from Sheen and were met by thousands of riders and men on foot. The Londoners presented Richard with a sword, the keys of the city and a horse. They gave Anne a horse with a golden saddle. The streets of London were decorated with banners and crowded with people and a number of pageants were staged, including one where a choir of boys, dressed as angels, placed crowns on Anne and Richard's heads. The couple then processed to Westminster Abbey, where they dismounted and ceremonially performed their devotions. At Christmas 1393 the couple were again entertained by the Londoners, who presented Anne with 'a large and remarkable bird with an enormously wide gullet'. This was possibly a pelican and Anne's reaction to the gift unfortunately does not survive. Thanks to Richard's favourable reaction to the show put on for him by the city, Anne was able to persuade him to remit some of the £40,000 owed to him by the Londoners.

Anne did not long survive Richard's reconciliation with his capital city. Whilst staying at her favourite palace of Sheen, she fell ill suddenly with the plague and died on 7 June 1394 at the age of just twenty-eight. Richard was grief-stricken and he ordered that Sheen, the palace where they had been happiest, be demolished so that he would never have to visit it without her. Richard gave Anne a grand funeral in Westminster Abbey and commissioned a fine double tomb for Anne and himself which showed the couple's effigies, touchingly, holding hands. Anne of Bohemia and Richard II were devoted to each other and Anne brought out the best in the King. After her death, Richard's hold on his throne rapidly spiralled out of his control and his second queen, Isabella of Valois, never exercised any authority over the increasingly autocratic and unpredictable king.

The marriage of ISABELLA OF VALOIS (1389–1410) and Richard II was one of the strangest royal marriages and caused comment by contemporaries. In June 1393, a peace treaty with France was drawn up, but Richard's parliament refused to ratify it. Richard II, who was very far removed from his martial father and grandfather, remained anxious to make a lasting peace with France, and his second marriage was a substitute for this aborted treaty. In spite of his grief on the death of Anne of Bohemia, Richard needed a new wife so that he could father an heir. Within months of Anne's death, he sent envoys to ask for the hand of Yolande of Aragon in marriage. He was persuaded to break off negotiations when Charles VI of France offered his own daughter, Isabella, as a bride.

Isabella of Valois, the eldest child of Charles VI of France and his wife, Isabella of Bavaria, was born in 1389. Richard was attracted to marriage to Isabella primarily due to the promise of peace that it offered. It is also possible that the bride's extreme youth appealed to him, as it would give him time for his grief for Anne of Bohemia to mellow. Certainly, when challenged on the wisdom of marrying a bride so far from being old enough for childbearing, Richard contended that she would become older with every day that passed. This was a clever response but one that satisfied no one, and the marriage was deeply unpopular in England. Richard was the only surviving child of the Black Prince and had no direct or obvious successor, meaning that there was a great urgency for him to father an heir. The marriage was not universally unpopular and the scholar Philippe de Mézières wrote an open letter to Richard setting out the benefits of the marriage and pointing out that Richard had no guarantee of issue with an adult queen. He highlighted the benefits of being able to train Isabella as an English queen from an early age, suggesting that a camel had to be trained from infancy to obey man. He concluded that 'would it not be better that the lady he chooses as helpmeet and wife, from her childhood, before reaching the age of discretion and before acquiring harmful habits of mind, should be well instructed under the prudent and wise guidance of the royal majesty'. It is unlikely that this letter dispelled many doubts about the marriage, but Richard himself remained committed to the match.

Negotiations for the marriage proceeded slowly, but Richard and Charles eventually agreed a twenty-eight-year truce in March 1396. According to Froissart, at the same time, the English ambassadors requested that they be allowed to see Isabella, in order to report on her appearance and conduct to their master. This was granted, although the French, concerned by Isabella's extreme youth, pointed out that they muste be content howe so ever they founde her, for they sayde she was but a yonge chylde of eyght yere of age, wherefore they sayd, there coulde nat be in her no great wysdome nor prudence; howbeit, she was indoctryned well ynough, and that the lords founde well whan they sawe her. The erle Marshall, beynge on his knees, sayde to her: Fayre lady, by the grace of God ye shall be our lady and quene of Englande. Than aunswered the yonge lady well advisedly, without counsayle of any other persone: Syr, quod she, and it please God and my lorde my father that I shall be quene of Englande, I shall be glad therof, for it is shewed me that I shall be than a great lady.

The ambassadors left convinced that Isabella 'was lykely to be a lady of hygh honoure and great goodnesse'.

Richard sailed to Calais in 1396 for a meeting with the French king. The two kings had much in common, and the visit was a cordial one. Over dinner one night in a rich tent, Charles commented to Richard that he wished Isabella was older, so that she would love Richard more. To this, Richard replied that he was pleased with her as she was. Froissart recorded the couple's first meeting: immediately after dinner, Isabella was led in accompanied by a great number of ladies and was ceremonially handed over to her new husband, receiving English attendants, led by the Duchesses of Lancaster and Gloucester, in place of her French ladies. She was seated in a rich litter and, together with Richard and the English nobility, travelled back towards Calais. For Isabella, at the age of only seven, this must have been a bewildering experience, but her first meeting with her husband went well. The couple were married in Calais and then sailed for England. The crossing was marred by storms and many of Richard's ships were lost. According to the sixteenth-century historian John Hayward, many people in England saw the stormy arrival of Richard's second queen as a bad omen. Other bad omens were also seen at the time, including a plank of wood that bled and flies swarming thickly in one of Richard's palaces. In a superstitious age, this did not augur well for either Richard's marriage or his reign.

Richard gave Isabella a grand entry into London. This must have been a terrifying experience for her, as the people of the town, eager to catch a glimpse of their young queen, crowded thickly around her. Isabella was unscathed, but at least nine people were crushed to death on London Bridge, a tragedy that marred the occasion. Isabella's coronation at Westminster Abbey went ahead as arranged. At only seven years old, it was never intended that she would be ready for either marriage or queenship, and she was sent with her own household to Windsor in order to grow up. Isabella was allowed to keep some of her remaining French attendants and her countrywoman, Lady de Coucy, was appointed as her governess.

Due to Isabella's youth, she played no role in the politics of Richard II's troubled reign. Richard was fond of his young bride and visited her regularly. Isabella was glad of this attention, and she became devoted to him. It is likely that she was not aware of the growing resentment towards him in England. Richard had been slowly working towards revenge against the five Lords Appellant since he had wrested control back from them. Soon after his marriage, he heard of a plot by his uncle, the Duke of Gloucester, and the Earl of Arundel to imprison him and Isabella and rule England as regents. Richard, who was with Isabella when he heard of the plot, left her at Eltham and made a pretence of going hunting. He then rode to Havering where Gloucester was staying and asked him to come with him to London. Gloucester was surprised but obeyed and rode to London with the King. As they entered the city, the duke was accosted by a large group of armed men. Richard rode away from the trap, leaving Gloucester to be arrested and taken to Calais, where he was murdered. Richard saw this as just revenge against his troublesome uncle, but there were murmurings amongst the other noblemen in England. Richard failed to heed this and, soon after Gloucester's arrest, had the Earl of Arundel executed. A further Appellant, the Earl of Warwick, was also arrested, although his death sentence was commuted to life imprisonment following a plea for mercy from Isabella.

The remaining two Appellants, Henry, Earl of Derby, and the Earl of Nottingham, gave Richard the opportunity he needed to complete his revenge when they quarrelled in 1398. Both accused the other of treason, and it was agreed that the dispute should be settled by combat. On 16 September 1398, as the two men prepared to do battle, Richard dramatically stopped the proceedings and exiled Nottingham for life and Derby for six years. The lenience of Derby's sentence was due to the powerful position of his father, John of Gaunt, in Richard's government. By September, John of Gaunt was already ailing, and in February 1399, he died. Richard immediately seized John of Gaunt's extensive lands and declared that Derby, who was still in exile on the Continent, could never return to England. Richard felt that that was the end of the matter and made plans for an expedition to Ireland.

Before he left for Ireland, Richard held a grand tournament and feast in London. The tournament was intended to highlight the splendour of Richard's reign, and Isabella was present. In spite of the expense laid out in the tournament, it was poorly attended, and according to Froissart, this was due to Richard's treatment of the Earl of Derby. Isabella played the part of queen well, but soon after the tournament, she returned to Windsor, where Richard took his leave of her. Neither can have realised that this would be the last time that they would meet.

Soon after Richard left for Ireland, Derby sailed from France in order to claim his inheritance as Duke of Lancaster. He received a rapturous reception in England and decided to make an attempt on his cousin's crown. Richard had left his remaining uncle, the Duke of York, as regent of England in his absence, and as soon as he heard of Derby's plans, York had Isabella conveyed to the safety of Wallingford Castle. Richard made an attempt to regain his throne and sailed home from Ireland. He was deeply unpopular however and, on 20 August 1399, was captured attempting to seek refuge in Wales and taken to the Tower of London on the orders of the triumphant Earl of Derby. He was soon compelled to abdicate, and Derby took the throne as Henry IV.

The deposition of her husband left Isabella in a difficult position, and she was moved by Henry from Wallingford to Havering-at-Bower, where she could be kept under close watch. According to Froissart, her state was 'tourned and broken', and she was stripped of the French and English ladies of her household with whom she was familiar and furnished with an entirely new household loyal to Henry. This must have been an unsettling time for Isabella, especially as her new servants were ordered to provide no information about Richard's whereabouts or mention his name. The French ambassadors received a similar prohibition when they were permitted to visit Isabella shortly after Richard's capture. Froissart records that the ambassadors travelled to see the young queen in her household:

[She] received them sweetly, and demaunded of them howe the Frenche kinge her father dyd and the quene her mother. They saide, Well, and so communed with her a great season. They kepte well their promesse, for they spake no worde of kynge Rycharde. Than they tooke leave of the quene and retourned to London: than shortely after they wente to Eltham to the kynge, and there dyned and the kyng gave them fayre presents and jowelles, and right amiably they toke their leave of the kynge, who sayd to them: Syrs, ye may say whan ye come into Fraunce, that the quene of Englande shall have no hurte nor trouble, but shall always kepe her estate as to her belongeth, and shall enjoy all her right, for as yet she shall nat knowe the mutacyons of the worlde.

Henry's words satisfied the French ambassadors and her family as to her treatment, but for Isabella, the lack of news of Richard was alarming, and she determined to take action herself.

Whilst Isabella was staying at Sunning near Reading, a group of Richard's supporters obtained a man to impersonate the deposed King and spread rumours that he had escaped and was raising an army. These supporters came personally to Isabella and informed her that Richard already had 100,000 men and that he had good hopes of victory. According to John Hayward, Isabella was jubilant at this news:

Shee defaced King Henries armes and plucked away his cognisance from those his servants that attended uppon her, and having in some sorte satisfied her womanish anger with this harmelesse spight, she and the lords departed together, first to Wallingforde, and from thence to Abington, stirring the people by the waye to take armour and to rise in ayde of King Richard, who was (saide they), and is, and should be their prince.

By the time that Isabella and the lords who accompanied her had reached Chichester in Sussex, they had amassed a large army. When they attempted to enter the city, they were attacked by the townspeople and heavily defeated. The false Richard, who attempted to flee to Scotland following news of the defeat, was captured and executed, and Isabella found herself once again a prisoner of

Henry IV. Isabella's rebellion had far greater consequences, and soon afterwards, Richard was murdered at Pontefract Castle. Isabella was not, at first, aware that she had become a widow, and she continued to look towards Richard's restoration to the throne.

Isabella remained a prisoner during the early years of Henry's reign as the new King had no intention of allowing such a valuable bargaining counter to leave his kingdom. When her father heard of Richard's death, he demanded that Isabella be returned to France. Froissart claimed,

> The Englysshemen wolde in no wyse delyver her, but sayd she shulde lyve styll in Englande upon her dowrie; and that though she had lost her husbande, they wolde provide for her another, that shulde be fayre, yong, and gentyll, with whom she shuld be better pleased than with Richard of Burdeaux, for he was olde, and this shuld be the prince of Wales, eldest sone to kyng Henry.

When word reached Isabella that a new match had been proposed for her, she finally realised that her husband was dead. According to John Hayward, she plunged her household into mourning and 'estranged her selfe from all occasions of pleasure or comforte, and was accompanied with a heavy traine composed to sorrow both in behaviour and attire'. Isabella spent her time loudly lamenting her husband's fate and cursing Henry IV. She surprisingly requested an audience with Henry IV himself, which was granted, and she used this opportunity to attack him openly to his face. Upon being admitted to the King's presence, Isabella wept before declaring,

> 'In seeking to obtaine our purpose of others, it is an ordinarie endeavour to move ether by prayers pittie, or by promises hope, or by threats feare. But as with men cruell and ambitious and in theire owne opinion mightie, these meanes are of litle force, soe with them whose miserie is beneath all releife they cannot bee of any use. Being now therefore in that distresse that there remaineth to mee nether thing to desire nor thought to obtaine, I am come only to putt you in remembrance, what benefittes with what ingratitude you have required, that in my heaviest misshape, I may conceive this vaine satisfaction to have reproved you openly to your face.'

As the daughter of the King of France, Isabella knew that she had little to fear, and she gave vent to her anger and grief. She criticised Henry's ingratitude to Richard, accusing him of greed in seeking further honours. She ended saying,

'And albeit ambition (an unquiet humour) hath hitherto blinded your judgement, yet shame will shortlie cause you to discerne that you possesse onlie an appearance of honor sett upon you by a few flatterers which will easily bee escared [defaced] by those infamies which our just complaintes shall blazen through the world. Your owne conscience alsoe shall torment you and compel you to condemne your selfe to the severest punishments which treason and parricide cann deserve. And albeit it may seeme by successe that god in his secrett judgement hath furthered your proceedings, yet assure your selfe hee hath not favored them. But your dominion begunne with crueltie shall in you, or in your progenie, end with contempt. As for my dishonour, I will not offend the law of modestie in being overcarried with remembrance therof, being fullie purposed to make light accounte of any disgrace of fortune afterward, yet I make litle doubte but it shall alsoe appeare to be instantly recompenced with revenge.'

Isabella's speech appears prophetic, and the authenticity of her words is doubtful. It is clear that she revered Richard's memory and cursed Henry IV, and Hayward's account may record something of her own thoughts.

Isabella's hostility and her family's demands for her return finally convinced Henry IV that she would never marry his son. When she was still only twelve years old, Isabella was returned to France with all the jewels and plate that she had brought with her to England. For Isabella, it must have been a sombre homecoming to the country that she had left when barely out of her infancy. She quickly settled back into her life as a princess of France and, in 1407, married Charles, heir to the Duke of Orléans. Like her first, Isabella's second marriage was destined to be brief, and on 1 September 1410, she bore a daughter, before dying a few hours later. It was a sorry end for a queen who had shown so much promise.

Isabella of Valois was one of the most unlucky of any medieval queen, and her brief life, in which she was used as a pawn by male relatives and other figures, was a far cry from the powerful lives led by earlier Plantagenet queens, such as Eleanor of Aquitaine. With the usurpation of the crown in 1399 by Henry IV, the direct line of descent from the Empress Matilda came to an end. Henry IV was a direct male-line descendant of the Empress, but by seizing the crown, he founded his own Lancastrian dynasty, which saw four women married to the three Lancastrian kings.

5

The Lancastrian Queens

With his usurpation of the throne in 1399, Henry IV diverted the line of succession to the descendants of John of Gaunt, the third surviving son of Edward III, in preference to Richard II, the sole heir of Edward III's eldest son, and to the descendants of his second surviving son. The Lancastrian dynasty saw four women married to its kings, and whilst the first, Mary de Bohun, was never a queen, the remaining three women all helped to develop the role of queen in response to the very particular circumstances they faced. Henry IV's reign was dogged by rebellion as he sought to establish the legitimacy of his dynasty. His son, Henry V, was undisputed king as long as he lived, but the long reign of his son and successor, Henry VI, marked the end of the dynasty. The four Lancastrian kings' wives led very different lives, but each sought to maintain and extend the prestige of the Lancastrian dynasty in England.

MARY DE BOHUN (*c.* 1368–94), the first wife of Henry IV, was never queen and would have had no idea that her husband, and later her son and grandson, would wear the crown of England. Mary was the daughter of Humphrey de Bohun, Earl of Hereford, and his wife, Joan Fitzalan. Her mother was the daughter of the Earl of Arundel by his wife Eleanor of Lancaster. Mary and her elder sister Eleanor were their parents' only surviving children, and on their father's death in January 1373, they inherited his extensive estates. In 1376, Mary's elder sister married Thomas of Woodstock, Duke of Gloucester, the youngest son of Edward III and Philippa of Hainault.

Mary lived with her mother both before and in the early years of her marriage. There is evidence that she was educated and her family were patrons of a number of books produced during the fourteenth century. Both Mary and her sister continued this family tradition. Mary's family commissioned two psalters as wedding presents for her and Henry on their marriage, and it is likely that it was known that these gifts would be appreciated by the couple. Henry IV also loved learning. Before he became king, he attended lectures at the University of Paris, and once he became king, he commissioned a study to be built for him at Eltham Palace, with cupboards specifically built for his books. Their shared love of learning brought the couple together during their marriage.

As one of the greatest heiresses in England, Mary de Bohun was much sought after as a bride. According to Froissart, her brother-in-law, the Duke of Gloucester, wishing to keep Mary's inheritance to himself, attempted to force her to become a nun. Mary had no vocation, and in July 1380, whilst Gloucester was out of the country, John of Gaunt, the third surviving son of Edward III, purchased the right to her marriage from the King for 5,000 marks. This presented Gloucester with a *fait accompli*, and on or around 5 February 1381, Mary married John's eldest son, Henry, Earl of Derby, at her family's manor of Rochford Hall in Essex.

Mary was very wealthy, and this was part of the attraction for John of Gaunt in purchasing the rights to her marriage. John himself had taken the English heiress, Blanche of Lancaster, as his first wife, and he wanted to ensure that his son was similarly provided for. It has been suggested that Mary's wealth was not the only reason for the marriage. Whilst Mary's inheritance was extensive, she was not the only unmarried heiress in England. John of Gaunt was a product of the famously happy marriage between Edward III and Philippa of Hainault. His first marriage was also a fond one, and he is famous for marrying his long-term mistress and the mother of several of his illegitimate children, Catherine Swynford. It is possible that John chose Mary because Henry had already shown an interest in her. The couple's mothers were cousins and the pair knew each other in childhood. They shared a number of interests and enjoyed music, with both able to sing and play. Surviving depictions of Mary show that she conformed to the contemporary ideal of beauty, with fair skin, blond hair and delicate features. Henry was also personable enough, and according to his sixteenth-century biographer, John Hayward, 'he was verie courteous and familiar respectively towards all men, whereby hee procured great reputation and regarde'. Froissart considered that Henry, at the time of his marriage, 'though he were but yonge, yet he was of great wysdome, and likely to come to great honour'.

At the time of her marriage, Mary was too young to live with her husband and remained with her mother. On 10 March 1386, Henry officially received Mary's inheritance, and it is likely that the couple had begun to live together shortly before this. The couple travelled around together and spent a considerable amount of time in each other's company, with Mary bearing children frequently. Their eldest child, the future Henry V, was born at Monmouth Castle on 16 September 1386. Young Henry's birth was followed in late summer or autumn 1387 by that of a second son, Thomas, in London. A third son, John, was born on 20 June 1389, and a fourth, Humphrey, in the autumn of 1390. Mary's first daughter, Blanche, was born in the spring of 1392, and her youngest child, Philippa, in the early summer of 1394. Remarkably for the time, all six children survived to adulthood, and Mary de Bohun spent her brief life in a domestic sphere, devoting herself to childbearing.

Mary was anxious for the safety of her husband during the troubled years of the reign of Richard II. Henry left Monmouth shortly after the birth of his eldest son in order to attend a parliament at which he openly declared his opposition to the King. The opposition to Richard was led by Mary's brother-in-law, the Duke of Gloucester, who declared the King's favourites to be traitors. This caused the King to storm out of parliament in an attempt to dissolve it, only for the lords and commons to continue sitting. Richard re-entered parliament on 24 October and, around that time, declared his twelve-year-old cousin, Roger Mortimer, Earl of March, who was a grandson of the second surviving son of Edward III, to be his heir. This disappointed the hopes of John of Gaunt and Mary's own husband, and it was a melancholy and angry Henry who returned to Mary in late November 1386. The couple spent the summer of the following year together at Kenilworth before moving to London in the autumn to await the birth of their second child. Mary spent only a brief time in London, and as the political situation deteriorated, she and her children left the capital for the safety of the countryside.

Mary's constitution was weakened by her frequent childbearing, and in the early spring of 1394, whilst still only in her mid-twenties, she passed away either during or shortly after the birth of her youngest child, Philippa. Henry was not with Mary at the time, but he gave her a grand funeral on 6 July 1394 in the Lady Chapel at the Lancastrian Collegiate Church in Leicester. Mary's funeral was held the day after that of Henry's stepmother, Constanza of Castile, who had died at around the same time, and both events were attended by Henry and his father in an attempt to mark the prestige of the Lancastrian dynasty. Henry mourned Mary sincerely and wore black for an entire year as a mark of respect. Mary de Bohun was not the only love of his life, and he went on to make a second love match to Joan of Navarre.

JOAN OF NAVARRE (1368–1437), the second wife of Henry IV, came from a particularly noble background and was the daughter of Charles the Bad, King of Navarre, and his wife Joan, daughter of King John of France. Her father, as his nickname suggests, lived a turbulent life. He was the eldest son of Jeanne, Queen of Navarre, who had been the only surviving child of King Louis X of France, the eldest son of Philip IV. On her father's death, Jeanne had been passed over in the succession of France in favour of her two uncles and then her father's cousin, but had been allowed to inherit her father's second kingdom of Navarre.

Charles was frequently at war with France, and in 1381, his three children, who were lodged in one of his castles in Normandy, were captured by the regents of France in an attempt to ensure his good behaviour. Joan could have been in a very difficult position on finding herself as a hostage in Paris, particularly since Charles had no intention of being bound by any terms and, instead, tried to poison the regents. Joan and her two elder brothers did not suffer for their father's actions, and the French regents, who were their maternal uncles, treated them honourably. Charles was anxious to secure his children's return, and they were released on the intervention of the King of Castile, a man that Joan had been betrothed to in her childhood.

Joan did not spend long in Navarre because, on her return, her father opened negotiations for her to marry John IV, Duke of Brittany. John was nearly thirty years older than Joan and had been married twice before: first, to Mary of England, the daughter of Edward III, and then to Joan Holland, a half-sister of Richard II. Neither marriage produced children and, following the death of Joan Holland in 1384, John sought an urgent remarriage. In June 1384, Breton envoys arrived in Navarre to fetch Joan, and on 2 September, she and John were married by proxy. Joan sailed for Brittany immediately afterwards and was married in person to John at Saille on 11 September. She rapidly fulfilled her primary role as Duchess of Brittany, and whilst her first child, a daughter born in 1388, died in infancy, on 24 December 1389, she bore her first son. Joan bore her husband three further sons and three daughters, providing for the succession in Brittany.

Joan's time as Duchess of Brittany was dominated by childbearing, but she was also able to build some political role for herself. Shortly before her husband's death, she wrote to his brother-in-law, Richard II, on his behalf, regarding some lands that the English king had withheld:

I desire every day to be certified of your good estate, which our Lord grant that it may ever be as good as your heart desires, and as I should wish it for myself. If it would please you to let me know of it, you would give me great rejoicings in my heart, for every time that I hear good news of you I am most perfectly glad at heart. And if to know tidings from this side would give you pleasure, when this was written my lord, I and our children were together in good health of our persons, thanks to our Lord, who by his grace ever grant you the same. I pray you, my dearest and most redoubted lord, that it would ever please you to have the affairs of my said lord well recommended, as well in reference to the deliverance of his lands as other things, which lands in your hands are the cause why he sends his people so promptly towards you. So may it please you hereupon to provide him with your gracious remedy, in such manner that he may enjoy his said lands peaceably; even as he and I have our perfect surety and trust in you more than in any other. And let me know your good pleasure, and I will accomplish it willingly and with a good heart to my power.

The outcome of Joan's suit is unknown, but the fact that the letter was written shows the trust placed in her by her husband. John IV died on 1 November 1399, leaving Joan as regent of Brittany.

Joan's first marriage was an arranged one, and whilst she was fond of her husband, it is unlikely that she was in love with him. She had already met the man that would become her second husband, and she and Henry IV of England made a love match. The couple were almost exactly the same age, and the King, with his Plantagenet good looks, must have seemed like a welcome contrast to John IV when Joan first met him. No details of the first meeting between the couple exist, but they had probably already met by 1396 when both attended Richard II's marriage to Isabella of Valois at Calais. On that visit, Henry spent almost a month on the Continent, and the couple would have met frequently. Joan and her first husband also visited England in April 1398, and again, she would almost certainly have had an opportunity to renew her acquaintance with Henry. A letter written by Joan to Henry in 1400 suggests that the relationship was more than merely a formal one:

Since I am desirous to hear of your good estate, which our Lord grant that it may ever be as good as your noble heart knows best how to desire, and, indeed, as I would wish it for myself, I pray you, my most dear and honoured lord and cousin, that it would please you very often to let me know the certainty of it, for the very great joy and gladness of my heart; for every time that I can hear good news of you, it rejoices my heart very greatly. And if of your courtesy you would hear the same from across here, thanks to you, at the writing of these presents, I and my children were together in good health of our persons, thanks to God, who grant you the same, as Johanna of Bavalen, who is going over to you, can tell you more fully, whom it please you to have recommended in the business on which she is going over. And if anything that I can do over here will give you pleasure, I pray you to let me know it, and I will accomplish it with a very good heart, according to my power.

Joan's concern for Henry's welfare and the personable tone in which she wrote makes it clear that the couple were fond of each other, and Joan gave up much to be with Henry.

Henry IV came to the throne following the deposition of his cousin, Richard II. His kingship was not universally recognised, and for the first few years of his reign, he was on the verge of war with France.

As a result of this, the relationship between Joan and Henry was at first conducted with secrecy. Whilst Joan and Henry renewed their acquaintance shortly after her husband's death, it was only on 20 March 1402 that a papal bull permitting the marriage was obtained. On 2 April 1402, the couple were married by proxy at Eltham Palace. Joan was heavily censured when the match was publicised, and whilst she and her two daughters were allowed to sail to England in December 1402, she was forced by the nobles of Brittany to relinquish her regency and the custody of her sons.

Coupled with her grief at the loss of her sons, Joan's crossing must have been an ordeal, as John Hayward recounts:

> As shee crossed the seas for England, her passage was verie dangerous by reason of tempestuous wether, which accident was esteemed ominous in both King Richard's wives. The king received her at Winchester, and there having spent some time in devises of pleasures, upon the viith of Februarie the marriage was solemnized between them, and upon the xxvith of the same moneth shee was with all ceremonies of state, crowned at Westminster.

Henry rushed to meet Joan as soon as she had landed, and they settled into married life together.

Henry was determined to ensure that Joan lived in some state, and on 8 March 1403, he granted her a dower of 10,000 marks. Coupled with her Breton dower, this made Joan an exceptionally wealthy woman. She also built a relationship with her stepchildren, and Henry's youngest sons, Humphrey and John, presented her with a rich pair of tablets as a wedding present. In a letter that Joan wrote to her stepson John in 1415, she referred to him as her 'dearest and best-beloved son', and Henry's children helped to fill some of the gap left by her separation from her own sons.

Joan and Henry's relationship was not without difficulties, as, whilst he was a kind and attentive husband, he cannot have been easy to live with. By around 1408, he had contracted a skin disease that appears to have been similar to leprosy, and he became a virtual recluse, shutting himself away with Joan. It must have been sad for Joan, who had known Henry in the prime of his life, to see him struck down with the disfiguring disease. According to John Hayward,

Henry's troubles were compounded by his guilt at his usurpation of the crown, and his mind was 'perpetuallie perplexed with an endless and restless chardge, ether of cares, or greifes, or of suspicions and feares'. For Joan, it may perhaps have been a relief when he died in 1413.

Joan made no attempt to return to either Navarre or Brittany on Henry's death, as she considered England to be her home. She was often referred to as queen mother during her stepson Henry V's reign, and she continued to play a public role as a member of the English royal family, taking a prominent place in a procession from St Paul's to Westminster in celebration of Henry V's victory at Agincourt against the French. This went against Joan's personal feelings, as her son-in-law, the Duke of Alençon, and her brother, Charles of Navarre, were both killed fighting for the French. Joan's own son, Arthur, was captured and brought as a prisoner to England, although this did at least allow her to renew her acquaintance with him.

Henry V's French wars took a harsh toll on his finances, and he looked with interest at Joan's vast wealth. On 27 September 1419, the English council made an order depriving Joan of all her possessions and revenues, and four days later, she was arrested for witchcraft at her palace of Havering-atte-Bower. Joan had always been on good terms with Henry V, and her arrest must have been a terrible shock to her. The charges stemmed from a confession by her confessor, John Randolf, who claimed that he had tempted Joan to use witchcraft to try to kill the King. Joan had no reason to kill her stepson, and there is no doubt that the accusations were trumped up in order to allow the King to claim her wealth. This can be seen in the lenient treatment she received, and whilst a prisoner, she maintained a luxurious existence. Joan's household accounts survive and, in the first months of her imprisonment, she kept a stable, an indication that she was able to continue to ride. She also employed nineteen grooms and seven pages and lived in some state, purchasing expensive goods including furs, lace, gold chains and a gold girdle. She stocked a large wine cellar at Leeds Castle, where she was imprisoned, and entertained visitors. In spite of this, the stigma of being an imprisoned witch remained, and it cannot have been an easy period of her life.

Henry V did not believe in his stepmother's guilt, and whilst he was happy to keep her in prison and make use of her wealth during his lifetime, in 1422, as he lay dying of dysentery in France, he felt remorse and ordered that she be released and have her goods returned to her. This allowed Joan to resume her life as an independent and wealthy widow. She remained in contact with the English court, and in 1437, her step-grandson, Henry VI, made her a New Year's gift of a bejewelled tablet, suggesting that he was fond of her. She employed the renowned composer John Dunstable during the late 1420s and was in contact with her grandson Giles, who was present in England between 1432 and 1434. Joan became increasingly religious, and in 1427, she went on a pilgrimage to Walsingham. She virtually disappears from the sources following her release from prison, and she died at Havering in July 1437 and was buried with Henry IV at Canterbury. This would have been Joan's wish, as the early years of her marriage with Henry were probably the happiest times of her life.

Whilst Joan of Navarre made a love match with Henry IV, her successor as queen, Catherine of Valois, was married to Henry V for purely political reasons. Catherine brought the kingdom of France as her dowry, but her most lasting legacy is that she brought the Tudor dynasty to prominence and the connection with Catherine helped bring them the crown of England.

CATHERINE OF VALOIS (1401–37) was the youngest of the twelve children of Charles VI of France and Isabella of Bavaria. She was the younger sister of Richard II's second queen, Isabella of Valois, and was born on 27 October 1401 in Paris. Catherine had a troubled childhood, and by the time of her birth, her father was insane for long periods. Her mother was notorious for her lovers, and according to one story, Isabella and her lover, the Duke of Orléans, stole the King's revenues, leaving the infant Catherine and her elder sister Michelle so poor that they nearly starved. The sisters were housed in the same palace as their insane father and only survived thanks to the charity of their servants. When Charles returned to his senses, Isabella and Orléans fled to Milan. They attempted to abduct the royal children, and Catherine and her siblings were only saved by the Duke of Burgundy overtaking them on the road out of France.

Henry V had originally been suggested as a husband for Catherine's eldest sister, Isabella, whilst the widowed queen was held in England. This came to nothing, but in 1413, Henry himself suggested a marriage with Catherine. Initial overtures were unsuccessful, but the subject of the marriage was raised again in 1415 when Henry V demanded Catherine's hand in marriage along with a dowry of 2 million crowns and the return of the entire Angevin empire. These demands were extortionate and not intended to be accepted. Whilst the French attempted to negotiate, Henry would not budge, using the rejection of his demands as an excuse to invade France. He was rapidly successful and, on 25 October 1415, won his greatest victory at Agincourt. During the battle, the French suffered huge losses, and three French dukes, ninety counts, 1,500 knights, and between 4,000 and 5,000 men at arms are believed to have died. Catherine shared her family's alarm at Henry V's invasion, but there were also domestic issues to contend with.

In 1417, Charles VI entered a period of relative sanity. Isabella had begun a new love affair not long before, and this was reported to the King. He reacted angrily and had the lover tortured and killed before imprisoning Isabella at Tours. Isabella did not remain a captive for long, as, later the same year, the Duke of Burgundy rescued her, and she set herself up as regent of France at Troyes. She gained control over the once-more-mad Charles and her last unmarried daughter, Catherine.

Henry V always claimed to be King of France through his descent from Isabella of France, the daughter of Philip IV of France, and he continued his war over the next few years, inflicting huge losses on the French. After the fall of Rouen to the English, it was agreed that he would meet with Isabella and the Duke of Burgundy at Meulan. Catherine, who was the beauty of her family, was brought to the meeting, and according to *Hall's Chronicle*, when he arrived, Henry kissed and embraced both Catherine and her mother.

> The next day after they had assembled againe, & the Frenche part brought with them the lady Katherin, only to thentent that the king of Englnd seyng and beholding so fayre a lady and so minion a damsel, should so be inflamed and rapte in loye, that he to obtayne so beautiful an espouse should the soner agre to a gentle peace & louvyng [loving] composicion.

Henry was indeed eager to marry Catherine, but not, as the French hoped, without first being granted the crown of France.

Henry V arrived at the meeting at Meulan as a conqueror, and Isabella of Bavaria was in no position to bargain with him. It was agreed that Henry would marry Catherine and in return, Charles VI would make him his heir, disinheriting Catherine's brother, the Dauphin. In order to ensure that France remained firmly in English hands, it was also agreed that Henry would be appointed as regent of France for the remainder of Charles's life. On a personal level, the agreement may have been satisfying for both Catherine and Henry, and some reports claim that Henry had fallen in love with Catherine. This may be true, but the match was primarily political and essential to Henry's French ambitions. Shakespeare may well sum up Henry's true feelings for Catherine in his play *Henry V* with the line given to Henry that Catherine was 'our capital demand, comprised within the fore-rank of our articles'. Catherine's own feelings about the match are not recorded, but she does not appear to have been concerned about the disinheritance of her brother. Henry was a dashing figure, and the eighteen-year-old Catherine may have been pleased with the idea of marriage to him. She was, in any event, a dutiful daughter and did as her mother bid her.

In May 1420, Henry arrived in Troyes in order to seal his treaty with Isabella and marry Catherine. The couple were married in St Peter's church in the city, and they soon afterwards made a triumphant entry to Paris accompanied by Catherine's parents. Catherine and Henry kept a grand court at the Louvre, whilst Catherine's parents stayed, ignored, in the Hotel St Pol. The couple then travelled to Rouen, where they celebrated Christmas before travelling to Calais and sailing for Dover. They were greeted by jubilant crowds intent on celebrating Henry's victories. On 24 February 1421, Catherine was crowned at Westminster Abbey. It was at her coronation banquet that she made her only recorded act of queenly intercession, when she asked for the captive James I of Scotland to be released from his imprisonment.

Catherine spent little time with her new husband, as, immediately after her coronation, Henry set out on a progress around England, initially leaving her in London. The reason for this separation is not clear, and Catherine had rejoined him at Leicester by Easter 1421. Henry set off north, whilst Catherine moved on to Lincoln to await his return. The couple then returned to London, where they parted, with Henry returning to his wars in France. Catherine had conceived a child shortly after her arrival in England, and Henry's parting words to her were that she should, under no circumstances, bear their child at Windsor, a castle in which he believed no lucky king of England had been born. With Henry gone, Catherine chose to ignore this advice, and on 6 December 1421, she gave birth to the future Henry VI at the castle. Henry V was destined never to see his son, and Catherine spent some months recovering from the birth before sailing to join him in France in May 1422.

The couple spent a few weeks together in France before Henry set off to besiege the town of Meaux. Whilst in France, Catherine was reunited with her parents, and the three travelled to Senlis to await Henry's return. Whilst she was there, Catherine heard that Henry had contracted dysentery and had been taken by litter to Vincennes. She must have spent an anxious few weeks with her parents before news reached her that he had died on 31 August 1422. Catherine was further shocked by the news that Henry had left her with neither the regency of England nor France, nor custody of her son. Catherine joined Henry's funeral procession at Rouen and made the long sombre journey back to England.

Catherine rejoined her son upon her return to England, and she was still with him in September 1422 when news arrived that her father had died and that her son, Henry VI, had been proclaimed king of France. Catherine devoted the early years of her widowhood to her son's upbringing, despite not being named as his guardian. The *Chronicle of London* gives one example of Catherine's continuing association with her son in November 1423:

The king and the queen his mother removed from Windsor towards the parliament at London, which began at Westminster on the 21st day of October before, and on the aforesaid 13th day of November at night the king and queen were lodged at Staines, and upon the morrow, which was Sunday, the king was borne towards his mother's chair, and he shrieked and cried and sprang and would not be carried further. Wherefore he was borne again into the inn, and there he abode on Sunday all day; and on the Monday he was borne to the chair, and then he was glad and happy in spirits. In the evening he came to Kingston and there rested the night, and on the Tuesday he came to Kennington and on Wednesday he came to

London with a glad countenance and happy spirits, and was borne
in his mother's bosom in a chair through London to Westminster,
and on the morrow was brought into parliament.

This story was intended to show the piety of Henry VI, who, even as
an infant, refused to break the Sabbath. It also demonstrates the close
relationship between Catherine and her son in his early years.

Whilst she enjoyed playing a role in Henry VI's upbringing,
Catherine had been only twenty-one at Henry V's death, and she
was not prepared to shut herself away. Within a few years of Henry
V's death, she became romantically involved with Edmund Beaufort,
a cousin of her late husband. Whilst details of the relationship are
scant, it is possible that the couple became lovers, and there is no
doubt that they planned to marry. Any man that Catherine married
would become the King's stepfather, and Henry's minority council
were anxious that he would also seek to become regent. In 1426,
parliament made a formal request to the regency council that they
cease their refusals to allow Catherine to remarry. It is likely that
Catherine petitioned parliament for their aid herself. Henry VI's
council was determined to prevent Catherine from marrying, and in
the parliament of 1429 to 1430, a statute was passed legislating on the
remarriage of dowager queens. The new law ordered that anyone who
dared marry the Queen without the King's express permission would
have his lands and property confiscated and effectively meant that
Catherine could not remarry until Henry VI obtained his majority.
Further restrictions were placed on Catherine around this time, and
between 1427 and 1430, her household was merged with that of her
son.

The opposition of the regency council and the statute prohibiting
her remarriage made it impossible for Catherine to marry someone as
prominent and influential as Edmund Beaufort. She did not, however,
abandon her desire to remarry. At some point around 1428 or 1429,
Catherine, 'folowyng more her awne appetite, then frendely counsaill
and regardyng more her priuate affeccion, than her open honour,
toke to husband priuily'. The object of Catherine's affection was
Owen Tudor, a Welshman in her household. Despite later attempts
by the Tudor dynasty to present Owen as of noble lineage, he was of
low birth and may have been the keeper of Catherine's household or

of her wardrobe. The origins of their love affair are obscure but one legend claims that Owen fell into Catherine's lap during a dance. Few details of the marriage survive, and it was not common knowledge until after Catherine's death. Catherine bore Owen four children: Edmund, Jasper, Owen, and a daughter who died in infancy.

Catherine apparently found happiness in her second marriage, but this did not last long. According to some accounts, Henry VI's governors discovered the marriage in the late summer of 1436 and sent Catherine, under restraint, to Bermondsey Abbey. Alternatively, Catherine, already in ill health, may have decided to retire to the abbey to die. Whatever the reason for her stay at Bermondsey, she did not long survive and died on 3 January 1437 aged just thirty-five. On Catherine's death, Owen Tudor was arrested and imprisoned in Newgate in accordance with the statute of 1430. He was finally released in July 1439, when he was pardoned by Henry VI and taken into his household. Henry VI was fond of his half-brothers, Edmund and Jasper, and he created them, respectively, Earls of Richmond and Pembroke. He arranged for Edmund to marry the royally descended Margaret Beaufort, a union which produced the future King Henry VII. It was through Catherine that the Tudor family gained its closeness to the throne of England and the status with which to claim it.

Catherine's story does not quite end with her death. She was buried in Westminster Abbey with Henry V, but at some point, her mummified body was disinterred and put on display. On 23 February 1669, the diarist Samuel Pepys visited the abbey and recorded that 'here we did see, by particular favour, the body of Queen Katherine of Valois, and had her upper part of her body in my hands. And I did kiss her mouth, reflecting upon it that I did kiss a Queen, and that this was my birthday, 36 years old, that I did first kiss a Queen'. This was a bizarre postscript to the life of an extraordinary queen. Both during and after her life, Catherine was essentially a cipher through which the crowns of England and France were transmitted. Catherine of Valois was a politically important figure who wielded little power herself. This was in stark contrast to her successor, Margaret of Anjou, who was amongst the most politically influential of all English queens.

MARGARET OF ANJOU (1430–82) has one of the worst reputations of any queen of England. She was the fourth child of Rene of Anjou and his wife, Isabel, Duchess of Lorraine. Margaret had little contact with either of her parents in her early childhood, and on 2 July 1431, her father was captured at the Battle of Bulgneville and spent some years in prison. In November 1435, Rene's elder brother died, and he inherited the county of Anjou, as well as the titles to the crowns of Jerusalem and Naples. He was already titular King of Sicily. In spite of this wealth of titles, Rene only controlled Anjou and Lorraine, which he ruled on behalf of his wife. Margaret's mother was determined to increase the family's prestige, and in 1435, she set out with an army to conquer Naples, leaving her children in the care of their paternal grandmother, Yolande of Aragon. Yolande was an example to Margaret of the power that a woman could wield, and she had already ruled Anjou for several years by the time she took custody of her grandchildren. She had also raised the French king, Charles VII, marrying him to her daughter, Marie. Margaret lived with Yolande until her death in November 1442. By that time, both her parents had returned to Anjou, and Margaret returned to her mother's care.

The war between England and France continued throughout Margaret's childhood, with the English losing much of what they had won under Henry V. In 1444, a meeting was held at Tours in an attempt to agree a peace. According to *Hall's Chronicle*, it was suggested at the meeting that a marriage between Henry VI and a French princess be arranged. Charles VII had no intention of allowing his English nephew to marry any of his daughters, and Margaret, as the niece of the Queen of France, was nominated. Margaret's father was happy with the match, and he was badly in need of funds, 'callyng himself kyng of Sicile, Naples, and Hierusalem, hauyng onely the name and stile of the same, without any pay profite, or fote of possession'. The English agreed to surrender lands in Anjou and Maine to Rene in return for Margaret's hand in marriage. To his embarrassment, Rene was unable to pay for Margaret's journey to England, and 'Kyng Reyner her father, for all his long stile, had to short a purse, to sende his doughter honourably, to the kyng her spouse'. Henry and Margaret were married by proxy at Tours on 23 May 1444, with the Earl of Suffolk playing the role of Henry VI. This was followed by celebrations before Margaret returned home with her mother to prepare for her journey. In March 1445, she set out for England accompanied by an escort of 1,500 people, paid for by Henry VI.

Henry VI had requested a portrait of Margaret as soon as marriage negotiations opened, and he was eager to meet her when she landed in England. According to the report of the Milanese ambassador to England, Henry rushed down to see Margaret unofficially as soon as she arrived:

> When the queen landed in England the king dressed himself as a squire, the Duke of Suffolk doing the same, and took her a letter which he said the King of England had written. While the queen read the letter the king took stock of her, saying that a woman may be seen very well when she reads a letter, and the qyeen never found out it was the king because she was so engrossed in reading the letter, and she never looked at the king in his squire's dress, who remained on his knees all the time. After the king had gone the Duke of Suffolk said: 'Most serene queen, what do you think of the squire who brought the letter?' The queen replied: 'I did not notice him, as I was occupied in reading the letter he brought'. The duke remarked: 'Most serene queen, the person dressed as a squire was the most serene King of England', and the queen was vexed at not having known it, because she had kept him on his knees.

The couple's first meeting was not encouraging, but their official meeting soon afterwards was more successful. Margaret was a beauty, with the Milanese ambassador commenting that she 'is a most handsome woman, though somewhat dark'. Whilst he has a reputation for being somewhat simple, Henry was a kindly man. The historian Polydore Vergil summed up his character:

> King Henry [VI] was a man of mild and plain dealing disposition who preferred peace before wars, quietness before troubles, honesty before utility, and leisure before business; and, to be short, there was not in this world a more pure, more honest and more holy creature. There was in him honest reproachfulness, modesty, innocence, and perfect patience, taking all human chances, miseries, and all afflictions of this life in so good part as though he had justly by some offence deserved the same. He ruled his own affections so

that he might more easily rule his own subjects; he hungered not after riches, nor thirsted for honour and worldly estimation, but was careful only for his soul's health.

Henry was also described as 'tall of stature, slender of body [and] of comely visage', and Margaret must have felt that she had done well in her husband. The couple were married at Tichfield Abbey on 22 April before travelling up to London, where Margaret was crowned.

Margaret was a much more forceful personality than Henry, and she rapidly gained influence over him, persuading him in December 1445 to surrender the county of Maine to France. The loss of any territory won in Henry V's wars was deeply unpopular in England and created hostility towards Margaret. This increased when, in July 1449, her uncle, Charles VII, declared war on England, ending the truce sealed by her marriage. Margaret worked closely with the Duke of Suffolk, Henry's hated chief minister, and there were rumours that the pair were lovers, with *Hall's Chronicle* referring to him as 'the Quenes dearlynge'. This was slander, but it was widely believed.

Whilst Margaret was never popular in England, she was able to carry out the traditional role of queen during the early years of her marriage. Henry had founded Eton College in September 1440 and King's College, Cambridge, in February 1441, and following his example, Margaret founded Queen's College, Cambridge. She was conventionally pious and made two pilgrimages to Becket's shrine at Canterbury. She made a further pilgrimage of thanksgiving to Walsingham in the spring of 1453, shortly after she discovered that she was pregnant for the first time.

Margaret had little time to enjoy her pregnancy, as, on 16 July 1453, the English army was decisively defeated in France at the Battle of Castillon, leaving England in control only of Calais on the Continent. Henry was devastated by the news, and it triggered an attack of the mental disorder that had so plagued the life of his maternal grandfather, Charles VI of France. On 15 August 1453, the King felt unusually tired and went to bed early. According to Whethamstead's Register, during the night 'a disease and disorder of such a sort overcame the king that he lost his wits and memory for a time, and nearly all his body was uncoordinated and out of control that he could neither walk, nor hold his head upright, nor easily move from where he sat'. Whilst seemingly conscious, he was unable to take in anything around him. On 13 October 1453, whilst Henry was still unresponsive, Margaret gave birth to her only child in London, a son whom she named Edward.

From the moment of Edward of Lancaster's birth, he became Margaret's focus, and she sought to ensure his inheritance at all costs. As soon as he was born, the old rumours surfaced that Margaret had been unfaithful to the King, and in 1460, Margaret's enemy, the Earl of Warwick, wrote that 'our king is stupid and out of his mind; he does not rule but is ruled. The government is in the hands of the queen and her paramours'. According to *Hall's Chronicle*, many people in England believed that Edward was either a changeling, introduced into the Queen's bedchamber because she could not conceive a child of her own, or that he was Margaret's son by the Duke of Somerset, a cousin of Henry VI's. These rumours had no basis in fact, but they were damaging, and Margaret immediately attempted to secure Henry's recognition of her son. Once she had recovered from the birth, she moved her household to Windsor, where Henry was staying. According to a newsletter written by John Stodeley in January 1454,

As touchyng tythynges, please it you to write that at the Princes coming to Wyndesore, the Duc of Buk' toke hym in his armes and presented hym to the Kyng in godely wise, besechyng the Kyng to blisse hym; and the Kyng gave no answere. Natheless the Duk abode stille with the Prince by the Kyng; and whan he coude no maner answere have, the Quene come in, and toke the Prince in hir armes and presented hym in like forme as the Duke had done, desiryng that he shuld blisse it; but alle their labour was in veyne, for they departed thens without any answere or counteaunce saving only that ones he loked on the Prince and caste doune his eyene ayen, without any more.

Henry's lack of response to his son was disastrous for Margaret's reputation, and the rumours about her son's birth persisted. In February 1454, she decided to act, and presented a bill of five articles to parliament in London, claiming the regency of England for herself. Even in this she was unsuccessful, and Henry's cousin, the Duke of York, was named as Protector of England on 27 March 1454. Margaret was firmly allied with York's enemy, the Duke of Somerset, and this appointment horrified her, but there was nothing she could do except rejoin Henry at Windsor and await the outcome of events. Once at Windsor, Margaret renewed her efforts to wake Henry, and in late December 1454, he suddenly recovered. Margaret brought their son to him 'and then he askid what the Princes name was, and the Queen told him Edward; and than he hild up his hands and thankid God thereof. And he seid he never knew til that tyme, nor wist not what was seid to him, nor wist where he had be whils he hath be seke til now'. Margaret was overjoyed that Henry finally recognised their son, and the couple travelled to London, where they relieved York of his protectorate. Henry's recovery was only partial, and it was Margaret who emerged as the real power behind the throne.

The Duke of York had no intention of surrendering power, and following Henry's return to London, he moved north to raise troops. In late May 1455, Henry set out from London to attend a parliament at Leicester, whilst Margaret remained behind in London. On 21 May, Henry's men were attacked by an army led by York at St Albans. This was the first battle of the Wars of the Roses and saw the beginning of a civil war that would nearly bring the crown and nobility to its ruin. During the course of the battle, Somerset and other leading Lancastrians were killed, and Henry was taken prisoner by York and escorted back to London. Margaret withdrew with her son to the Tower, but she was powerless to do anything to stop York, and on 17 November 1455, his second period of protectorate was declared. Margaret continued to build up her own powerbase, and in October 1458, an attempt was made to assassinate York's nephew, the powerful Earl of Warwick, at Westminster. Warwick fled to Calais, where he began raising troops. His father, the Earl of Salisbury, raised an army in the north and York began recruiting in Wales. Margaret herself, alarmed by the sudden activity of the Yorkist party, travelled to Cheshire to raise troops in her son's name. She won a victory over the Yorkists in October 1459 when they fled in the face of her army in the Welsh Marches. In June 1460, the tide turned again, and Margaret's army was defeated by Warwick and Salisbury at Northampton. During the battle, Henry was taken prisoner and Margaret and her son were forced to flee to the safety of Harlech Castle.

The recapture of Henry VI emboldened the Duke of York, and

on 10 October 1460, he arrived at a parliament in London and sat down in the King's empty throne, signalling his decision to claim the crown of England. York had a strong claim to the throne because, when Henry IV had usurped the crown from Richard II in 1399, he had ignored the rights of Edmund Mortimer, the great-grandson of Edward III's second son, Lionel of Clarence. Edmund Mortimer died childless and his claim passed to the Duke of York himself, the son of Mortimer's sister, Anne. York was therefore a descendant of Edward III's second son, whilst Henry VI was only a descendant of his third. York set out his claim to parliament, and it was agreed that, whilst Henry would retain the throne for the remainder of his life, York would be acknowledged as his heir, in preference to Edward of Lancaster. This was something to which Margaret could never agree, and she marched north with 20,000 men. On 31 December 1460, she met an army commanded by York and Salisbury at Wakefield where she won a decisive victory. York was killed in battle, and Salisbury, who was captured, was summarily executed on Margaret's orders. Margaret was determined to have her revenge, and according to *Hall's Chronicle*, her men 'came to the place wher the dead corps of the duke of Yorke lay, and caused his head to be stryken of, and set on it a croune of paper, and so fixed it on a pole, and presented it to the Quene'. Margaret had York and Salisbury's heads set on poles above the gates of York before marching south in triumph.

Margaret met a second Yorkist army at St Albans soon after Wakefield and was once again victorious, rescuing Henry VI, who had been brought out of London to lead the Yorkist forces. Whilst Margaret and Henry had initially had a fond marriage, following the birth of Edward of Lancaster and Henry's acquiescence to his disinheritance, Margaret became more ambivalent towards her husband and he was no longer the focus of her efforts. In spite of this, he was an important figurehead and possession of the King was crucial to her efforts to ensure her son's position. Margaret continued her journey south towards London, and once outside the city, she issued a manifesto to the citizens, demanding entry to the capital:

And whereas the late Duke of York of extreme malice, long hid under colours, imagined by divers and many ways and means the destruction of our lord's good grace, whom God of his mercy ever preserve, hath now late, upon an untrue pretence, feigned a title to my lord's crown, and royal estate, and pre-eminence, contrary to his allegiance and divers solemn oaths of his own offer made, uncompelled or constrained, and fully proposed to have deposed him of his regality, ne had been [had it not been for] the sad [firm], unchangeable and true dispositions of you and others, his true liegemen, for the which your worshipful dispositions we thank you as heartily as we can. And howbeit, that the same untrue, unsad and unadvised person, of very pure malice, disposed to continue in his cruelness, to the utterest undoing, if he might, of us, and of my lord's son and ours the prince, which, with God's mercy, he shall not be of power to perform, by the help of you and all my lord's faithful disposed subjects, hath thrown among you, as we be certainly informed, divers untrue and feigned matters and surmises; and in especial that we and my lord's said son and ours should newly draw toward you with an unseen power of strangers, disposed to rob and to despoil you of your goods and havings [property]; we will that you know for certain that, at such time as we or our said son shall be disposed to see my lord, as our duty is and so binds us to do, you, nor none of you, shall be robbed, despoiled, nor wronged by any person that at that time we or our said son shall be accompanied with, or any other sent in our or his name, praying you, in our most hearty and desirous wise, that above all earthly things you will diligently intend [attend] to the surety of my lord's royal person in the mean time; so that through malice of his said enemy he be no more troubled, vexed, nor jeoparded. And, so doing, we shall be unto you such lady as of reason you shall be largely content.

The Londoners were not convinced by Margaret's promise, and they sent out a delegation headed by the Duchesses of Bedford and Buckingham and Lady Scales to beg her not to allow her army to enter. Margaret made the greatest error of her life in agreeing, and she took her army back towards the north without securing the capital. A few days later, the Duke of York's eldest son, Edward, Earl of March, entered the city, and on 4 March, he was proclaimed king as Edward IV. On 29 March, Margaret's army was decisively defeated by the new King at Towton, leaving Margaret, Henry and their son as fugitives.

Margaret waged a campaign from Scotland against Edward IV for the next two years, even visiting France in an attempt to secure aid. In May 1464, she was defeated in battle on the edge of Hexham Forest. This was the final straw for Margaret, and she and her son abandoned their army, and Henry VI himself, and sailed to France. Whilst she had abandoned her husband's kingdom, Margaret had not abandoned the cause, and she continued to seek aid in France for some years. In 1465, she was dealt another blow when news arrived that Henry had been captured hiding in northern England and that he had been taken as a prisoner to the Tower of London.

For Margaret, the turning point came in 1470. Relations between Edward IV and his closest ally, the Earl of Warwick, had become increasingly strained throughout the 1460s, and in 1470, Warwick fled to France. Margaret's cousin, Louis XI, had been looking for an opportunity to attack Edward IV, who had allied himself with the French king's rival, the Duke of Burgundy, and he offered to reconcile Margaret and Warwick so that they could launch a joint attack on England. For Margaret, negotiations with her opponent were a bitter pill to swallow, but she was a pragmatist. On 22 July 1470, the pair underwent a formal reconciliation. It was agreed that Warwick would restore Henry to the throne with French aid and that, in return, Edward of Lancaster would marry Warwick's daughter, Anne Neville. True to his word, Warwick sailed to England and caused Edward IV to flee, restoring Henry VI to the throne. Margaret was jubilant at the news, and she and her son and daughter-in-law prepared to sail to England, only to find themselves delayed by bad weather.

Margaret and her party finally landed in England on 18 April 1471. On the very day that Margaret landed, Warwick fought a battle with the recently returned Edward IV at Barnet. The Lancastrians suffered a heavy defeat, and Warwick was killed. Edward IV returned to London in triumph and moved Henry VI from the palace rooms of the Tower back to the prison. Margaret was devastated, and Polydore Vergil documents her reaction:

When she heard these things the miserable woman swooned for fear, she was distraught, dismayed and tormented with sorrow; she lamented the calamity of the time, the adversity of fortune, her own toil and misery; she bewailed the unhappy end of King Henry, which she believed assuredly to be at hand, and, to be short, she behaved as one more desirous to die than live.

Margaret had no alternative but to continue her fight. She raised an army in the West Country before marching to Tewkesbury to confront Edward IV. According to *Hall's Chronicle*, as they prepared for battle, Margaret and her son rode amongst their troops to encourage them. Margaret then retired from the battlefield to await news of the day's events. Her hopes were dashed later that day when she heard that her army had been destroyed and that her son was amongst the Lancastrian dead. With the loss of her only child, Margaret was entirely broken, and she was captured by Edward IV at a religious house near the battlefield. She was led back to London as the prize prisoner in Edward IV's victory parade before being imprisoned in the Tower. On the very night of her arrival in the ancient fortress, Margaret was also widowed, as Henry VI was quietly murdered. With the deaths of her husband and son, Margaret had no relevance in English politics and nothing to fight for. After a few months, Edward IV, recognising her powerlessness, turned her over to the custody of her friend, the Duchess of Suffolk, at Wallingford.

At a meeting between Edward IV and Louis XI at Picquigny on 25 August 1475, in which a truce was agreed between the two monarchs, Louis agreed to ransom Margaret for the sum of 50,000 crowns. In late January 1476, Margaret left England for the last time. It was a broken woman who returned to the land of her birth, and after receiving the promise of a modest pension from her father, she retired to his castle at Reculee. In July 1480, Margaret's father died, and she found herself entirely dependent on the grudging generosity of the French king. She died miserable and poor on 25 August 1482 at Dampierre Castle.

The four queens of the House of Lancaster enjoyed varying fortunes as the dynasty came to prominence in a wave of popular support and, ultimately, suffered an ignominious end. Of the four women, only Margaret of Anjou asserted political dominance, and she was amongst the unhappiest of any English queen. As the Wars of the Roses continued to cause devastation and havoc in England, the successors to the Lancastrian queens, the queens of the House of York, fared little better as their fortunes, and those of their dynasty, ebbed and flowed.

6

The Yorkist Queens

The fortunes of the Yorkist dynasty proved to be as turbulent as those of the preceding House of Lancaster. Edward IV, the first Yorkist king, spent the first few years of his reign in uncertainty, due, to a large extent, to his marriage to the commoner, Elizabeth Woodville. His short-lived successor, Edward V, failed to establish himself and was deposed by his uncle, Richard III. Richard had great difficulty in establishing his regime, and at the Battle of Bosworth in 1485, he was killed by the forces of Henry VII, the first Tudor king.

The three Yorkist queens faced many of the concerns that had plagued their Lancastrian predecessors as the Wars of the Roses came to a close. Elizabeth Woodville, the first Yorkist queen, endured her husband's deposition in 1470 before his triumphant return and then found that her unpopularity brought her children and family to near ruin. Her sister-in-law, Anne Neville, who had previously almost been a Lancastrian queen due to her marriage to Edward of Lancaster, was marginalised by her childlessness and is an obscure figure. Finally, Elizabeth of York, the daughter of Edward IV and Elizabeth Woodville, whilst in truth the first Tudor queen, had a life entirely dominated by her father's dynasty and her position as the heir to the House of York.

ELIZABETH WOODVILLE (1437–92) was the first Englishwoman to be acknowledged as queen of England since Edith of Mercia in the eleventh century. She was the daughter of Jacquetta de St Pol, Duchess of Bedford. Jacquetta came from an ancient family in Luxembourg and could trace her descent back to Charlemagne. In 1433, she had married Richard, Duke of Bedford, the younger brother of Henry V.

After her husband's death, Jacquetta caused a scandal, which *Hall's Chronicle* describes, when she married Richard Woodville, a lowly member of her household:

> The duchesse of Bedford sister to Lewes, erle of Sainct Paule, myndyng also to marye rather for pleasure than for honour, without counsayl of her frenders, maryed a lusty knight, called Sir Richarde Wooduile, to the great displeasure of her vncle the bishop of Tyrwyne, and the erle her brother: but they now coulde not remedie it, for the chauce was cast and passed.

Regardless of the scandal, it was a very happy union, and Elizabeth, who was born at Grafton in Northamptonshire in 1437, was the eldest child of thirteen.

No details survive of Elizabeth's childhood. By the mid-1450s, she had married Sir John Grey, the son of Sir Edward Grey and his wife, Lady Ferrers. Elizabeth bore two children in quick succession: Thomas in around 1455 and Richard in the late 1450s. Sir John Grey was the heir to both his parents and the marriage was a good match for Elizabeth. On 17 February 1461, however, he was killed fighting for the Lancastrians at the second battle of St Albans.

The loss of her husband was devastating. Her family were staunchly Lancastrian in their sympathies, and within weeks of being widowed, Elizabeth was dealt a further blow with the capture of her father and eldest brother by the Yorkists at the Battle of Towton. With her fortunes at their lowest ebb, she returned to her mother at Grafton whilst her estates were confiscated by the new Yorkist king, Edward IV. Elizabeth resolved to personally approach the King to petition for the return of her lands, positioning herself and her sons under an oak tree that she knew the King would pass whilst he was out hunting. Elizabeth's surviving portraits show that she was both blond and beautiful. Edward was smitten with the young widow and fell in love with her at first sight.

Whilst Edward IV was very taken with Elizabeth, he had no intention of marrying her, as recounted by a contemporary, Dominic Mancini:

> When the king first fell in love with her beauty of person and charm

of manner, he could not corrupt her virtue by gifts or menaces. The story runs that when Edward placed a dagger at her throat, to make her submit to his passion, she remained unperturbed and determined to die rather than live unchastely with the king. Whereupon Edward coveted her much the more, and he judged the lady worthy of a royal spouse, who could not be overcome in her constancy even by an infatuated king.

Although of lowly birth herself, Elizabeth was descended from noble ancestors, and she had a high opinion of her honour. She was determined not to become the King's mistress, even when he threatened to rape her at knifepoint, instead telling him plainly 'that as she wist herself too simple to be his wife, so thought she herself too good to be his concubine'. When she made this comment, Elizabeth can never have expected that Edward would marry her, and at most, she may have hoped for an introduction to a more suitable second husband. Edward was, however, besotted with her, and on or around 1 May 1464, the couple were married in a secret ceremony.

Edward's decision to marry Elizabeth was impulsive, and he did not think through the consequences of his hasty action. Whilst the couple enjoyed the first few days of their married life, Edward's cousin and chief advisor, the Earl of Warwick, was in France attempting to arrange a marriage between Edward and the sister-in-law of the King of France. Following Warwick's return, Edward was forced to admit at a council meeting that he was already married. Edward's mother, Cecily Neville, was aghast and publicly declared that Elizabeth was not good enough for her son. More damagingly, in a fit of pique, she also claimed that Edward was not the son of her husband and was instead the product of an adulterous affair. There was no truth to this, but it demonstrates the fury with which news of Edward's marriage was greeted. Edward's brother, George, Duke of Clarence, objected to the marriage, saying that Edward should have married a virgin rather than a widow with children. It was Warwick's opposition that was most damaging to Edward and Elizabeth.

Elizabeth was secure in Edward's devotion to her, and aware that there was little her enemies could do to change the situation, she was not unduly concerned. Once news of their marriage became public, Edward was determined to promote his wife, and he gave her a grand coronation on 26 May 1465, a ceremony that was delayed in order to give Elizabeth's grand maternal relatives time to arrive from Luxembourg. Elizabeth intended that her family should benefit from her good fortune, and she arranged marriages for her many siblings. Elizabeth's sisters married the Earls of Essex and Kent, the wealthy Lord Strange and the heir to Lord Herbert. Elizabeth's youngest sister, Catherine, made by far the grandest match when she married the Duke of Buckingham. Elizabeth also arranged rich marriages for her brothers, with the marriage of one brother causing particular comment. According to the *Annales Rerum Anglicarum,* in January 1465, 'Catherine, Duchess of Norfolk, a slip of a girl of about eighty years old, was married to John Woodville, the queen's brother, aged twenty years, a diabolical marriage'. In February 1467, Elizabeth obtained the marriage of Edward's niece, Anne Holland, for her eldest son, Thomas Grey. The rise of the Woodvilles was resented in England, but Elizabeth ploughed on regardless, persuading Edward to ennoble her father as Earl Rivers and her eldest son as the Marquis of Dorset.

Elizabeth kept a tight control over her household and finances during her time as queen, and she was a very effective manager. Her household was smaller than Margaret of Anjou's, and she was less extravagant in her spending. She had an income of £4,500 and made a point of living within her means, appointing only seven maids instead of Margaret of Anjou's ten. In spite of this economy, Elizabeth enjoyed luxury goods and sums spent on furs and goldsmith's works are noted in her accounts for 1466–67. She guarded her rights, as can be seen from a letter that she wrote to Sir William Stoner, threatening him for exploiting one of her forests:

Trusty and well beloved, we greet you well. And whereas we understand, by report made unto us at this time, that you have taken upon you now of late to make masteries within our forest and chase of Barnwood and Exhill, and there, in contempt of us, uncourteously to hunt and slay our deer within the same, to our great marvel and displeasure; we will you wit that we intend to sue such remedy therein as shall accord with my lord's laws. And whereas we furthermore understand that your purpose, under colour of my lord's commission, in that behalf granted unto you, as you say, hastily to take the view and rule of our game of deer within our said forest and chace; we will that you show unto us or our council your said commission, if any such you have, and in the mean season, that you spare of hunting within our said forest and chace, as you will answer at your peril.

Elizabeth had suffered poverty following the death of her first husband, and this coloured her management of her affairs once she became queen.

Elizabeth also found time to carry out acts of patronage. In 1465, she was granted a licence by Edward to patronise Queen's College, Cambridge. Elizabeth proved enthusiastic in her support of the college and was often referred to as the college's true founder in documents of the period, reflecting the size of her contribution. She had strong religious beliefs and founded a chapel in Westminster Abbey. In March 1546, she obtained a royal licence to support sixty priests at Leadenhall in London. As a further demonstration of their faith, Edward and Elizabeth went on pilgrimages to Walsingham and Canterbury. They named their youngest child Bridget after a popular Swedish saint and Elizabeth saw charitable and religious patronage as part of her duty as queen.

Elizabeth fulfilled another aspect of the role of queen admirably. She bore her first child by Edward, a daughter named Elizabeth, on 11 February 1465, and this was soon followed by the births of two further daughters. Elizabeth was a fond mother and raised all her children in her household, with the exception of her eldest son by Edward. Both Elizabeth and Edward were pleased with their daughters, but they required a son, and Elizabeth was pregnant again in 1470 when Edward was forced to abandon his kingdom and his throne.

Both the Earl of Warwick and Edward's brother, the Duke of Clarence, had been furious when they heard of Edward's marriage, and by 1469, their hostility had turned into rebellion. Elizabeth was visiting Norwich with her daughters when Warwick and Clarence launched their attack on Edward. The rebellion was intended as an attack on Elizabeth's family, as a proclamation made by Warwick, Clarence and the Archbishop of York on 12 July 1469 made clear:

The king our sovereign lord's true subjects of divers parts of this his realm of England have delivered to us certain articles [remembering] the deceitful, covetous rule and guiding of certain seditious persons, that is to say, the Lord Rivers, the Duchess of Bedford his wife, William Herbert, Earl of Pembroke, Humphrey Stafford, Earl of Devonshire, Lord Scales [Elizabeth's eldest brother] and Audley, Sir John Woodville and his brothers, and others of this mischievous rule, opinion and assent, which have caused our sovereign lord and his realm to fall into great poverty and misery, disturbing the administration of the laws, only tending to their own promotion and enrichment.

Edward's forces were no match for Warwick's, and he was defeated at the Battle of Edgecote on 26 July and captured soon afterwards. Elizabeth was terrified and worse news followed when she heard that her father and brother John had been captured by Warwick's forces near Coventry and executed without trial. The Woodville family were always particularly close and Elizabeth plunged into mourning. Warwick was unable to hold the King for long, and Edward and Elizabeth were soon reunited, but any joy was short-lived. After a brief exile, Warwick and Clarence returned to England allied with Margaret of Anjou and the Lancastrians in September 1470, and deposed Edward IV, reinstating Henry VI as king of England.

Edward did not have the military strength to give battle against the Lancastrians and, instead, fled to Burgundy on hearing of Warwick's landing. Elizabeth was in London at the time of Warwick's invasion, and she immediately began to provision the Tower for a potential siege. As news reached her of Warwick's strength, it was obvious that she could not hold the Tower, and Elizabeth, her mother and daughters entered the sanctuary at Westminster Abbey. Soon afterwards, Warwick entered the city in triumph. It must have been a miserable party who awaited the outcome of events in sanctuary in late 1470, although the mood was lightened somewhat on around 1 November when Elizabeth gave birth to her first son by the King, whom she named in honour of his father.

On 11 March 1471, Edward sailed for England with an army. He had always been popular in London, and on 11 April, he was admitted to the city and promptly re-proclaimed as king, removing Henry VI from the royal apartments of the Tower and returning him to his prison rooms. Elizabeth was overjoyed by Edward's return, and she left sanctuary for what must have been an emotional reunion. Edward did not remain in the city for long and soon marched out at the head of an army to meet Warwick at the Battle of Barnet. Edward won the day and, on 4 May 1471, obtained his final victory over the Lancastrians, defeating the forces of Margaret of Anjou at Tewkesbury. With this victory, Edward was finally secure on his throne, and Elizabeth was equally secure in her position as his queen.

On her release from sanctuary, Elizabeth showed Edward their infant son for the first time, and his father declared him Prince of Wales. In 1473, Elizabeth accompanied the prince to Ludlow, where she was to rule Wales on his behalf for a time. She was responsible for appointing her son's council whilst at Ludlow, and she appointed both her eldest brother, who had succeeded their father as Earl Rivers, and her second son, Sir Richard Grey, to prominent posts. Elizabeth was back in London by 1475, and that summer, when Edward set out to invade France, he paid her the compliment of naming their four-year-old son regent, a move that made Elizabeth the effective ruler of England. Edward IV was notoriously unfaithful to Elizabeth throughout their marriage, something that she always pretended to ignore. The couple remained in love, and young Edward's birth was followed by the births of Margaret in 1472, Richard in 1473, Anne in 1475, George in 1477, and Catherine in 1479. Elizabeth bore her youngest child, Bridget, in November 1480, when she was forty-three years old. Elizabeth's youngest son, George, died in infancy, but her second son by Edward was created Duke of York.

Edward was some years younger than Elizabeth, but throughout his reign, he enjoyed fine food and drink and overindulged himself, growing immensely fat. By Christmas 1482, his health had begun to fail, and on 9 April 1483, he died, shortly before his forty-first birthday. This was devastating for Elizabeth, but she was forced to ignore her grief in order to ensure the succession of her twelve-year-old son, Edward V. According to the *Crowland Chronicle Continuations*, Elizabeth met with her late husband's council at Westminster soon after his death and, in order to allay fears about Woodville dominance, agreed to instruct her son to bring no more than 2,000 men with him to London. At the time, she must have felt that she had nothing to fear.

Edward V set out from Ludlow accompanied by his uncle, Earl Rivers, and half-brother, Sir Richard Grey, soon after news of Edward IV's death reached him. Unbeknownst to Elizabeth, Edward V's paternal uncle, the Duke of Gloucester, and his friend, the Duke of Buckingham, who fiercely resented his marriage to Elizabeth's sister Catherine, set out to meet the young king at around the same time, arriving at Northampton as the King reached Stony Stratford. Out of politeness, Rivers and Grey met with the two dukes, and they spent the evening together, feasting and drinking. It was late before the feasting came to an end, and Elizabeth's two kinsmen agreed to spend the night at the dukes' residence. They were horrified to find, in the morning, that they had been placed under arrest as they slept whilst the two dukes rode to intercept the young king. Edward V, who was fond of his mother and maternal family, put up a spirited defence when his paternal uncle informed him that his uncle and two half-brothers had intended to rule the country through him. He declared that 'what my brother Marquis has done I cannot say. But in good faith I dare well answer for mine uncle Rivers and my brother here, that they be innocent of any such matters'. Edward's loyalty to the Woodvilles deeply troubled the two dukes as they accompanied the King to London.

According to Dominic Mancini, Elizabeth heard the news of Gloucester's actions just after midnight the next day, and she and her eldest son, Dorset, immediately 'began collecting an army, to defend themselves and to set free the young king from the clutches of the dukes. But when they exhorted certain nobles who had come to the city, and others, to take up arms, they perceived that men's minds were not only irresolute, but altogether hostile to themselves'. With no other option, Elizabeth, Dorset, and her five daughters and youngest son, Richard, Duke of York, fled once again to the sanctuary at Westminster. Elizabeth must have felt very alone, and her contemporaries believed that she was overreacting, with the chancellor visiting her at Westminster to give her the great seal as a demonstration that she had nothing to fear. This did little to reassure her, and soon afterwards, the chancellor came to her again on the orders of Gloucester to obtain the surrender of her youngest son.

Elizabeth had no intention of handing over her youngest son without a fight, and she was very concerned about what Gloucester intended towards her family. On his second visit to Elizabeth, the chancellor informed her that her younger son, Richard, Duke of York, should be with his elder brother to provide the young king with a companion. Elizabeth retorted that it would be better for both children to be with their mother. The chancellor, believing that he was dealing with a hysterical and melodramatic woman, offered a pledge for her youngest son's safety, to which Elizabeth replied that 'each of these children is the other's defence while they be asunder, and each of their lives lie in the other's body. Keep one safe and both be sure, and nothing for them both more perilous than to be both in one place'. Alone and friendless, Elizabeth knew that it was only a matter of time before she would be forced to comply, and shortly afterwards, when Gloucester surrounded the abbey with soldiers, she tearfully gave in, relinquishing her youngest son.

Elizabeth was right to be uneasy about Gloucester's intentions towards her sons. Six days after she surrendered her youngest son, on 22 June, a sermon was preached at Paul's Cross claiming that Edward IV was a bastard born as a result of an adulterous affair and that he and Elizabeth had never been married. The assertion that Edward IV was illegitimate was quickly dropped, perhaps due to the outrage of his mother, Cecily Neville, and instead, the focus of Gloucester's attack was that Elizabeth had never truly been the King's wife. According to the chronicler, Philippe de Commines, the Bishop of Bath 'revealed to the Duke of Gloucester [in 1483] that King Edward, being very enamoured of a certain English lady, promised to marry her, provided that he could sleep with her first, and she consented. The bishop said that he had married them when only he and they were present'.

The lady in question was Eleanor Butler, a noblewoman who had died in 1468. If the claims that Edward had secretly married her were true, then his later marriage to Elizabeth would be invalid and their children illegitimate. It seems very unlikely that Edward ever did enter into a full marriage with Eleanor, and a precontract with her, which, once consummated, could be as valid as a marriage is also debateable. Few people in England believed the claim, and most saw it for the pretext that it was, a device used by Gloucester to claim the throne as Richard III. Soon after his accession, Elizabeth's two sons disappeared into the Tower and were never seen again. Their fate is fiercely debated, although, at the time, it was widely believed that they were murdered by their uncle. Elizabeth is likely to have believed this, and the fact that she later came to terms with Richard is no indication that she believed her sons to be still alive. She already knew that he was the murderer of her second son, Sir Richard Grey, and her eldest brother, Earl Rivers, who were executed by the new king on trumped up charges.

With the accession of Richard III, Elizabeth was demoted from Queen Dowager to merely Dame Elizabeth Grey. For a woman as proud as Elizabeth, this rankled, and she began plotting against the new king, conspiring from sanctuary with Margaret Beaufort, the mother of Henry Tudor, the leading Lancastrian claimant to the throne. The two women shared a physician, who passed messages between them, and within months of the deposition of her son, Elizabeth had agreed that, if Henry Tudor promised to marry her eldest daughter, Elizabeth of York, she would support his bid for the throne. Both Elizabeth and Dorset were heavily involved in a rebellion that broke out in October 1483, which was intended to support an invasion by Henry Tudor from Brittany. Richard's decisive action brought matters under control, and Elizabeth, faced with the defeat of her Lancastrian ally, instead made terms with the King, agreeing to come out of sanctuary with her daughters in return for a promise from Richard that he would do her and her family no harm. This is surprising, as Elizabeth had every reason to hate Richard. However, she was several years older than him and must have felt that she was unlikely to survive him. Elizabeth's ambition was also pricked by Richard's scheme to marry her eldest daughter, although this came to nothing.

Elizabeth was living in London when word reached her in August 1485 that Henry Tudor had launched a second invasion of England, having sworn that, if he was victorious, he would marry Elizabeth of York. With his victory over Richard III at Bosworth, he claimed the throne as Henry VII, something that, along with the death of Richard III in battle, must have been gratifying to Elizabeth. Soon after his accession, Henry VII repealed the Act declaring Elizabeth's marriage invalid and reinstated her as Queen Dowager. He married Elizabeth of York the following year.

Elizabeth was not on entirely good terms with Henry VII, and there is some evidence that she conspired against him, perhaps in the hope that her grandson, Prince Arthur, could become king in his father's place. According to the historian Francis Bacon, in the early years of Henry VII's reign, a pretender called Lambert Simnel emerged, claiming to be Edward IV's nephew, the Earl of Warwick. Simnel had been well-schooled in how to behave:

> So that it cannot be, but that some great person that knew particularly and familiarly Edward Plantagenet [Warwick], had a hand in the business, from whom the priest might take his aim. That which is most probable, out of precedent and subsequent acts, is, that it was the Queen Dowager, from whom this action had the principal source and motion. For certain it is, she was a busy negotiating woman, and in her withdrawing-chamber had the fortunate conspiracy for the king against King Richard the third been hatched; which the king knew, and remembered perhaps but too well; and was at this time extremely discontent with the king, thinking her daughter, as the king handled the matter, not advanced but displeased: and none could hold the book so well to prompt and instruct this stage-play as she could.

When news of the plot became known, Henry seized Elizabeth's property and sent her to Bermondsey Abbey, officially claiming that this was in punishment for her delivering her daughters to Richard III. Elizabeth was a spent force, and she remained at Bermondsey in forced retirement from May 1487 until her death on 8 June 1492. As befitted her status, she was given a grand funeral and was buried beside her second husband, Edward IV. Elizabeth Woodville lived a life of great turbulence, her fortunes greatly affected by the troubled times in which she lived. Her successor as queen, Anne Neville, lived an equally turbulent and tragic life.

ANNE NEVILLE (1456–85) was a figure of major importance in the Wars of the Roses. Married first to a Lancastrian prince and then to a Yorkist one, she participated in many of the major political events of the late fifteenth century. Anne was the daughter of the famous Richard Neville, Earl of Warwick, and his wife Anne Beauchamp, who was the heiress to the earldoms of Warwick and Gloucester, and the rich Despenser estates. Anne's father, who was known as 'The Kingmaker' for his role in bringing Edward IV to the throne and then deposing him in favour of Henry VI, had no male heir and was ambitious for his two daughters, Anne, who was born in 1456, and Isabel, who was five years older.

In May 1457, Warwick was appointed captain of Calais and moved his household to France. His wife accompanied him, and it is possible that the couple took their two daughters. The family returned to England in 1460. By 1465, Warwick's young cousin, Richard, Duke of Gloucester, had joined the household. Anne's feelings for the King's youngest brother are nowhere recorded, but he was only four years older than her, and she would have had some contact with him in childhood. Gloucester and his elder brother George, Duke of Clarence, were the most eligible men in England, and in 1464, Warwick suggested a double marriage between them and his two daughters. Nothing came of either match in 1464, perhaps because the scheme was vetoed by the King.

Whilst Anne's marriage was allowed to drop, Warwick was determined to secure Clarence for his eldest daughter, and the King's attempts to thwart him were another reason for the earl to be discontented. Clarence was also disillusioned with his brother, and in early July 1469, Warwick, Clarence and Warwick's wife and daughters crossed the channel to Calais in the company of Warwick's brother, the Archbishop of York. Safely out of the reach of Edward IV, Isabel and Clarence were married on 11 July. Soon after the ceremony, Warwick, Clarence and the Archbishop issued a proclamation opposing the King, before sailing for England to raise troops. Anne, her mother and sister probably remained in Calais during Warwick and Clarence's first invasion. At some point after Edward's defeat and capture, the three women returned to England, and they were present in London for the Christmas celebrations where Edward, Warwick and Clarence were publicly reconciled. The public show of unity convinced no one that the rivalry between Warwick and the King was at an end, and Anne and her family returned to Warwick soon after Christmas, deeply concerned about the future.

In early 1470, violence again erupted between Warwick and Clarence and Edward IV. Edward inflicted a heavy defeat on Warwick's forces at Stamford, and Warwick and Clarence fled. On their way to the coast, the fugitives passed through Warwick, where they were joined by Anne and her mother and sister. The family then took ship, intending to land at Calais. They were nonplussed on 16 April to find Calais defended against them. Unable to land, matters became worse the following day when Isabel went into labour with her first child. With few women present to attend her, it is likely that both Anne and her mother assisted in Isabel's labour. It must have been a major trauma for everyone present, and Isabel's child was either stillborn or died soon after birth.

Whilst they were considering their next move, the family remained at sea, engaging in piracy against Burgundian ships, the allies of Edward IV. They finally landed in France, where Warwick allied himself with the Lancastrians in an attempt to oust Edward IV. According to the *Crowland Chronicle Continuations*, Anne was central to her father's plans:

> King Louis received them with kindness and, in the end, they were reconciled with Queen Margaret and her son, Prince Edward, and promised, henceforth, fruitfully to support their cause and the cause of King Henry. Furthermore, so that their renewed love and faith might be made more certain in time to come, a marriage contract was made between the prince and Lady Anne, the Earl of Warwick's younger daughter.

It is likely that Warwick wanted to witness the marriage, as a token of Margaret's good faith, but the couple, who were both descended from John of Gaunt, were forced to wait for a dispensation from the Pope, which had still not arrived by 9 September when Warwick finally sailed.

Anne spent the weeks of her betrothal largely with her fiancé's mother, Margaret of Anjou. Margaret kept her word and, following the arrival of the dispensation, the couple were married on 13 December at Amboise. By then, news of Warwick's success in deposing Edward IV and reinstating Henry VI had reached France, and Anne and her new husband were fêted by Louis XI in a grand reception held in their honour in Paris. Anne and Edward spent some time getting to know each other, and then, in late March 1471, travelled, with their respective mothers, to Harfleur with the intention of sailing to England. They were delayed by bad weather, but finally sailed the following month, with Anne travelling in the ship carrying her husband and mother-in-law. Whilst the weather had calmed to some extent, it was still a dangerous crossing and the fleet was scattered at sea, with Anne's ship landing in Weymouth and her mother's at Portsmouth. Within days of landing, Anne was horrified to hear that her father had been killed by Edward IV at the Battle of Barnet. When Anne's mother heard the news, instead of joining her daughter at Weymouth as arranged, she fled to the sanctuary of Beaulieu Abbey. Anne remained with Margaret whilst the Battle of Tewkesbury was fought, and she must have been shocked to hear that she was widowed that day so soon after her marriage.

Edward IV captured Margaret and Anne near the battlefield and took them triumphantly back to London. Margaret was imprisoned in the Tower, but Anne was, instead, passed into Clarence's custody. Clarence had recently been reconciled with his brother, and a legend has grown up around Anne's time in his household. According to the *Crowland Chronicle Continuations*,

> Richard, Duke of Gloucester, sought to make the same Anne his wife; this desire did not suit the plans of his brother, the Duke of Clarence (married previously to the earl's elder daughter) who therefore had the girl hidden away so that his brother would not know where she was, since he feared a division of the inheritance. He wanted it to come to himself alone, by right of his wife, rather than to share it with someone else. The Duke of Gloucester, however, was so much the more astute, that having discovered the girl dressed as a kitchen-maid in London, he had her moved into sanctuary in St Martin's.

Clarence had good reason for keeping Anne unmarried, and he vetoed any suggestion of a marriage between her and his brother.

It is unlikely that Richard and Anne made a love match, as is indicated by Richard's interest in her inheritance. There is no evidence of the date of Anne's second marriage, but by 16 February 1472, they were betrothed, and they married soon afterwards. The marriage brought Richard and his brother Clarence into open rivalry, with the elder brother refusing to give up any of Warwick's estates. A series of hearings were held in the early spring to decide the matter, and a settlement was agreed where Clarence gave up some lands in return for receiving the Neville titles of Earl of Warwick and Earl of Salisbury. Edward IV personally brokered the settlement, which disinherited Anne Beauchamp, who remained in sanctuary at Beaulieu. Anne's feelings on the treatment meted out to her mother are not recorded, but she was apparently happy to occupy her mother's estates. Neither Clarence nor Richard were entirely happy with the settlement, and the matter continued to fester.

Anne Beauchamp keenly resented her treatment, and a petition by her to parliament survives, protesting her innocence:

> It hath pleased the king's highness, by some sinister information to his said highness made, to direct his most dread letters to the abbot of the monastery of Beaulieu, with right sharp commandment that such persons as his highness sent to the said monastery should have guard and strait keeping of her person, which was and is to her great heart's grievance, she specially fearing that the privileges and liberties of the church, by such keeping of her person, might be interrupted and violated, where the privileges of the said sanctuary were never so largely attempted unto this time, as is said; yet the said Anne and Countess, under protestations by her made, hath suffered strait keeping of her person and yet doth, that her fidelity and liegeance to the king's highness the better might be understood, hoping she might the rather have had largess to make suits to the king's highness in her own person for her livelihood and rightful inheritance, with all revenues and profits thereto pertaining, with her jointure also, and dower of the earldom of Salisbury, fully and wholly hath been restrained from her, from the time of the death of her said lord and husband unto this day.

Anne Beauchamp's claims were a threat to both Clarence and Richard. Early in June 1473, Richard's agents removed Anne Beauchamp from Beaulieu and took her to his castle at Middleham. She probably thought that she was being offered her freedom and the return of her status and estates, but in reality, she was imprisoned by her son-in-law. The extent to which Anne Neville was involved in this is unclear, but both she and Richard feared the possibility of Anne Beauchamp remarrying. Anne may well have been complicit in the imprisonment of her mother in order to safeguard her inheritance.

There is no record of any protest by her when her mother, who was still very much alive, was declared legally dead by Act of Parliament in May 1474, in order to allow her sons-in-law to inherit her property.

Anne Neville virtually disappears from the sources during her time as Duchess of Gloucester, and she spent most of her time on her estates in the north. On 22 December 1476, her sister died in childbirth, and Clarence, who had never fully regained the King's trust, was executed in the Tower just over a year later. Anne and Richard rarely visited court, and Anne's time was occupied in running her household. At some point during the 1470s, she bore her only child, Edward of Middleham. He is first recorded in contemporary records in February 1478, when he was created Earl of Salisbury, and it is likely that he was born between 1473 and 1476. There is no evidence that Anne ever conceived another child, and it is likely that she was in ill health by the late 1470s. By 1484, when she was still only in her twenties, she was popularly considered to be past childbearing.

Richard and Anne were together at Middleham on 9 April 1483 when Edward IV died. On hearing the news, Richard acted decisively, travelling to intercept his nephew, Edward V's, journey from Wales. Anne joined her husband in London on 5 June 1483. Officially, she was there to attend Edward V's coronation, but it is likely that she had some idea of her husband's real intentions. Anne and Richard stayed at Baynard's Castle whilst they were in London, and the couple were both there when Richard accepted the throne on 26 June, becoming king as Richard III. Anne shared Richard's coronation on 6 July, in which the couple processed through the streets of London, with Anne attended by a great train of ladies and wearing a coronet of gems in her hair. Once they had been crowned, the couple attended a grand banquet, and sitting as an anointed queen, Anne may have felt that her father's hopes for her had finally been fulfilled.

Richard III's usurpation of the crown did not have universal public support, and immediately following his coronation, he went on a progress to show himself to the people. He set out on 20 July, travelling first to Windsor. Anne did not set out with Richard, and she may have been delayed by ill health. She had rejoined him at Warwick by August, and the pair travelled slowly northward through Coventry, Leicester and Nottingham. On 24 August, they were joined at Pontefract by their son. The royal party reached York on 29 August, where they found cheering crowds waiting for them and the city decorated in celebration of their visit. Richard was so delighted with this that he decided to create his son Prince of Wales in the city. Following the ceremony, Richard, Anne and Edward of Middleham walked in procession through the streets of York with Anne holding her son's hand. The couple were fond parents to their only child, and as they slowly moved southwards again, Anne decided to remain at Middleham with him.

Anne had rejoined Richard by March 1484 when the couple set out on another progress. During their journey, they visited Cambridge, where Anne made a generous endowment to Queen's College. They then travelled to Nottingham, where they received devastating news, as recorded in the *Crowland Chronicle Continuations*:

> In the following April, on a day not far off King Edward's anniversary, this only son, on whom, through so many solemn oaths, all hope of the royal succession rested, died at Middleham Castle after a short illness, in 1484 and in the first year of King Richard's reign. You might have seen the father and mother, after hearing the news at Nottingham where they were staying, almost out of their minds for a long time when faced with sudden grief.

The couple attempted to comfort each other in their grief, suggesting that they were close. However, the loss of their only son and Anne's inability to bear more children caused a rift between them that eventually drove them apart.

Anne spent Christmas 1484 at court in increasingly bad health. It cannot have been a happy occasion for her, and she suffered from comparisons with Richard's young niece, Elizabeth of York, who appeared wearing the same dress as Anne. Over Christmas, rumours arose that Richard wished to marry Elizabeth, intending to either divorce Anne or await her death. *Hall's Chronicle*, which, as a Tudor source, is admittedly hostile to Richard, claimed that Richard intended to hasten Anne's death. He complained publicly that she was barren, and around that time, ceased to sleep with her. He also apparently spread a rumour that she had already died, hoping that the shock of hearing it would hasten her death. *Hall's Chronicle* states that when the quene heard tell that so horrible a rumour of her death was sprong emongest the comminallie she sore suspected and judged the world to be almost at an ende with her, and in that sorofull agony, she with lamentable countenaunce of sorofull chere, repaired to the presence of the kyng her husband, demaundynge of hym, what it should meane that he had judged her worthy to die. The kyng aunswered her with fake words, and with dissimulynge blandimentes and flattering lesynges comforted her, biddynge her to be of good comforte, for to his knowledge she should have none other cause.

Anne died on 16 March 1485 on the day of a total eclipse of the sun. She was still only twenty-nine years old and her last months were not happy, with the likelihood that Richard would have divorced her had she lived longer. By the time of Anne's death, Richard's kingship was already unstable, and he was forced, on 30 March 1485, to make a public denial that he had murdered Anne. The crown brought Anne Neville nothing but misery. Her successor as queen, Elizabeth of York, was happier.

ELIZABETH OF YORK (1466–1503) was, for much of her life, the most important political figure in England and crucial to the success of any man who claimed the English crown. Elizabeth was the eldest child of Edward IV and Elizabeth Woodville and was born at Westminster Palace on 11 February 1466. Her childhood was dominated by marriage negotiations, and she was first betrothed at the age of four to Warwick's nephew, George Neville, who was created Duke of Bedford for the occasion. This marriage came to nothing, but in 1475, it was instead agreed that Elizabeth would marry the Dauphin of France.

With the exception of her father's exile and her time in sanctuary with her mother in 1470 and 1471, Elizabeth had a happy and secure childhood. This came to an abrupt end in April 1483 with Edward IV's death, and following the seizure of Edward V by Richard III, she once again fled with her family to sanctuary. It was from sanctuary that Elizabeth watched the events that placed her uncle on the throne, and on 25 June 1483, Elizabeth and all her siblings were declared to be illegitimate by parliament. Elizabeth may have known something of her mother's plot with Margaret Beaufort to marry her to Margaret's son, Henry Tudor, if he was able to claim the throne. With the disappearance of her brothers into the Tower and their likely murders, Elizabeth was widely regarded as the heiress to the House of York, and there is evidence that she desired to become queen of England, presumably seeing it as her birthright. Henry Tudor's first invasion of England ended in failure, and Elizabeth Woodville gave up hope of the deposition of Richard III, instead moving the family out of sanctuary in March 1484 and entrusting her daughters to Richard III's care. Elizabeth met with Richard III soon afterwards and was placed in the household of his queen, Anne Neville.

Upon Elizabeth's arrival at court, rumours began to spread that Richard III intended to divorce his wife and marry his niece. By marrying Elizabeth, Richard hoped to have his kingship popularly recognised as legitimate. Elizabeth's feelings about the marriage are unclear. It is often claimed that she found the idea totally abhorrent, and certainly, this was the view that Tudor historians were keen to portray. However, a now lost letter supposedly written by Elizabeth to the Duke of Norfolk in February 1485 suggests a different story. In the letter, Elizabeth asked Norfolk to mediate with Richard for her on the subject of their marriage, and she wrote that she feared that Anne Neville would never die. This letter no longer exists and must be considered highly suspect. If it is genuine, it demonstrates an aspect of Elizabeth's character that has been lost to history, and she may have been as ambitious as her mother. Whether she welcomed the marriage to her uncle or not, it was not to be. Richard was forced to publicly deny that he had considered making an incestuous marriage after there were murmurs of rebellion in the country in disgust.

The last months of Richard III's reign were filled with suspicion, and Elizabeth's conduct was closely watched. During the summer of 1485, the country was poised for Henry Tudor's expected invasion, and Elizabeth was sent north to Sheriff Hutton with her cousin, the Earl of Warwick, the son of the Duke of Clarence, to ensure that they were out of Henry's reach. On 22 August 1485, Richard was defeated and killed at the Battle of Bosworth and Henry Tudor was declared king as Henry VII. The new king sent Sir Robert Willoughby to Sheriff Hutton to bring Elizabeth and Warwick back to London. Warwick was sent as a prisoner to the Tower, whilst Elizabeth was lodged at her mother's house in the capital.

Henry VII claimed the crown through three separate titles: his maternal descent from the House of Lancaster, by right of conquest, and through his proposed marriage to Elizabeth of York. According to the historian Francis Bacon, his claim through Elizabeth was the one most favoured by the people of England. This unnerved Henry, and 'it lay plain before his eyes, that if he relied upon that title, he could be but a king at courtesy, and have rather a matrimonial than a regal power; the right remaining in his queen, upon whose decease, either with issue, or without issue, he was to give place and be removed'. Henry was anxious not to be seen only as a king through marriage and so delayed his marriage to Elizabeth, refusing to marry her until after his coronation on 30 October 1485.

Henry and Elizabeth began living together as husband and wife before their marriage, and she was in the early stages of pregnancy when they married on 18 January 1486. News of the marriage was received joyfully in England according to *Hall's Chronicle*:

> By reason of whiche marriage, peace was thought to discende oute of heuen [heaven] into England, considering that the lynes of Lancastre and Yorke, being both noble families equivalent in ryches, fame and honour, were now brought into one knot and connexed together, of whose two bodyes one heyre might succeed, whiche after their tyme should peaceably rule and enjoye the whole monarchy and realme of England.

The marriage was portrayed as bringing peace out of the turmoil of the Wars of the Roses, and Elizabeth, who had been deeply affected by the troubles, must have been proud of her role in bringing the civil war to an end.

There is some debate as to the relationship between Henry and Elizabeth. Francis Bacon believed that Henry 'shewed himself no very indulgent husband towards her, though she was beautiful, gentle, and fruitful. But his aversion towards the house of York was so predominant in him, as it found place not only in his wars and councils, but in his chamber and bed'. Bacon believed that Henry hated Elizabeth and was a cold and indifferent husband. It is certainly true that Henry gave Elizabeth no political role, and it was to his mother, Margaret Beaufort, that he turned for advice. However, throughout their marriage, the couple were rarely apart, and Henry was genuinely grief-stricken at her death. The marriage was political in origin, but it appears that affection developed between the couple.

The birth of Elizabeth's first child was greatly anticipated in England. Henry was acutely aware of the symbolic importance of the child who would be the heir to both Lancaster and York, and he asked Elizabeth to bear the child at Winchester, which was believed to have been King Arthur's capital. Through his grandfather, Owen Tudor, Henry claimed descent from Welsh royalty, and he was eager to stress his links with the mythical British king. On 20 September 1486, Elizabeth gave birth to a son who was named Arthur. The prince was given a grand christening in Winchester Cathedral with a great procession beginning and ending in Elizabeth's chamber. For Elizabeth, the birth was a triumph, and she had fulfilled her dynastic purpose. The christening was also a tribute to Elizabeth and her family, and her mother, Elizabeth Woodville, stood as godmother to the prince. Elizabeth's sister, Cecily, and her sister-in-law, the Marchioness of Dorset, carried the baby and his train.

The early years of Henry's reign were troubled by rebellions, and one of the most serious erupted in June 1487, when a rebel army landed in England led by Lambert Simnel, a boy who claimed to be Elizabeth's cousin, the Earl of Warwick. Elizabeth did not believe that Simnel was her cousin, and it is likely that she knew that the real Warwick was imprisoned in the Tower. For her safety, Henry sent Elizabeth to Greenwich whilst he marched north to confront the rebels, whom he crushed in battle at Stoke. With his victory, Henry finally felt secure enough to crown Elizabeth. On 23 November 1487, Elizabeth, Margaret Beaufort, and a company of ladies sailed from Greenwich in a procession of decorated boats, with one shaped like a red dragon. The procession docked at the Tower, where Henry met Elizabeth and escorted her inside. Two days of celebrations and feasting followed, and on 25 November, Elizabeth was crowned in Westminster Abbey, wearing a gown of purple velvet.

Much of Elizabeth's time as queen was spent in childbearing. She bore a daughter, Margaret, in 1489, followed by a second son, Henry, in 1491. Elizabeth was particularly fond of her second son, who she raised herself, and he bore a remarkable resemblance to her father, Edward IV. A second daughter, Elizabeth, was born the year after

Henry's birth, and a further son in 1497. Mary was born in 1498 and Edmund in 1499. Elizabeth's eighth and last child, Catherine, was born in 1503. Elizabeth was a fond mother to her children, and it is possible that the death of her daughter Elizabeth in 1497 caused the premature birth of her third son, who died before he was given a name. Elizabeth grieved for both these children and went on a pilgrimage to Walsingham in their memory. When her fourth son, Edmund, died in infancy, he was given a grand funeral in London.

Elizabeth played an active role in the negotiation of her children's marriages. Both she and Henry were overjoyed in 1497 when they secured the betrothal of their eldest son, Arthur, to Catherine, the youngest daughter of Ferdinand, King of Aragon, and Isabella, Queen of Castile. This match was proof of the strength of the Tudor dynasty and provided international recognition of Henry's kingship. A letter from Elizabeth to Isabella of Castile survives in which Elizabeth sought to reassure Catherine's mother of the warm welcome her daughter could expect in England:

> Although we before entertained singular love and regard to your highness above all other queens in the world, as well for the consanguinity and necessary intercourse which mutually take place between us, as also for the eminent dignity and virtue by which your said majesty so shines and excels that your most celebrated name is noised abroad and diffused every where; yet much more had this our love increased and accumulated by the accession of the most noble affinity which has recently been celebrated between the most illustrious Lord Arthur, prince of Wales, our eldest son, and the most illustrious princess the Lady Catherine, the infanta, your daughter. Hence it is that, amongst all other cares and cogitations, first and foremost we wish and desire from our heart that we may often and speedily hear of the health and safety of your serenity, and of the health and safety of the aforesaid most illustrious Lady Catherine, whom we think of and esteem as our own daughter, than which nothing can be more grateful and acceptable to us. Therefore we request your serenity to certify of your estate, and of that of the aforesaid most illustrious Lady Catherine, our common daughter. And if there be any thing in our power which would be grateful or pleasant to your majesty, use us and ours as freely as you would

your own; for, with most willing mind, we offer all that we have to you, and wish to have all in common with you.

Catherine of Aragon arrived in England in October 1501 and was placed in Elizabeth's care until her marriage. Catherine and Arthur were given a great state wedding before being sent to Ludlow to rule Wales. Disaster struck on 2 April 1502 when Arthur died suddenly. The news of his death was brought first to Henry, who sent for Elizabeth so that he could tell her himself. Both parents were grief-stricken, but Elizabeth tried to comfort Henry, pointing out that they were young enough to have more children and that they still had one son. Henry was calmed by Elizabeth's words, and she left him to return to her own chamber, where she gave way to her grief, falling on the floor and sobbing. Elizabeth's ladies rushed to Henry and he immediately joined his wife and comforted her in turn. No further proof of the close relationship that had developed between the couple is needed than their shared grief at the death of their eldest son.

Elizabeth conceived another child soon after Arthur's death and, on 10 February 1503, bore a daughter, whom she named Catherine. Elizabeth was a day short of her thirty-seventh birthday, an advanced age for childbearing at the time, and the labour was difficult. The next day, she quietly died, with her baby daughter following her to the grave shortly afterwards. Henry was devastated by Elizabeth's death, and he gave her a splendid funeral. In spite of the fact that she had played no political role, she was an admirable queen, and it was always through her that her son, Henry VIII, and her later descendants claimed their right to the crown.

The three Yorkist queens were all English by birth and upbringing, and whilst they sought to carry out the traditional role of queen, they also opened up the possibility of an Englishwoman becoming queen of England. This was a precedent followed in the Tudor dynasty, and of the six wives of Henry VIII, all but two were members of the English nobility.

Genealogical Tables

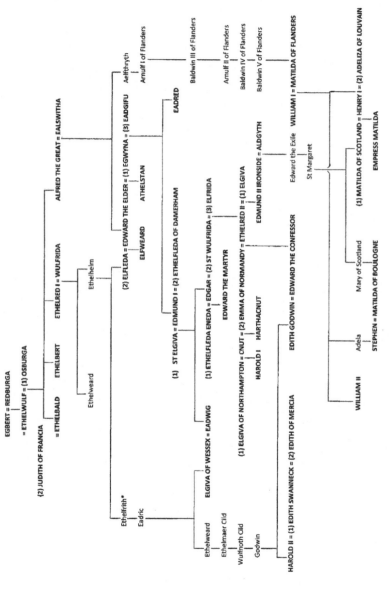

50. The Anglo-Saxon and Norman queens.

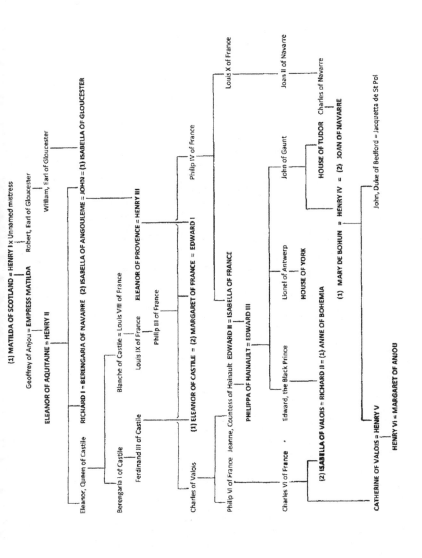

51. The Plantagenet and Lancastrian queens.

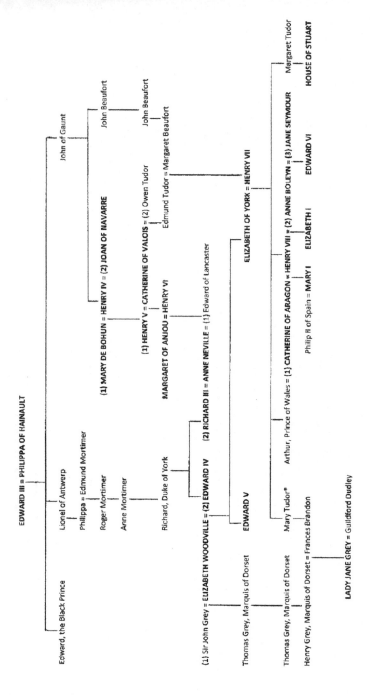

52. Yorkist queen consorts and Tudor queen regnants.

* Mary Tudor was actually the youngest surviving child

Notes & Bibliography

Due to the large scope of this work, it would be impossible to list all primary and secondary sources consulted. The main works used for each queen are listed below. Place of publication is London unless otherwise stated.

1 The Early & Mythical Queens

Sources used include
Bede, *Ecclesiastical History of the English People*, Sherley-Price, L., Latham, R. E., and Farmer, D. H. (eds) (1990).
Dio, C., *Roman History, vol. VIII*, Cary, E. (ed.) (1925).
Fairweather, J. (ed.), *Liber Eliensis: A History of the Isle of Ely* (Woodbridge, 2005).
Giles, J. A. (ed.), *Six Old English Chronicles* (1848) (which includes Geoffrey of Monmouth's *British History*, Nennius and the *Chronicle of Ethelweard*).
Gregory of Tours, *The History of the Franks*, Thorpe, L. (ed.) (1974).
Malory, T., *Morte d'Arthur*, Strachey, E. (ed.) (1868).
Roger of Wendover, *Flowers of History*, Giles, J. A. (ed.) (1849).
Tacitus, *Complete Works*, Hadas, M. (ed.) (New York, 1942).
William of Malmesbury, *The Kings Before the Conquest*, Stephenson, J. (ed.) (1854).

There are short biographies of many early queens in Hall, Mrs M., *The Queens Before the Conquest* (1854). Information on Rowen is from Geoffrey of Monmouth and Nennius. Sexburga is described in the *Chronicle of Ethelweard*. There are a number of works on Boudica, including Hingley, R., and Unwin, C., *Boudica: Iron Age Warrior Queen* (2005) and Bedoyere, G.

de la, *Defying Rome* (Stroud, 2003). There is one biography of Cartimandua: Howarth, N., *Cartimandua: Queen of the Brigantes* (Stroud, 2008). Bedoyere 2003 details Caratacus and Venutius. Klein, S. S., *Ruling Women: Queenship and Gender in Anglo-Saxon Literature* (Notre Dame, 2006) discusses Bertha. Pope Gregory's letter is from Hall 1854. Kirby, D. P., *The Earliest English Kings* (2000) discusses Cynethryth.

2 The Anglo-Saxon Queens

The leading sources are

Asser, *Life of King Alfred*, Keynes, S., and Lapidge, M. (eds) (2004).

Douglas, D. C., and Greenaway, G. W. (eds), *English Historical Documents vol. II: 1042–1189* (1981).

Florence of Worcester, *Chronicle*, Stevenson, J. (ed.) (1853).

Sawyer, P. H. (ed.), *Anglo-Saxon Charters* (1968) (charter numbers are abbreviated to S1454, for example).

Sturluson, Snorri, *Heimskringla: History of the Kings of Norway*, Hollander, L. M. (ed.) (Austen, 2002).

Swanton, M. (ed.), *The Anglo Saxon Chronicles* (2001) (*ASC*).

Whitelock, D. (ed.), *English Historical Documents vol. I: 500–1042* (1979).

William of Malmesbury, *The Deeds of the Bishops of England*, Preest, D. (ed.) (Woodbridge, 2002).

Norton, E., *She Wolves: The Notorious Queens of England* (Stroud, 2008) contains short biographies of some Anglo-Saxon and later queens. Where appropriate, spellings of Anglo-Saxon names have been modernised and simplified.

Redburga

Egbert's campaigns are in the *ASC*. Asser describes Queen Edburga. Woodruff, D., *The Life and Times of Alfred the Great* (1974) details Egbert's kingship. The *Annals of St Bertin* are in Whitelock. William of Malmesbury (Preest) comments on Ethelwulf's upbringing.

Osburga

Asser and Florence of Worcester are the main source for Osburga. Woodruff 1974 also describes her.

Judith of Francia

Nelson, J. L., *Charles the Bald* (1992) and Kirby 2000 detail Judith's life. The *Annals of St Bertin* are in Whitelock. Judith's coronation is discussed in Nelson, J. L., *Politics and Ritual in Early Medieval Europe* (1986) and Stafford, P., 'Charles the Bald, Judith and England' in Gibson, M. T. and Nelson, J. L. (ed.), *Charles the Bald: Court and Kingdom* (Aldershot, 1990). William of Malmesbury (Stephenson) discusses Ethelbald's rebellion. A surviving charter of Ethelbald is S151.

Wulfrida

Stenton, F., *Anglo-Saxon England* (Oxford, 1971) discusses the Viking raids. Asser describes Ethelred's kingship and death. Yorke, B., 'Edward as Æthling', in Higham, N. J. and Hill, D. H. (eds), *Edward the Elder* (2001) suggests that Wulfrida may have been crowned. Charter 56 in Pierquin, H. (ed.), *Recueil General Des Chartes Anglo-Saxonnes 604–1061* (Paris, 1912) is witnessed by Wulfrida. Ethelwold's rebellion is in *ASC* Winchester 901.

Ealswitha

The main source for Ealswitha is Asser. The charters attested by Mucil are S340 and S1201. *ASC* Winchester 903 calls Ealswitha's brother an ealdorman. Charter S1442 names him as a member of the Mercian royal family.

Egwyna

The main sources for Egwyna are William of Malmesbury (Stephenson) and Florence of Worcester. Sharp, S., 'The West Saxon Tradition of Dynastic Marriage: with special reference to Edward the Elder' in Higham and Hill 2001 discusses Egwyna.

Elfleda

Stafford, P., 'The King's Wife in Wessex, 800–1066', in Damico, H., and Olsen, A.H. (eds), *New Readings on Women in Old English Literature* (Bloomington, 1990) discusses Elfleda. Nelson 1986 suggests that Elfleda may have been crowned. Coatsworth, E., 'The Embroideries from the Tomb of St Cuthbert' in Higham and Hill 2001 notes Elfleda's commission of the embroidery.

Edgiva

The main source for Edgiva is William of Malmesbury (Stephenson). Hart, C., 'Two Queens of England' (*Ampleforth Journal* 82, 1977) and Stafford,

P., *Queens, Concubines and Dowagers* (1983) give information on Edgiva. Charters from Edmund and Eadred's reign are S489, S562 and S1511. Eadred's Will is S1515. The *Life of Dunstan* is in Whitelock. St Ethelwold is described in Ælfric's *Life of St Æthelwold* (Whitelock) and Wulfstan of Winchester, *The Life of St Æthelwold* (Oxford, 1991). Dunstan's exile is in *ASC* 957. The New Minster Charter is in Miller, S. (ed.), *Charters of the New Minster, Winchester* (Oxford, 2001). The *Liber Eliensis* records Edgiva's bequests to Ely Abbey.

St Elgiva

S755 contains a grant made by Edgar to his maternal grandmother, Wynfleda. Florence of Worcester and William of Malmesbury (Stephenson and Preest) are the main sources for Elgiva. Campbell, A. (ed.), *The Chronicle of Æthelweard* (1962) notes her death.

Ethelfleda of Damerham

ASC Worcester 946 records Ethelfleda's marriage and Edmund's death. Ethelfleda's Will is S1494.

Elgiva of Wessex

Elgiva's Will is S1484. William of Malmesury (Stephenson) and the *Chronicle of Æthelweard* are the main sources for Elgiva. Elgiva's relationship with Bishop Ethelwold is in Yorke, B., 'Æthelwold and the Politics of the Tenth Century', in Yorke, B. (ed.), *Bishop Æthelwold: His Career and Influence* (Woodbridge, 1997). Florence of Worcester, William of Malmesbury (Preest) and *ASC* Worcester 958 describe the attacks on Eadwig, and Elgiva's divorce. The grants to Elgiva are S737 and S738.

Ethelfleda Eneda

Ethelfleda's background is described in William of Malmesbury (Stephenson).

St Wulfrida

Yorke, B., 'The Legitimacy of St Edith' (*The Haskins Society Journal* 11, 1998) describes Wulfrida. Stubbs, W. (ed.), *Memorials of St Dunstan* (Rolls Series, 1874) contains the *Life of St Dunstan*, which describes Edgar's affair with a nun. Elfrida's conflict with Wulfhilde is in '*La Vie de Sainte Vulfhilde Par Goscelin De Cantorbéry*' (*Analecta Bollandiana* 32).

Elfrida

William of Malmesbury (Stephenson) describes Elfrida. Her first marriage is in Gaimar's *Lestoire des Engles Solum,* Hardy, T. D., and Martin, C. T. (eds) (1888), Hart, C., 'Athelstan 'Half-King' and his Family' (*Anglo-Saxon England* 2, 1973) and Macray, W. D. (ed.), *Chronicon Abbatiae Rameseiensis* (1886). Elfrida's dower is S725. Edgar's changes to the monasteries are in Symons, D. T. (ed.), *Regularis Concordia: The Monastic Agreement of Monks and Nuns of the English Nation* (1953). The *Life of St Oswald* is in Whitelock. The earliest account of Edward's murder is in *ASC* 979 (version E). Osbern's *Life of St Dunstan* is in Stubbs 1874. The renewal of the freedom of Taunton is in Robertson, A. J. (ed.), *Anglo-Saxon Charters* (Cambridge, 1939). Elfrida's letter is from Harmer, F. E. (ed.), *Anglo-Saxon Writs* (Manchester, 1952).

Elgiva

Ethelred's reign is described in Lavelle, R., *Aethelred II* (Stroud, 2002) and Williams, A., *Æthelred the Unready: The Ill-Counselled King* (2003). Stafford 1983 comments on Elgiva.

Emma of Normandy

Works on Emma include Stafford, P., *Queen Emma and Queen Edith* (Oxford, 1997), O'Brien, H., *Queen Emma and the Vikings* (2005) and Strachan, I., *Emma the Twice-Crowned Queen* (2004). The leading source is Campbell, A. (ed.), *Encomium Emmae Reginae* (Cambridge, 1998) (the *Encomium*). Emma's background is in Wace, *The History of the Norman People* (Woodbridge, 2004). The letter from Pope John XV is in Whitelock. The quotation suggesting Edward was named as heir is from Barlow, F. (ed.), *The Life of King Edward who Rests at Westminster* (1962) (*King Edward*). *ASC* Peterborough 1013 records Ethelred's exile. *ASC* Peterborough 1017 notes Cnut's marriage to Emma. Archbishop Wulfstan's letter is in Whitelock. The reburial of St Alfheah is in *ASC* 1023 Winchester. Emma's plot to make Harthacnut king of Denmark is in the *Heimskringla*. *ASC* Worcester 1035 records Cnut's death. Emma's letter to her sons is from the *Encomium*. The seizure of Emma's goods by Edward is in *ASC* Peterborough 1042 and William of Malmesbury (Preest).

Aldgyth

William of Malmesbury (Stephenson) is the main source for Aldgyth.

Elgiva of Northampton

Campbell, M. W., 'Queen Emma and Ælfgifu of Northampton: Canute the Great's Women' (*Medieval Scandinavia* 4, 1971) details Elgiva. The main source for Elgiva is the *Heimskringla*. Florence of Worcester describes Elgiva's family background and the rumours about the births of her sons.

Edith Godwin

The main work on Edith is Stafford 1997. Barlow, F., *The Godwins* (2002) and Mason, E., *The House of Godwine* (2004) feature Edith. The main source for Edith is *King Edward*. William of Malmesbury (Stephenson) describes Edith's education and marriage. Florence of Worcester and William of Malmesbury (Stephenson) recount the attempt to divorce Edith. William of Poitiers (Douglas and Greenaway) states that Edward made William his heir. John of Worcester, *Chronicle,* McGurk, P. (ed.) (Oxford, 1998) notes Edith's death and burial.

Edith Swanneck

Walker, I. W., *Harold: The Last Anglo-Saxon King* (Stroud, 1997) and Barlow detail Edith.

Edith of Mercia

The main work on Edith is Beech, G., 'England and Aquitaine in the Century Before the Norman Conquest' (*Anglo-Saxon England* 19, 1990), which suggests that she died in France. Walker also details Edith's life. Orderic Vitalis, *The Ecclesiastical History, vol. II*, Chibnall, M. (ed.) (Oxford, 1968) describes Edith's family. Edith's father's exiles are in *ASC* Peterborough 1055 and *ASC* Worcester 1058. Gruffydd's death is in *ASC* Peterborough 1063. Florence of Worcester claims that Edith's brothers left Hastings to move her from London. The death of Edwin and the capture of Morcar are in *ASC* Worcester 1072. William of Malmesbury (Stephenson) notes young Harold's role in the King of Norway's campaigns.

3 The Norman Queens

The leading primary sources for the Norman queens are
Orderic Vitalis, *The Ecclesiastical History, vols III-VI,* Chibnall, M. (ed.) (Oxford, 1973–83).
Potter, K. R. (ed.), *Gesta Stephani* (Oxford, 1976).
Van Houts, E. (ed.), *The Normans in Europe* (Manchester, 2000).
William of Malmesbury, *Gesta Regnum Angorum, vol. I*, Mynors, R. A. B. (ed.) (Oxford, 1998).

William of Malmesbury, *Historia Novella,* King, E., and Potter, K. R. (eds) (Oxford, 1998).

Wood, M. A. E. (ed.), *Letters of Royal and Illustrious Ladies, 3 vols* (1846).

There are short biographies of most of the post-Conquest queens in Strickland, A., *Lives of the Queens of England, 12 vols* (1844).

Matilda of Flanders

Fettu, A., *Queen Matilda* (Orep, 2005) details Matilda. William of Poitiers is from Douglas and Greenaway. Orderic Vitalis vol. II details Matilda's background, family and piety. William of Malmesbury (Mynors) comments on Matilda's wisdom. Strickland notes Matilda's love for the English ambassador. Matilda's gift of a flagship to William is in 'The Ship List of William the Conqueror' (Van Houts 2000). The foundation charter for Lewes priory is in Douglas and Greenaway. Matilda's coronation is discussed in Gathagan, L. L., 'The Trappings of Power: the Coronation of Matilda of Flanders' (*The Haskins Society Journal* 13, 1999). The quotation on Matilda's love for Robert is from Orderic Vitalis vol. III.

Matilda of Scotland

The only biography of Matilda is Huneycutt, L. L., *Matilda of Scotland: A Study in Medieval Queenship* (Woodbridge, 2003), which also contains a translation of the *Life of St Margaret*. Menzies, L., *St Margaret, Queen of Scotland* (London, 1925) details Matilda's early life. Orderic Vitalis vol. IV records Matilda's time at Romsey. Eadmer, *History of Recent Events in England,* Bosanquet, G. (ed.) (1964) recounts the controversy over whether Matilda was a nun. William of Malmesbury (Mynors) records that Matilda wore the veil to reject suitors. John of Worcester describes Matilda's coronation. Matilda's letters are from Wood.

Adeliza of Louvain

Thompson, K., 'Queen Adeliza and the Lotharingian Connection' (*Sussex Archaeological Collections* 140, 2002) and Wertheimer, L., 'Adeliza of Louvain and Anglo-Norman Queenship' (*Haskins Society Journal* 7, 1997) contain details of Adeliza. John of Worcester notes Adeliza's parentage. Adeliza's marriage and coronation is in *ASC* Peterborough 1121. William of Malmesbury (King and Potter) notes the visit of the Empress Matilda to Arundel.

Matilda of Boulogne

Tanner, H. J., 'Queenship: Office, Custom, or Ad Hoc? The Case of Queen Matilda III of England (135–1152)', in Wheeler, B., and Parsons, J. C. (eds), *Eleanor of Aquitaine: Lord and Lady* (Basingstoke, 2002) details Matilda. Her activities are described in Green, J. A., *The Aristocracy of Norman England* (Cambridge, 1997), Crouch, D., *The Reign of King Stephen* (Harlow, 2000) and Matthew, D., *King Stephen* (2002). Matilda is prominent in the *Gesta Stephani*. William of Malmesbury (King and Potter) records that Henry I arranged Matilda's marriage and that of her parents. Given-Wilson, C., *The Royal Bastards of Medieval England* (1984) describes Stephen's illegitimate son. Henry of Huntingdon, *Chronicle*, Forester, T. (ed.) (1853) describes Stephen's seizure of the crown. Orderic Vitalis vol. VI records Matilda's siege of Dover. Henry of Huntingdon (Douglas and Greenaway) describes the Battle of Lincoln and its aftermath. The *Gesta Stephani* discusses Matilda of Boulogne's triumphant entry to London after the Empress's expulsion and the siege of Winchester. Robert of Gloucester's capture is from William of Malmesbury (King and Potter).

Empress Matilda

The most detailed biography of Matilda is Chibnall, M., *The Empress Matilda* (Oxford, 1991). Two other biographies are Pain, N., *Empress Matilda: Uncrowned Queen of England* (1978) and Bradbury, J., *Stephen and Matilda* (Stroud, 2005). There is a chapter on Matilda in Fraser, A., *The Warrior Queens* (1988). *ASC* Peterborough 1109 records the arrangements for Matilda's first marriage. Robert of Torigni is quoted from Van Houts. Details of the Emperor Henry V are from Mommsen, T. E., and Morrison, K. F. (eds), *Imperial Lives and Letters of the Eleventh Century* (New York, 2000). This work includes a translation of the *Life of the Emperor Henry IV*, which describes Henry V's seizure of the Imperial crown and a letter of Henry IV's, which is quoted from. *ASC* Peterborough 1127 records that Matilda's second marriage was unpopular in England. John of Worcester describes Matilda's landing in England in 1139 and her activities at Bristol. The *Gesta Stephani* and William of Malmesbury (King and Potter) describe the Council at Winchester. Chibnall, M., 'The Charters of the Empress Matilda', in Garnett, G., and Hudson, J. (eds), *Law and Government in Medieval England and Normandy* (Cambridge, 1994) discusses whether Matilda was called Queen. Matilda's letter is from Wood.

4 The Plantagenet Queens

The main sources used are

Capgrave, J., *Chronicle of England*, Hingeston, F. (ed.) (1858).

Crawford, A. (ed.), *Letters of the Queens of England* (Stroud, 2002).

Froissart, J., *Chronicle, 6 vols*, Berners, Lord (trans.) (1901).

John of Salisbury, *The History Pontificalis of John of Salisbury*, Chibnall, M. (ed.) (Oxford, 1986).

Myers, A. R. (ed.), *English Historical Documents, vol. IV: 1327–1485* (1969).

Nicholson, H. (ed.), *Chronicle of the Third Crusade: A Translation of the 'Itinerarium Peregrinorum et Gesta Regis Ricardi* (Aldershot, 1997).

Paris, M., *Monachi Sancti Albani, Chronica Majora, vol. II*, Luard, H. R. (ed.) (1874).

Paris, M., 'The Chronica Majora 1247–1250', in Vaughan, R. (ed.), *Chronicles of Matthew Paris* (Gloucester, 1984).

Richard of Devizes, *The Chronicle of the Time of King Richard the First*, Appleby, J. T. (ed.) (1963).

Roger de Hoveden, *The Annals*, in Riley, H. T. (ed.) (Felinfach, 1997).

Rothwell, H. (ed.), *English Historical Documents, vol. III: 1189–1327* (1975).

William of Newburgh, *The History of English Affairs*, Walsh, P. G. and Kennedy, M. J. (eds), Book I (Warminster, 1988).

Eleanor of Aquitaine

There are a number of works on Eleanor of Aquitaine, including Meade, M., *Eleanor of Aquitaine* (1977), Boyd, D., *Eleanor: April Queen of Aquitaine* (Stroud, 2004), Huneycutt, L. L., 'Alianora Regina Anglorum: Eleanor of Aquitaine and her Anglo-Norman Predecessors as Queen of England', in Wheeler, B., and Parsons, J. C. (eds), *Eleanor of Aquitaine: Lord and Lady* (Basingstoke, 2002), Kelly, A., *Eleanor of Aquitaine and the Four Kings* (Cambridge, 1950), Martindale, J., 'Eleanor of Aquitaine: The Last Years', in Church, S. D. (ed.), *King John: New Interpretations* (Woodbridge, 2003) and Weir, A., *Eleanor of Aquitaine* (1999). Eleanor's comments that she had married a monk are from William of Newburgh. The crusade is described in Odo of Deuil, *De Profectione Ludovici VII in Orientem*, Berry, V. G. (ed.) (New York, 1948) and John of Salisbury. Gerald of Wales (Douglas and Greenaway) describes Henry II and his visit to Paris. Roger de Hoveden describes the death of the Young King. Matthew Paris (Luard) describes Eleanor's release from prison and the early days of Richard's reign. Richard of Devizes records

John's conduct during Richard's absence. Richard's imprisonment and release is in Matthew Paris (Luard). Eleanor's letters are from Crawford.

Berengaria of Navarre

There are two biographies of Berengaria: Mitchell, M., *Berengaria: Enigmatic Queen of England* (Burwash Weald, 1986) and Trinidade, A., *Berengaria: In Search of Richard the Lionheart's Queen* (Bodmin, 1999). Berengaria's marriage is described in the *Gesta Regis Ricardi*. Richard of Devizes records Alais's affair with Henry II. The same two sources note the conquest of Cyprus and the crusade. The Bishop of Lincoln's rebuke to Richard is from Douie, D. L., and Farmer, H. (eds), *The Life of St Hugh of Lincoln, vol. II* (1962). Pope Innocent's letters are from Cheney, C. R., and Cheney, M. G. (eds), *The Letters of Pope Innocent III (1198–1216) Concerning England and Wales* (Oxford, 1967). Berengaria's letters are from Wood.

Isabella of Gloucester

Patterson, R. B. (ed.), *Earldom of Gloucester Charters* (Oxford, 1973) describes Isabella's life. Charters referred to are from this source. Richardson, H. G., 'The Marriage and Coronation of Isabelle of Angoulême' (*English Historical Review* 61, 1946) describes Isabella of Gloucester's background and her marriage to John. Roger de Hoveden details the marriage of Isabella and John. Richardson, H. G., 'King John and Isabelle of Angoulême' (*English Historical Review* 65, 1950) claims that no dispensation was sought. Warren, W. L., *King John* (1997) details John's activities during Richard's reign and his attempts to marry Alais of France.

Isabella of Angoulême

Works on Isabella include Cazel, F. A., and Painter, S., 'The Marriage of Isabelle of Angoulême' (*English Historical Review* 63, 1948), Cazel, F. A., and Painter, S., 'The Marriage of Isabelle of Angoulême' (*English Historical Review* 67, 1952), Richardson 1946, Richardson 1950, and Vincent, N., 'Isabella of Angoulême: John's Jezebel' in Church, S. D. (ed.), *King John: New Interpretations* (Woodbridge, 2003). She is described in Snellgrove, H. S., *The Lusignans in England 1247–1258* (Albuquerque, 1950). Matthew Paris (Luard) describes Isabella's marriage and the Dauphin's invasion. Isabella's letters are in Crawford and Wood.

Eleanor of Provence

The leading biography of Eleanor is Howell, M., *Eleanor of Provence* (Oxford, 1998). Other works include Goldstone, N., *Four Queens: The Provençal Sisters who Ruled Europe* (New York, 2007), Howell, M., 'Notes and Documents: The Resources of Eleanor of Provence as Queen Consort' (*English Historical Review* 102, 1987) and Biles, M., 'The Indominable Belle: Eleanor of Provence, Queen of England' in Bowers, R. H. (ed.), *Seven Studies in Medieval English History and Other Historical Essays* (Jackson, 1983). Strickland claims that Eleanor composed a poem about a Cornish hero. Eleanor's letters are from Wood 1846 and Crawford 2002. Ridgeway, H. W., 'Foreign Favourites and Henry III's Problems of Patronage, 1247–1258' (*English Historical Review* 104, 1989) details the favouritism of the Savoyards. Henry III's letter to Alexander III is in Shirley, W. W. (ed.), *Royal and Other Historical Letters Illustrative of the Reigh of Henry III, vol. II* (1866). Matthew Paris (Vaughan) describes the Lusignans. Matthew Paris (Rothwell) records Edward's move toward the Lusignan faction and Louis's refusal to receive them. Stubbs, W., 'Annales Londoniensis' in *Chronicles of the Reigns of Edward I and Edward II, 2 vols* (1882) notes Edward's reconciliation with his father. The *Annals of Dunstable* (Rothwell) describe Edward's raid on the Temple and Eleanor's attempt to leave the Tower. The *Annales Londoniensis* describe Edward's escape from prison.

Eleanor of Castile

Works on Eleanor include Parsons, J. C., *Eleanor of Castile* (New York, 1998), Powrie, J., *Eleanor of Castile* (Studley, 1990), and a collection of essays in Parsons, D., (ed.), *Eleanor of Castile 1290–1990* (Stamford, 1991). Prestwich, M., *Edward I* (1997) also details Eleanor. Eleanor's letters are from Wood 1846. Capgrave describes the assassination attempt. Camden, W., *Britannia*, Piggot, S. (ed.) (Newton Abbott, 1971) recounts that Eleanor sucked poison from Edward's wounds. Parsons, J. C., 'The Court and Household of Eleanor of Castile in 1290' (Pontifical Institute of Medieval Studies 37, 1977) contains Eleanor's household accounts.

Margaret of France

There are no works specifically on Margaret but details of her life are in Prestwich. The *Chronicle of Peter Langcroft* is in Rothwell. The Song of the Scottish Wars is in Wright, T., (ed.), *The Political Songs of England* (1839). Edward's letters are from Chaplais, P., 'Notes and Documents of Some Private

Letters of Edward I' (*English Historical Review* 77, 1962). Margaret's letters are from Crawford 2002. Margaret's death is in Stubbs, W., 'Annales Paulini' in *Chronicles of the Reigns of Edward I and Edward II, 2 vols* (1882).

Isabella of France

There are two biographies of Isabella: Doherty, P., *Isabella and the Strange Death of Edward II* (2003) and Weir, A., *Isabella: She-Wolf of France, Queen of England* (2005). Articles on Isabella are Bond, E. A., 'Notices of the Last Days of Isabella, Queen of Edward the Second, Drawn from an Account of the Expenses of her Household' (*Archaeologia* 36, 1853) and Menache, S., 'Isabella of France, Queen of England – A Reconsideration' (*Journal of Medieval History* 10, 1984). The leading primary sources are Froissart and Maxwell, H. (ed.), *The Chronicle of Lanercost* (Glasgow, 1913). Details of Isabella's early life and marriage are from *The Chronicle of Lanercost*. The *Annales Paulini* record that Edward sent his wedding presents to Gaveston. Capgrave records Gaveston's conduct at the coronation. Isabella's letter to Edward is from Crawford. *The Chronicle of Lanercost* describes the murder of Gaveston. Conway Davies, J., *The Baronial Opposition to Edward II* (1967) records Isabella's efforts in securing the see of Durham for her candidate. Capgrave describes the Leeds Castle incident. Fryde, N., *The Tyranny and Fall of Edward II* (Cambridge, 1979) records the invasion of Gascony and the *Annales Paulini* relates the seizure of Isabella's lands. *The Chronicle of Lanercost* and Froissart describe Isabella's time in France. Mortimer's life is described in Mortimer, I., *The Greatest Traitor* (2003). Isabella's proclamation is from Crawford. The *Pipewell Chronicle* (Rothwell 1975) describes Edward II's abdication. The *Chronicle of Geoffrey Le Baker* (Myers 1969) details the execution of Kent and Edward III's attack on Mortimer. The quotation from the Bard is from Gray, T., *The Complete Poems,* Starr, H. W. and Hendrickson, J. R. (eds) (Oxford, 1966).

Philippa of Hainault

The only biography of Philippa is Hardy, B. C., *Philippa of Hainault and Her Times* (1910). Packe, M., *King Edward III* (1983) also details her life. The main source is Froissart, who Philippa knew personally. Le Bel, J., *Chronique de Jean Le Bel,* Viard, J., and Deprez, E. (eds) (Paris, 1904) records Isabella of France's visit to Hainault. The *Pipewell Chronicle* (Rothwell 1975) details parliament's agreement to the marriage. Magrath, J. R., *The Queen's College, vol. I* (Oxford, 1921) details Philippa's foundation of Queen's College, Cambridge. Ormrod,

W. M., *The Reign of Edward III* (1990) describes Edward's affair with Alice Perrers.

Anne of Bohemia

There are no works specifically on Anne of Bohemia, although Bevan, B., *King Richard II* (1990) and Saul, N., *The Three Richards* (2005) detail her life. The main sources are Froissart and Hector, L. C., and Harvey, B. F. (eds), *The Westminster Chronicle 1381–1394* (Oxford, 1982). Froissart discusses the Great Schism. Hayward's account of Anne's sea crossing is in Hayward, J., *The Life and Raigne of King Henrie IIII*, Manning, J. J. (ed.) (1991). Anne's books are discussed in Bell, S. G., 'Medieval Women Book Owners: Arbiters of Lay Piety and Ambassadors of Culture', in Erler, M. and Kowaleski, M. (eds), *Women and Power in the Middle Ages* (Athens, 1988). The *Westminster Chronicle* records the favouritism of Bohemians and Anne's death.

Isabella of Valois

Palmer, J. J. N., *England, France and Christendom 1377–99* (1972), Bevan and Saul contain details of Isabella's life. Hayward comments that the marriage was unpopular with Richard's uncles. Philippe de Mézières's letter is in Coopland, G. W. (ed.), *Letter to King Richard II* (Liverpool, 1975). Isabella's entry to London is from Strickland. Froissart describes Gloucester's plot and his murder. Hayward describes Henry IV's seizure of the crown.

5 The Lancastrian Queens

Major sources for the Lancastrians include Froissart, Capgrave, Hayward, and the selected documents in Myers 1969. Further sources include
Dockray, K. (ed.), *Henry VI, Margaret of Anjou and the Wars of the Roses: A Source Book* (Stroud, 2000).
Gairdner, J. (ed.), *The Paston Letters, 3 vols* (Westminster, 1896).
Hall, E., *Chronicle Containing the History of England*, Johnson, J., *et al* (eds) (1809).

Mary de Bohun

Details of Mary's life are in Mortimer, I., *The Fears of Henry IV* (2007) and Weir, A., *Katherine Swynford* (2007). The main sources are Froissart and Hayward.

Joan of Navarre

Strohm, P., 'Joanna of Navarre: That Obscure Object of Desire' in *England's Empty Throne* (1998) describes Joan. Kirby, J. L., *Henry IV of England* (1970) contains details of Joan's life. Joan's childhood and first marriage is discussed in Jones, M., *Ducal Brittany 1364–1399* (Oxford, 1970), Jones, M., *Between France and England* (Aldershot, 2000) and Strickland. Mortimer 2007 discusses Joan and Henry's love match. Joan's letters are from Wood. Henry's illness is noted in the *Eulogium Historiarum* (Myers 1969). Joan's imprisonment is in Myers, A. R., 'The Captivity of a Royal Witch: The Household Accounts of Queen Joan of Navarre' in *Crown, Household and Parliament in Fifteenth-Century England* (1985).

Catherine of Valois

Loades, D., *Tudor Queens of England* (2009) contains a section on Catherine. She is also described in Griffiths, R. A., and Thomas, R. S., *The Making of the Tudor Dynasty* (Stroud, 1985). Strickland details Catherine's troubled childhood. Shakespeare, W., 'Henry V' in Wells, S., and Taylor, G. (eds), *The Oxford Shakespeare: The Complete Works* (Oxford, 1998) is quoted. Henry and Catherine's progress is noted in the *Chronicle of John Strecche* (Myers 1969). The *Chronicle of London* is in Myers 1969. Griffiths, R. A., *King and Country: England and Wales in the Fifteenth Century* (1991) details Catherine's relationship with Edmund Beaufort. *Hall's Chronicle* discusses Catherine's second marriage. Pepys, S., *The Illustrated Pepys,* Latham, R. (ed.) (2000) is quoted.

Margaret of Anjou

Works on Margaret include Archer, R. E., 'Queen Margaret of Anjou, Queen Consort of Henry VI: A Reassessment' in *Crown, Government and People in the Fifteenth Century* (Stroud, 1995), Bagley, J. J., *Margaret of Anjou*, Erlanger, P., *Margaret of Anjou* (1970), Haswell, J., *The Ardent Queen*, and Maurer, H. E., *Margaret of Anjou* (Woodbridge, 2003). There is information on Margaret in Cron, B. M., 'The Duke of Suffolk, the Angevin Marriage, and the Ceding of Maine, 1445' (*Journal of Medieval History* 20, 1994), Laynesmith, J. L., *The Last Medieval Queens* (Oxford, 2004), Lee, P. A., 'Reflections of Power: Margaret of Anjou and the Dark Side of Queenship' (*Renaissance Quarterly* 39, 1986), Griffiths, R. A., *The Reign of King Henry VI* (Stroud, 1998), and Storey, R. L., *The End of the House of Lancaster* (Stroud, 1999). The couple's first meeting is described in Report to Bianca Maria Visconti Duchess of Milan, 24 October

1458 (Dockray). Polydore Vergil and *Wherhamsted's Register* are from Dockray. Warwick's comments on Margaret are from Dockray. Margaret's attempts to secure Henry's recognition of their son are from Paston letters 195 and 226. *Hall's Chronicle* details York's claims to the throne. Margaret's letter is from Wood. Paston letters 385 and 687 detail Margaret's defeat at Towton and captivity.

6 The Yorkist Queens

The main sources for the Yorkist Queens are
Bacon, F., *History of the Reign of King Henry VII*, Lumby, J. R. (ed.) (Cambridge, 1885).
Dockray, K. (ed.), *Edward IV: A Source Book* (Stroud, 1999).
Halliwell, J. O., *Warkworth's Chronicle of the First Thirteen Years of the Reign of King Edward the Fourth* (Llanerch, 1990).
More, T., *The History of King Richard III* (2005).
Mancini, D., *The Usurpation of Richard III*, Armstrong, C. A. J. (ed.) (Gloucester, 1984).
Pronay, N. and Cox, J., *The Crowland Chronicle Continuatios: 1459–1486* (1986).

Elizabeth Woodville
There are two recent works on Elizabeth Woodville: Baldwin, D., *Elizabeth Woodville* (Stroud, 2002) and Okerlund, A., *Elizabeth Wydeville: The Slandered Queen* (Stroud, 2005). Laynesmith also discusses Elizabeth. More recounts that Elizabeth considered herself too good to be Edward's concubine. *Warkworth's Chronicle* records the secret marriage. More and Mancini note Cecily Neville's fury. The *Annales Rerum Anglicarum* is from Dockray. Elizabeth's household is discussed in Myers 1985. Elizabeth's letter is from Wood. Edward and Elizabeth's pilgrimages to Walsingham and Canterbury are in Paston letter 676. The proclamation made by Warwick, Clarence and the Archbishop of York is from Dockray. Paston letter 654 records Elizabeth's move to sanctuary in 1470. More and the *Crowland Chronicle Continuations* relate Richard III's coup. More recounts Elizabeth's surrender of her youngest son. Philippe de Commines is quoted from Dockray.

Anne Neville
The only biography of Anne is Hicks, M., *Anne Neville* (Stroud, 2006). Further details about her are in Laynesmith 2004, Hicks, M., 'Warwick – The

Reluctant Kingmaker' (*Medieval History* 1, 1991), Hicks, M., *False, Fleeting, Perjur'd Clarence* (Bangor, 1992), Saul 2005 and Seward, D., *Richard III: England's Black Legend* (1997). The *Crowland Chronicle Continuations* details the feud between Edward and Warwick and Clarence. Anne Beauchamp's petition is from Wood. Hicks, M., 'One Prince or Two? The Family of Richard III' (*The Ricardian* 9, 1993) details Edward of Middleham's birth. *Hall's Chronicle* describes the coronation. The *Crowland Chronicle Continuations* notes the rivalry between Anne and Elizabeth of York.

Elizabeth of York

There are two biographies of Elizabeth: Okerlund, A., *Elizabeth of York* (Basingstoke, 2009) and Harvey, N. L., *Elizabeth of York* (1973). Nicolas, N. H. (ed.), *Privy Purse Expenses of Elizabeth of York* (1830) contains Elizabeth's expenses as queen and details of her life. Visser-Fuchs, L., 'Where Did Elizabeth of York Find Consolation?' (*The Ricardian* 9, 1993) records Richard III's plan to marry Elizabeth. Bacon describes Henry VII's accession and his marriage to Elizabeth. Elizabeth's letter is from Wood. Elizabeth's death is recorded in *Hall's Chronicle*. Her funeral is described in Baker, R., *A Chronicle of the Kings of England from the time of the Romans unto the Death of King James* (1696).

List of Illustrations

1. Extract from the manuscript of the ninth-century writer Asser, who recorded details of Queen Edburga, wife of King Beohtric. © Jonathan Reeve JR2236b39p652 1000110O.

2. Viking warriors. Scene from a viking-age picture stone from Stenkyrka, Gotland, Sweden. © Jonathan Reeve JR2230b39p473 700800.

3. Head of Alfred the Great from a silver penny. © Jonathan Reeve JR2237b39p670 800900.

4. A passage from a letter from Alfred the Great to Bishop Werferth. © Jonathan Reeve JR2233b39p599 800900.

5. The coffin of St Cuthbert, one of the most important medieval saints of England, venerated by many English queens. Elfleda, Edward the Elder's queen, is known to have been pious, and at some point during her time as queen, she commissioned embroideries to adorn the tomb of St Cuthbert. © Jonathan Reeve JR2232b39fp555 600700.

6. A Viking ship. Scene from a viking-age picture stone from Stenkyrka, Gotland, Sweden. © Jonathan Reeve JR2231b39fp488 700800.

7. Queen Bertha in stained glass at Canterbury Cathedral. Bertha has been credited with bringing Christianity to England, and her family insisted that she be granted the freedom to practise her faith in Kent. (Elizabeth Norton)

8. Queen Bertha from Canterbury Cathedral. The Frankish princess founded the first Anglo-Saxon Christian church in England. (Elizabeth Norton)

9. A folio from the manuscript by the early British chronicler Nennius (*Historia Brittonum*) and the earliest mention of King Arthur, who was a real historical figure, unlike his queen, Guinevere, who was purely mythical. © Jonathan Reeve JR2226b38fp122c 1000110O.

10. Offa's Dyke. The great barrier built between England and Wales stands today as a testament to King Offa's power. (Elizabeth Norton)

11. Silver penny of Cynethryth. Cynethryth was the most notorious of the early queens. The wife of King Offa of Mercia, Cynethryth (died after 798) is the only Anglo-Saxon queen to have minted her own coins. © Jonathan Reeve JR2235b39fp650 700800.

12. Offa from an thirteenth-century English manuscript. © Jonathan Reeve JR2223b99plateI 12001300.

13. A statue of King Alfred at Winchester. Alfred is remembered as having been one of the greatest kings England ever had, and most of the later kings and queens of England were his descendants. (Elizabeth Norton)

14. Winchester Cathedral. Winchester was the capital of the Anglo-Saxon kingdom of Wessex, and a number of early queens are associated with the cathedral and monasteries there. Alfred the Great's wife, Queen Ealswitha, is buried here in the New Minster beside her husband. It was rare for Anglo-Saxon queens to be buried with their husbands, and this is a further indication that Ealswitha enjoyed a happy life and a long and contented marriage. (Peter2010)

15. The ruins of St Oswald's Minster, Gloucester. The original church was built on the orders of Ethelfleda of Mercia, the daughter of King Alfred and an important Anglo-Saxon ruler in her own right. (Elizabeth Norton)

16. The *Anglo-Saxon Chronicle*. The *Anglo-Saxon Chronicle* mentions Ethelfleda of Damerham as Edmund I's queen. © Stephen Porter.

17. The coronation of King Edgar at Bath Abbey. Unusually for the Anglo-Saxon period, Elfrida, Edgar's queen, shared his coronation. (Elizabeth Norton)

18. Queen Emma's Mortuary Chest at Winchester Cathedral. The Queen shares her grave with her second husband, King Cnut, and son, King Harthacnut. (David Sawtell)

19. Queen Edith at King Edward the Confessor's deathbed from the Bayeux Tapestry. With special permission from the city of Bayeux.

20. A page from a gospel book belonging to St Margaret, a descendant of the Anglo-Saxon royal dynasty and the mother of Matilda of Scotland. (Elizabeth Norton)

21. The coat of arms of Matilda of Flanders, the first Norman queen of England, from Lincoln Cathedral. Matilda's descent from the English royal family and close relationship with the kings of France was a deciding factor in William the Conqueror's choice of her as a bride. © Gordon Plumb.

22. The coat of arms of Matilda of Boulogne, the wife of King Stephen, from Lincoln Cathedral. Stephen relied on his wife to aid him in his war with his cousin, the Empress Matilda, and Matilda of Boulogne proved herself to be an effective military commander. © Gordon Plumb.

23. A depiction of St Catherine in a stained-glass window from the church at Deerhurst in Gloucestershire. The saint is depicted in the dress of a medieval queen. (Elizabeth Norton)

24. Isabella of Angoulême from her tomb at Fontrevaud. © Elizabeth Norton.

25. Eleanor of Aquitaine from her tomb at Fontrevaud Abbey. The abbey became the mausoleum of the early Plantagenet kings and queens and was the place of both Eleanor of Aquitaine and Isabella of Angoulême's retirement and death. © Elizabeth Norton.

26. Coat of arms of Isabella of Angoulême, wife of King John, Lincoln Cathedral. © Gordon Plumb.

27. A medieval king and queen embracing from an thirteenth-century English manuscrpt. © Jonathan Reeve JR2224b99plateXIV 12001300.

28. The Eleanor Cross at Geddington. Only three of the monuments to Queen Eleanor of Castile now survive. (Elizabeth Norton)

29. and 30. The Eleanor Cross at Hardinstone. The Eleanor Crosses provided a lasting testament to Edward I's devotion to his wife, Eleanor of Castile. (Elizabeth Norton)

31. The Eleanor Cross at Waltham Cross. During her lifetime, Eleanor of Castile's reputation was poor, but the crosses served to create a posthumous reputation for queenly virtue. (Elizabeth Norton)

32. Eleanor of Castile, effigy on monument, Lincoln Cathedral. © Gordon Plumb.

33. Berkeley Castle. Edward II was imprisoned and murdered in the castle on the orders of his wife, Isabella of France, and her love, Roger Mortimer. (Elizabeth Norton)

34. Actual portraits of Richard II and Anne of Bohemia, though the results may be affected to some extent by their conformity to the type of features from which artists found it difficult to escape. From *Liber Regalis* (Coronation Book of Richard II) executed in 1377 or 1378. © Jonathan Reeve JR2152b97plate22 13501400.

35. The tomb of Joan of Navarre at Canterbury Cathedral. Joan and Henry IV made a love match, but Joan's time in England was far from easy, and she was the only queen to be punished for witchcraft. (David Sawtell)

36. The coronation of Joan of Navarre, Westminster Abbey February 1403. © Jonathan Reeve JR1724b90fp8 14001500.

37. Joan of Navarre at a joust on the occasion of her marriage to Henry IV in 1403. © Jonathan Reeve JR1724b90fp9 14001500.

38. Catherine of Valois, Henry V's queen, giving birth to Henry VI. © Jonathan Reeve JR1730b90fp88 14001500.

39. The marriage of Catherine of Valois to Henry V in the parish church of St John, Troyes, 2 June 1420, a direct result of the Treaty of Troyes ratifed less than a fortnight earlier on 21 May. © Jonathan Reeve JR1729b90fp85 14001500.

40. A queen depicted in a window in Fromond's Chantry, Winchester College. Work on the building was carried out during Catherine of Valois' time as queen and queen dowager. It is possible that the queen with her blond wavy hair was based upon Catherine, who was often depicted in a similar manner. © Gordon Plumb.

41. Elizabeth Woodville. (Ripon Cathedral portrait)

42. Richard III. The last Yorkist king married Anne Neville, the widow of the Lancastrian Prince of Wales, in order to secure a share of the great Warwick inheritance. (Ripon Cathedral portrait)

43. Warwick Castle. One of the residences of Anne Neville, the wife of Richard III. (Elizabeth Norton)

44. Margaret Beaufort from Christ's College, Cambridge. Margaret Beaufort passed her claim to the throne to her son, Henry Tudor, who took the crown as Henry VII. (Elizabeth Norton)

45. Anne Neville (centre), her first husband Prince Edward of Lancaster (left) and her second husband, Richard III (right). Anne and Richard are depicted with crowns and sceptres. © Jonathan Reeve JR1731b90fp109 14001500.

46. Henry VII. The first Tudor king was always sensitive to claims that he wore the crown in right of his wife. (Ripon Cathedral portrait)

47. Elizabeth of York was the daughter, sister, niece, wife and mother of kings of England, and it was through her that the Tudor dynasty gained its legitimacy. (Ripon Cathedral portrait)

48. This richly illuminated psalter belonged in turn to Elizabeth of York, then Catherine of Aragon. It notes the birth of Henry VII and Elizabeth of York's eldest son, Arthur. Marked in the psalter are the precious statements: 'Thys boke ys myn Elisabeth ye quene' and 'Thys boke ys myn Katherina the quene'. © Jonathan Reeve JR2153b97plate24 13501400.

49. Queen Philippa (left) and her headstrong eldest daughter, Princess

Isabella. Drawings of scenes depicted in tapestries made during the reign of Edward III and which hung in St Stephen's Chapel, Westminster, until they were destroyed when the old Palace of Westminster burned down. © Jonathan Reeve JR718b18p204 13001350.

50. The Anglo-Saxon and Norman queens. © Elizabeth Norton.

51. The Plantagenet and Lancastrian queens. © Elizabeth Norton.

52. Yorkist queen consorts and Tudor queen regnants. © Elizabeth Norton.

Index

Adela, Daughter of William I 77–8, 92, 94

Adeliza of Louvain, Second Queen of Henry I 88–93, 103, 105, 253

Alais of France 125, 133, 149, 256

Aldgyth, Queen of Edmund II 60–3, 81, 251

Alençon, Francis, Duke of, and later Duke of Anjou 203

Alfonso X, King of Castile 149, 153

Alfonso, Son of Edward I and Eleanor of Castile 153–4

Alfred the Great, King of Wessex 29–32, 35, 75, 82, 248

Alfred, Son of Ethelred II and Emma of Normandy 54, 57–8

Anne of Bohemia, First Queen of Richard II 181–8, 259

Anselm, St, Archbishop of Canterbury 83, 85–7

Arthur, Legendary King of Britain 14–16, 239

Arthur of Brittany, Grandson of Henry II 123–4, 137

Arthur, Prince of Wales, Son of Henry VII 239–41

Athelstan, King of England 34–7, 46, 51, 251

Augustine, St 101

Baldwin V, Count of Flanders 75

Beauchamp, Anne, Countess of Warwick 229, 233, 262

Beaufort, Edmund, Duke of Somerset 208, 260

Beaufort, Margaret, Countess of Richmond and Derby 209, 228, 236, 238–9

Becket, Thomas, Archbishop of Canterbury 109

Berengaria of Navarre, Queen of Richard I 120, 124–131, 256

Bernard of Clairvaux 113

Bertha, Queen of Kent 16–19, 248

Bohun, Mary de, First Wife of Henry IV 196–9, 259

Boudica, Queen of the Iceni 7–12, 247

Burgh, Hubert de 135

Caratacus 11–12, 248

Cartimandua, Queen of the Brigantes 7–12, 248

Catherine of Valois, Queen of Henry V 204, 209, 260

Charibert I, King of Paris 17

Charlemagne, Emperor of the Franks 21, 24, 89, 219

Charles the Bald, King of Francia 26, 53, 249

Christina, Daughter of Edward the Exile 81, 83, 85

Clarence, George, Duke of 221, 223, 230, 232, 237

Claudius, Emperor 8

Cnut, King of England, Denmark and Norway 54–63, 65, 251

Cordelia, Legendary Queen Regnant of Britain 7, 12–14

Corfe Castle 49

Crusades 113–14, 116, 120–1, 125, 127, 133, 143–4, 147, 152–3, 255–6

Cynethryth, Queen of Mercia 21–2, 248

d'Aubigny, William 91–3

David, King of Scotland 96, 99, 106, 177

Decianus, Catus 9

Despenser, Hugh, the Elder 166

Despenser, Hugh the Younger 163, 166

Dorset, Thomas Grey, First Marquis of 173, 222

Dunstan, St, Archbishop of Canterbury 38–40, 42–5, 47–50, 71, 250–1

Eadred, King of England 37–9, 42, 250

Eadric Streona 60–3

Eadwig, King of England 39–40, 42–4, 51, 250

Ealswitha, Queen of Alfred the Great (Eahlswith) 30–3, 42, 44, 249

Edburga, Queen of Wessex (Eadburh) 22–5, 30, 37, 248

Edgar, King of England 39–48, 50–1

Edgitha, Third wife of Edward the Elder (Eadgifu) 26–28, 29, 250–1

Edith of Mercia, Second Wife of Harold II 71–2, 74, 219, 252

Edith, St, of Wilton, Daughter of King Edgar 35, 250

Edith Godwin, Queen of Edward the Confessor 66–71, 252

Edith Swanneck, First Wife of Harold II 71–2, 252

Edmund I, King of England 37–41

Edmund, Eldest Son of King Edgar and Elfrida 48

Edmund II, King of England 62, 81

Edmund, Earl of Kent, Son of Edward I 168

Edward I, King of England 149, 156–7, 159, 162–3, 257–8

Edward II, King of England 159, 161–3, 171–3, 257–8

Edward III, King of England 162, 171–3, 179, 181–2, 196–9, 215, 258–9

Edward IV, King of England 216–20, 224–7, 229–34, 236, 239, 261

Edward V, King of England 219, 225–6, 234, 236

Edward of Lancaster, Prince of Wales 213, 215, 217, 219

Edward of Middleham, Prince of Wales 234–5, 262

Edward III 162, 171–3, 179, 181–2, 196–9, 215, 258–9

Edward the Confessor, King of England 59, 62, 66, 68, 70–1, 73, 78, 81, 85, 142, 147

Edward the Elder, King of Wessex 30, 34–7, 44, 249

Edward the Exile, Son of Edmund II and Aldgyth 62, 70, 81

Edward the Martyr, King of England 51

Edwin, son of Edward the Elder and Elfleda 35, 37

Edwin, Earl of Northumberland 73

Egbert, King of Wessex 22–4, 248

Egfrid, King of Northumbria 19–20

Egwyna, First Wife of Edward the Elder 33–5, 44, 249

Eleanor of Aquitaine, Queen of Henry II 111–125, 128–9, 133, 149, 152, 195, 254–5

Eleanor of Castile, First Queen of Edward I 144, 149–57, 159, 161, 257

Eleanor of England, Queen of Castile 124

Eleanor of Provence, Queen of Henry III 141–9, 154, 257

Elfleda, Second wife of Edward the Elder (Aelfflaed) 35–7, 44, 249

Elfrida, Daughter of Alfred the Great 33

Elfrida, Third wife of King Edgar (Aelfthryth) 39, 46–52, 250–1

Elfweard, King of Wessex 35–7

Elgiva, St, First Queen of Edmund I (St Aelfgifu) 40–1, 46, 48, 250

Elgiva of Wessex, Queen of Eadwig (Aelfgifu) 42–4, 250

Elgiva, First Wife of Ethelred II 51–2

Elgiva of Northampton, First Wife of Cnut (Aelfgifu) 56–7, 60, 62–6

Elizabeth of York, Queen of Henry VII 219, 228, 235–41, 262

Emma of Normandy, Second Wife of Ethelred II, Second Wife of Cnut 52–60, 63, 65, 251

Ethelbald, King of Wessex 27–8, 249

Ethelbert, King of East Anglia 21–2

Ethelbert, King of Kent 17–18, 28

Ethelbert, King of Wessex 28–9

Etheldreda, St 19, 88, 185

Ethelfleda, Lady of the Mercians 33, 35

Ethelfleda of Damerham, Second Queen of Edmund I (Aethelflaed) 41–2, 250

Ethelfleda *Eneda*, First Wife of King Edgar (Aethelflaed) 45, 48

Ethelgiva, Mother of Elgiva of Wessex 32–3, 42–3

Ethelred I, King of Wessex 29–31, 35, 42, 44, 66

Ethelred II, King of Wessex, 'The Unready' 50, 52

Ethelweard, Son of Alfred the Great 33, 42–3, 247

Ethelwold, Son of Ethelred I and Wulfrida 30

Ethelwold, St, Bishop of Winchester 38–9, 43

Ethelwulf, King of Wessex 24–8, 42

Eustace, Son of King Stephen and Matilda of Boulogne 93, 95, 97, 99–101

Gaveston, Piers 161, 163

Geoffrey, Count of Anjou 104, 116

Geoffrey, Earl of Brittany, Son of Henry II 123

Geoffrey FitzEmpress, Son of the Empress Matilda 104

Godwin, Earl of Wessex 58, 66–9

Godwin, Edith, *see* Edith Godwin

Goneril 13–14

Gruffydd, King of Wales 73

Guinevere, Legendary Queen of King Arthur 7, 14–16

Gunnor, Duchess of Normandy 52

Harold I, Harefoot, King of England 57

Harold II Godwinson, King of England 71

Harthacnut, King of England 56–7, 59, 63, 65–6, 251

Hengist 7

Henry I, King of England 62, 81, 85, 88–9, 91, 93–5, 97, 102–4, 131–2, 254

Henry II, King of England 110–11, 117, 120, 125, 131–2, 149, 255–6

Henry III, King of England 129–30, 135, 137, 139–41, 145, 149–50, 152–3, 257

Henry IV, Holy Roman Emperor 102–3

Henry IV, King of England 185, 191, 193–7, 199, 201, 204, 215, 254, 259–60

Henry V, Holy Roman Emperor 89, 102–3, 254

Henry V, King of England 196, 198, 203–7, 209–10, 219, 260

Henry VI, King of England 121, 196, 204, 207–11, 214–15, 217–18, 224, 230–1, 259–60

Henry VII, King of England 209, 219, 228, 237–8, 261

Henry, the Young King, Son of Henry II 119

Isabella of Angouleme, Second Wife of King John 135–41, 256

Isabella, Queen of Castile 240

Isabella of France, Queen of Edward II 157, 161–75, 205, 258

Isabella of Gloucester, First Wife of King John 131–41, 256

Isabella of Valois, Second Queen of Richard II 187–95, 201, 204, 259

Joan of Navarre, Second Wife of Henry IV 199–204, 260

Joanna, Queen of Sicily, Daughter of Henry II 117, 126–8

John, King of England 129, 131, 135, 199, 255–6

Judith of Francia 26–9, 53, 249

Lancelot, Sir 15–16

Lear, Legendary King of Britain 13–14

Louis VI, King of France 112

Louis VII, King of France 97, 109, 114

Louis IX, King of France 131, 141, 144–6, 152

Louis XI, King of France 217–18, 231

Lusignan, Hugh de, the elder, Count of Le Marche 136

Lusignan, Hugh de, the younger, Count of Le Marche 139

Mandeville, Geoffrey de, Earl of
    Essex 134
Margaret, St, Queen of Scotland
    81–3, 85, 253
Margaret of Anjou, Queen of Henry
    VI 209–18, 224–5, 231, 259–61
Margaret of France, Second Queen
    of Edward I 157–62, 257–8
Mary, Countess of Boulogne 101
Matilda, Duchess of Saxony,
    Daughter of Henry II 117, 119
Matilda, Empress, Lady of the
    English 75, 89, 93–4, 96, 101–11,
    195, 253–4
Matilda of Boulogne, Queen of
    Stephen 75, 93–101, 107, 254
Matilda of Flanders, Queen of
    William I 75–81, 253
Matilda of Scotland, First Queen of
    Henry I 81–8, 90, 93, 102, 111, 253
Montford, Simon de 145–7
Morcar, Earl of Mercia 73, 262
Mordred 15–16
Mortimer, Roger 168–9, 175, 198

Neville, Anne, Queen of Richard III
    217, 219, 229–37, 261–2
Neville, Cecily, Duchess of York 221,
    227

Offa, King of Mercia 21–3
Olaf Tryggvason, King of Norway 64
Osburga, First Queen of Ethelwulf
    (Osburgh) 24–7, 248

Paullinus, Suetonius, Governor of
    Britain 9–10
Perrers, Alice 181, 259

Peter of Savoy 142–3, 146
Philip IV, King of France 157, 161–2,
    176, 199, 205
Philip Augustus, King of France 119,
    121, 123, 130, 133–7
Philippa of Hainault, Queen of
    Edward III 173–81, 186, 196–7,
    258–9
Prasutagus, King of the Iceni 8

Raymond of Aquitaine 115
Redburga, Queen of Egbert of
    Wessex (Raedburgh) 22, 24, 248
Regan 13–14
Religious Reform Movement, Tenth
    Century 38, 181, 184
Richard I, Duke of Normandy 52, 75
Richard I, King of England 122–8,
    132–3, 136, 149
Richard II, Duke of Normandy 52–3,
    75
Richard II, King of England 181–2,
    185, 187, 190–1, 196, 198, 200–1,
    204, 215, 259
Richard III, King of England 77, 219,
    227–9, 234, 236–7, 261–2
Richard, Earl of Cornwall, Son of
    King John 141
Robert, Duke of Normandy, Eldest
    Son of William I 77, 79–81
Robert, Earl of Gloucester,
    Illegitimate Son of Henry I 92,
    97, 105
Rowen, Wife of King Vortigern 7,
    247

Sexburga, Queen Regnant of Wessex
    7, 247

Sigeferth of the Five Boroughs 60–1

Simnel, Lambert 229, 239

Stephen, King of England 77, 92–101, 105–8, 254

Sweyn Forkbeard, King of Denmark 54, 61, 63, 72

Sweyn, King of Norway, Son of Cnut and Elgiva of Northampton 63–5, 67

Sweyn, Son of Earl Godwin 67

Tostig, Son of Earl Godwin 69–70, 73

Tudor, Edmund 209

Tudor, Jasper 209

Tudor, Owen 208–9, 239

Vellocatus, Second Husband of Cartimandua 12

Venutius, King of the Brigantes 12, 248

Vikings 26–7, 29–33, 37–8, 40, 52–4, 60, 249, 251

Warwick, Richard Neville, Earl of, 'the Kingmaker' 214, 217, 221, 223, 229, 231

Wherwell Abbey 45, 69

William I 'The Conqueror', King of England 73–4, 82

William II 'Rufus', King of England 78, 81, 84–5

William IX, Duke of Aquitaine 111

William X, Duke of Aquitaine 112

William Aigret of Aquitaine 112

William 'The Aetheling', Son of Henry I and Matilda of Scotland 85, 87–8

William, Son of King Stephen 95, 97, 101

William FitzEmpress, Son of the Empress Matilda 104, 109

William, Eldest Son of Henry II and Eleanor of Aquitaine 117

William of Savoy, Uncle of Eleanor of Provence 141–2

Wilton Nunnery 36–7, 45–6, 66, 69–70, 72, 83–4

Winchester 24, 32–3, 38–9, 44, 47–8, 50, 54, 56–8, 60, 63, 70, 79, 90, 97–9, 106–7, 120–1, 130, 142, 144, 159, 202, 239, 249–51, 254

Woodville, Elizabeth, Queen of Edward IV 219, 229, 236–7, 239, 261

Wulfrida, Queen of Ethelred I (Wulfthryth) 29–30, 249

Wulfrida, St, of Wilton, Second Wife of King Edgar 45–6, 250

York, Richard, Duke of, Father of Edward IV and Richard III 213–15

York, Richard, Duke of, Son of Edward IV 226–7

Also available from Amberley Publishing

A radical retelling of one of the most important events in English history

'A gripping re-evaluation of those turbulent times... Rex vividly conjures up the ebb and flow of the battle' THE MAIL ON SUNDAY

Peter Rex tells the whole story of the Conquest of England by the Normans from its genesis in the deathbed decision of King Edward the Confessor in January 1066 to recommend Harold Godwinson as his successor, to the crushing of the last flickers of English resistance in June 1076.

£9.99 Paperback
57 illustrations (44 colour)
304 pages
978-1-4456-0384-1

Available from all good bookshops or to order direct
Please call **01453-847-800**
www.amberleybooks.com

Also available from Amberley Publishing

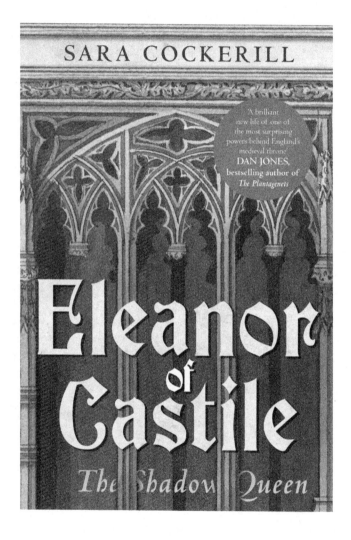

Available from all good bookshops or to order direct
Please call **01453–847–800**
www.amberleybooks.com

Also available from Amberley Publishing

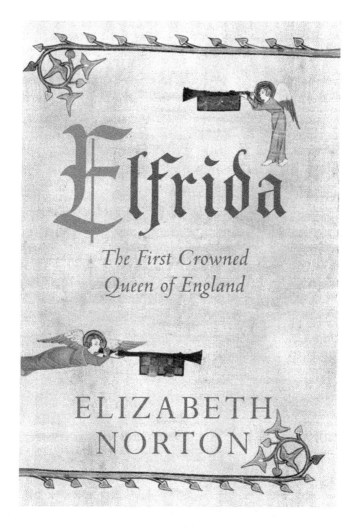

Elfrida

*The First Crowned
Queen of England*

ELIZABETH
NORTON

Also available from Amberley Publishing

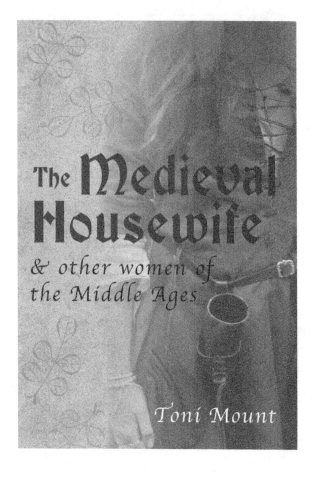

The Medieval Housewife & other women of the Middle Ages

Toni Mount

Also available from Amberley Publishing

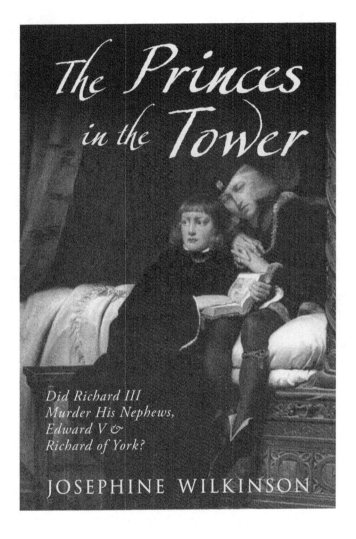

The Princes
in the Tower

Did Richard III
Murder His Nephews,
Edward V &
Richard of York?

JOSEPHINE WILKINSON

Available from all good bookshops or to order direct
Please call **01453-847-800**
www.amberleybooks.com

Richard III from Amberley Publishing

RICHARD III
David Baldwin

'A believably complex Richard, neither wholly villain nor hero'
PHILIPPA GREGORY

£9.99   978-1-4456-1591-2   272 pages PB   81 illus, 57 col

ANNE NEVILLE
Amy Licence

'Timely ... the real life of the daughter of Warwick the Kingmaker'
WI LIFE

£10.99   978-1-4456-3312-1   304 pages PB   30 col illus

CECILY NEVILLE
Amy Licence

£20.00   978-1-4456-2123-4   256 pages HB   35 illus

THE PRINCES IN THE TOWER
Josephine Wilkinson

£18.99   978-1-4456-1974-3   192 pages HB

RICHARD III
Terry Breverton

£16.99   978-1-4456-2105-0   200 pages HB   20 col illus

RICHARD III: THE YOUNG KING TO BE
Josephine Wilkinson

£9.99   978-1-84868-513-0   352 pages PB   40 illus, 25 col

THE MYSTERY OF THE PRINCES
Audrey Williamson

'Brilliant and readable'
THE TRIBUNE

£9.99   978-1-84868-321-1   192 pages PB   40 col illus

MARGARET OF YORK
Christine Weightman

'Brings Margaret alive once more'
THE YORKSHIRE POST

£10.99   978-1-4456-0819-8   256 pages PB   51 illus

ALSO AVAILABLE AS EBOOKS
Available from all good bookshops or to order direct
Please call **01453-847-800**
www.amberleybooks.com

Also available from Amberley Publishing

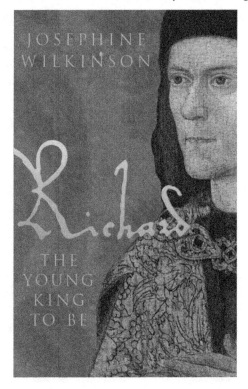

A major new biography of the young Richard III

Richard III is a paradox - the most hated of English kings, yet the most beloved, a deeply pious man, yet materialistic to the point of obsession, puritan, yet the father of at least two illegitimate children. This new biography concentrates on the much neglected early part of Richard's life - from his birth in 1452 as a cadet of the House of York to his marriage to the beautiful Anne Neville - and shows how his experiences as the son of an ambitious duke, a prisoner of war, an exile, his knightly training and awe of his elder brother, King Edward IV, shaped the character of England's most controversial monarch.

£9.99 Paperback
40 illustrations (25 colour)
352 pages
978-1-84868-513-0

Also available as an ebook
Available from all good bookshops or to order direct
Please call **01453-847-800**
www.amberleybooks.com

Also available from Amberley Publishing

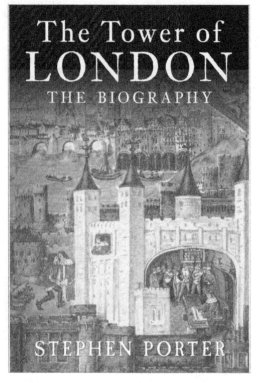

Fortress, palace & prison, the 1000 year story of the Tower

The Tower of London is an icon of England's history. William the Conqueror built the White Tower after his invasion and conquest in 1066, to dominate London and it has become infamous as a place of torture, execution and murder. The deaths of royals attracted most attention; the murder of Princes in the Tower, the beheading of Henry VIII's wives, Anne Boleyn and Katherine Howard, and Lady Jane Grey, Henry's great-niece, and queen for just nine days. Few prisoners recorded their experiences, but John Gerard, a Catholic priest imprisoned during Elizabeth I's reign, wrote of being questioned in the torture-room, which contained 'every device and instrument of torture'. After being hung from manacles, his wrists were swollen and he could barely walk. Stephen Porter's landmark new history traces the evolution of the Tower and it's changing role, the many personalities who lived or were imprisoned there, and the 'voices' of contemporaries during the Tower's long history.

£20 Hardback
112 illustrations (53 colour)
320 pages
978-1-4456-0381-0

Also available as an ebook
Available from all good bookshops or to order direct
Please call **01453-847-800**
www.amberleybooks.com

Also available from Amberley Publishing

Author of *The English Resistance*, 'Portrays William as he really was – a bloody, ruthless war criminal' FRANK MCLYNN

William
the
Conqueror

The Bastard of Normandy

ILLELM:
HAROLD

PETER REX

A new biography of the Norman king who conquered England in 1066, changing the course of the country forever

'Rex has a real ability to communicate difficult issues to a wide audience' BBC HISTORY MAGAZINE

Of Franco-Scandinavian descent through his father, Duke Robert 'the Magnificent', William the Conqueror's life is set against his true background, the turbulent Norman Duchy which, even after the Conquest of England, remained his primary concern. William is revealed as the brutal and violent product of his time, much given to outbursts of rage, capable of great cruelty, autocratic, avaricious and prone to a sort of grisly humour, yet, with all that he could also be a loyal friend and affectionate husband and father.

£12.99 Paperback
43 illustrations (30 colour)
304 pages
978-1-4456-0698-9

Also available as an ebook
Available from all good bookshops or to order direct
Please call **01453-847-800**
www.amberleybooks.com